The Practical Skeptic

CORE CONCEPTS IN SOCIOLOGY

Second Edition

Lisa J. McIntyre
Washington State University

**Mc
Graw
Hill**

Boston   Burr Ridge, IL   Dubuque, IA   Madison, WI   New York
San Francisco   St. Louis   Bangkok   Bogotá   Caracas   Kuala Lumpur
Lisbon   London   Madrid   Mexico City   Milan   Montreal   New Delhi
Santiago   Seoul   Singapore   Sydney   Taipei   Toronto

McGraw-Hill Higher Education &

A Division of *The McGraw-Hill Companies*

4 5 6 7 8 9 0 BAH/BAH 0 9 8 7 6 5 4 3 2

Library of Congress Cataloging-in-Publication Data

McIntyre, Lisa J.
    The practical skeptic : core concepts in sociology /
Lisa J. McIntyre.— 2nd ed.
      p. cm.
    Includes bibliographical references and index.
    ISBN 0-7674-2082-9
    1. Sociology. I. Title.
HM585 .M35 2001
301—dc21   00-069568

Sponsoring editor, Serina Beauparlant; *production editor,* April Wells-Hayes; *manuscript editor,* Barbara McGowran; *design manager,* Susan Breitbard; *text designer,* Joan Greenfield; *cover designer,* Laurie Anderson; *manufacturing manager,* Randy Hurst. The text was set in 10/12 Book Antiqua by TBH Typecast and printed on 50# Champion Offset by Banta Book Group.

Text credits appear on a continuation of the copyright page, page 258.

www.mhhe.com

Preface

It wasn't until I was about halfway through my first decade of teaching that I finally had the opportunity to teach Introduction to Sociology. Did I *want* to teach Intro? You bet! I was ecstatic. I had been teaching various upper-division classes—research methods, social theory, criminology, law and society—but I wanted to be the one who introduced sociology to students. I wanted to share with students the enthusiasm that I felt for the entire sociological enterprise and to expose them to the power of sociological thought.

I tried to create an introductory course that would speak to the typical first-year student who isn't planning on majoring in sociology and, indeed, may not even know what sociology is. Even among sociology majors, very few plan on becoming sociologists. Each semester, I ask my beginning students, "Why are you here? What is it about sociology that interests you?" The very charitable say, "I don't know what sociology is, but I am sure that it will be interesting." Mostly, students are honest: "I'm here to fulfill my general education requirements." A few are more specific: "I have to take a social science class and my advisor said that sociology is easier than economics or political science."

I knew that once these students discovered sociology, they would find merit in it. Even if they didn't major in sociology, they would come away from the class with some important life knowledge. I quote Robert Bierstedt in my syllabus: "Sociology owns a proper place not only among the sciences, but also among the arts that liberate the human mind" (1960, 3). I paraphrase Peter Berger to suggest that students will find one of the most important lessons of sociology to be that "things are not what they seem" (1963, 23)—that sociological training encourages people to look beyond the surface and to be suspicious of what "everybody knows." I tell them that it hardly matters what sort of career they are working toward: Learning how to be skeptical and how to think like a sociologist will help them understand and resolve complex and abstract problems on the job.

So, I knew how I wanted to structure the course—we would learn the basic concepts and then talk and read about how these worked in the real world. But I couldn't find a textbook whose author had anticipated my wishes. I wanted a book that would introduce students to sociology's foundational concepts—the scientific method, culture, social structure, socialization, deviance, inequality. I wanted a book that would not bury those concepts inside tons of empirical information but would present them in such a way that students could gain enough understanding to apply them to what they read elsewhere and what they encountered in life. It was the sociological perspective I wanted these students to come away with, not the details.

I was encouraged to pursue this vision by something I read in an article by Frederick Campbell, a sociologist from the University of Washington. In the book he co-edited with Hubert Blalock and Reece McGee, Campbell wrote that undergraduate courses in sociology ought to focus on *principles rather than facts:* "The mastery of sociology has a different meaning in the context of undergraduate education than in vocational training or a graduate program. A baccalaureate degree in sociology seldom prepares a student for a specific occupation or to pursue independent research. Emphasis on the subject matter, then, has little value if it means memorizing material that will soon go out of date for a job that does not exist. Mastery should move away from factual material and focus instead on the development of the mind" (1985, 13).

The longer I taught introductory sociology, however, the greater became my frustration with the available instructional material. So, one summer, I sat down to write some introductory and background materials for my students. My idea was that I would introduce them to the concepts that sociologists use, and we would then apply these to what we read in a variety of sociological articles and to what we encountered in real life (and in the media). My goal was to provide my students with the tools they needed to understand the social world through the eyes of sociologists. As everyone who has taught introductory courses probably knows, the foundational concepts of our discipline are not simple ones, and many students resist them. My goal was not to simplify the concepts but to make them accessible to students.

The set of essays I wrote that summer—on the history of sociology and the vocabulary of science, culture, social structure, socialization, deviance, and inequality—seemed to serve my students well. After students read them, we moved on with our shared vocabulary to other works by sociologists and to discussions of how these concepts applied to the real world. It worked. It was as Peter Berger had promised in his *Invitation to Sociology:* "It is not the excitement of coming upon the totally unfamiliar, but rather the excitement of finding the familiar becoming transformed in its meaning. The fascination of sociology lies in the fact that its perspective makes us see in a new light the very world in which we have lived all our lives" (1963, 21). Although I omitted much that is found in the typical sociology text (there are no chapters on family, religion, or politics), the concepts I did focus on (institutions, roles, values, and so on) allowed us to have relatively sophisticated discussions of those topics.

Be warned: I am not one of those sociologists who write in what Peter Berger called "a barbaric dialect." I've taken C. Wright Mills's caution to heart: "To get beyond sociological prose we must get beyond the sociologist's pose" (1959). Notwithstanding the fact that I once had a book rejected by a noted university press because it was "too much of a good read," I've persisted in my casual style and, whenever I couldn't help it, have indulged my odd sense of humor. Many sociological concepts are very complex, and I think I have done justice to that complexity, but I have tried to do it in ways that are accessible to students.

NEW TO THIS EDITION

This second edition of *The Practical Skeptic* owes much to many of the instructors who used the first edition in their introductory classes as well as, in many instances, their students. I found their comments both substantively helpful and psychically inspiring. The goals of the book remain the same: to introduce students to sociology in a way that makes the core concepts of our discipline accessible without losing the crucial complexity of these concepts in translation.

In this edition I have consolidated some of the materials on sociological methods and added a chapter on social institutions— how they come about and are sustained, and the roles that they play in society. The Stop and Review questions (and their answers) have been retained, but end-of-chapter review questions have been added.

INSTRUCTOR'S MANUAL WITH TEST ITEMS

I have written an instructor's manual with test items. In addition to the usual test items (containing multiple choice, true/false, and essay discussion questions), I have included discussion questions and activities, examples of lectures, and tips specifically targeting new instructors.

THE PRACTICAL SKEPTIC: READINGS IN SOCIOLOGY

Created to serve as a companion to the text, *The Practical Skeptic: Core Concepts in Sociology*, this reader, *The Practical Skeptic: Readings in Sociology*, includes classic sociological writings as well as recent writings on fascinating topics of interest to students. Corresponding to the conceptual organization of the text, each of the readings serves to illustrate key sociological concepts and ideas. A separate printed test bank for the reader is available. It contains multiple choice, true/false, and essay discussion questions for each reading.

ACKNOWLEDGMENTS

My largest thanks go to the hundreds of students who have read *The Practical Skeptic* and shared their views of the text with me.

I thank the reviewers of the second edition for their thoughtful reading: Jerry Barrish, Bellevue Community College; Debra Cornelius, Shippensburg University; Jamie Dangler, SUNY Cortland; Laurel R. Davis, Springfield College; Gloria Y. Gadsden, Fairleigh Dickinson University; Alan G. Hill, Delta College; Susan E. Humphers-Ginther, Moorhead State University; Katherine Johnson, Niagara County Community College; Barbara Karcher, Kennesaw State University; Debra C. Lemke, Western Maryland College; Patricia A. Masters, George Mason University; Susan McWilliams, University of Southern Maine; Dan Pence, Southern Utah University; Marcella Thompson, University of Arkansas; Georgeanna M. Tryban, Indiana State University; and Brenda S. Zicha, Charles Stewart Mott Community College.

I would also like to thank the reviewers of the first edition: Peter Adler, University of Denver; Sheila M. Cordray, Oregon State University; Mary Patrice Erdmans, University of North Carolina–Greensboro; Valerie Jenness, University of California–Irvine; Frances V. Moulder, Three Rivers Community–Technical College; Karl T. Pfeiffer, University of Alaska; Martha L. Shockey, St. Ambrose University; Lisa Troyer, University of Iowa; and Georgeanna M. Tryban, Indiana State University.

Contents

Preface   *iii*

Introduction   1

So, What Is Sociology?   2

The Value of Sociology to Students   3

Tips for Studying Sociology—and an Invitation   4

PART 1   GETTING STARTED IN SOCIOLOGY

Chapter 1   *Responding to Chaos: A Brief History of Sociology*   5

Inquiries into the Physical World   6

Technology, Urbanization, and Social Upheaval   10

The Origins of Modern Sociology in France: Émile Durkheim   12

EXCERPT: ÉMILE DURKHEIM, from *Suicide* (1897) and *The Rules of the Sociological Method* (1904)   14

The Origins of Modern Sociology in Germany: Ferdinand Tönnies, Max Weber, and Karl Marx   16

EXCERPT: FERDINAND TÖNNIES, from *Gemeinschaft and Gesellschaft* (1887)   17

Karl Marx   20

The Origins of Modern Sociology in England: Herbert Spencer   21

Sociology in the United States   23

The Place of Sociology in Modern Society   24

Chapter Review   25

Stop and Review: Answers and Discussion   25

Chapter 2   *The Sociological Eye*   *27*

The Focus on the Social   27

Skepticism   30

Box: Nail Down That Distinction Between Manifest and Latent Functions!   31

Chapter Review   33

Stop and Review: Answers and Discussion   *33*

Chapter 3   *Science and Fuzzy Objects: Specialization in Sociology*   *35*

Dividing Up the Task   37

Topic Area or Subject Matter   38

Theoretical Perspectives (Paradigms): Functionalist, Conflict, and Symbolic Interactionist   38

The Functionalist Paradigm   38
The Conflict Paradigm   39
The Symbolic Interactionist Paradigm   39

Which Paradigm Is Correct?   40

Levels of Analysis: Microsociology and Macrosociology   41

Chapter Review   42

Stop and Review: Answers and Discussion   *42*

Chapter 4   *Who's Afraid of Sociology?*   *44*

The Empirical World and Inconvenient Facts   44

Ethnocentrism   46

Avoiding Ethnocentrism Can Be Difficult   49

Cultural Relativism   50

Chapter Review   51

Stop and Review: Answers and Discussion   *51*

PART 2   TOOLS OF SOCIOLOGICAL RESEARCH

Chapter 5   *The Vocabulary of Science*   *52*

Variables   52

Hypotheses   54

Kinds of Variables: Independent Versus Dependent   56

Kinds of Relationships: Directionality   58

Operational Definitions   59

Tables and Figures   61

Chapter Review   67

Stop and Review: Answers and Discussion   67

Chapter 6   *Doing Social Research   74*

Two Traditions: Quantitative and Qualitative Research   74

First Things First: The Lit Review   75

The Survey   77

Types of Survey Questions   78
The Art of Asking Questions   80

Box: Six Guidelines for Crafting Survey Questions   80

The Experiment   81

Box: Five Rules for Doing True Experiments   84

Observation   84

Unobtrusive (Nonreactive) Research   85

Artifacts   86
Use of Existing Statistics   87
Content Analysis   87

The Importance of Triangulation   88

Sampling   89

Box: Ethics and Social Research   91

Chapter Review   91

Stop and Review: Answers and Discussion   92

PART 3   THE SOCIAL ENVIRONMENT

Chapter 7   *Culture   94*

Material and Nonmaterial Culture   95
Nonmaterial Culture   95
Symbols   95
Language   96
Norms   97
Types of Norms   98
Sanctions   98

Box: The Power of Informal Sanctions   99
  Values   100

Box: What Do Americans Value?   100

Box: Ponder   100

Box: Ideology   101
  Ideas and Beliefs   102

How It Adds Up   102

Box: Statements of Belief   102

Culture as a Product of Action   103

Culture as a Conditioning Element
of Further Action   104

Box: Problems Identified and Resolved
in All Known Cultures   105

Box: Varieties of Cultural Wisdom   106

Social Institutions   106

Social Change: Cultural Diffusion
and Leveling   107

Subcultures and Countercultures   107

EXCERPT: MARGARET VISSER, from *Much Depends
on Dinner* (1986)   108

Chapter Review   109

Stop and Review: Answers and Discussion   110

Chapter 8   *Social Structure   112*

Statuses   112

Roles   114
  Tricky Situation 1: Role Strain   115
  Tricky Situation 2: Status Inconsistency   115
  Tricky Situation 3: Role Conflict   116

Master Status   117

Groups   118
  Primary and Secondary Groups   119
  Formal Organizations and Bureaucracies   121
  Ideal-Type Bureaucracies   121

Chapter Review   124

Stop and Review: Answers and Discussion   125

Chapter 9   *Society and Social Institutions   127*

Societal Needs   130

The Nature of Social Institutions   133

Institutions Are Generally Unplanned;
They Develop Gradually   133

Institutions Are Inherently Conservative;
They Change, But Slowly   136

A Particular Society's Institutions Are
Interdependent; Because of This, Change
in One Institution Tends to Bring About
Change in Others   137

The Statuses, Roles, Values, and Norms
Associated with an Institution in One Society
Frequently Bear Little Resemblance to Those
in Another Society   138

BOX: Polygamy and Monogamy   139

Social Change: The Trend Toward
Increasing Specialization   139

Chapter Review   140

Stop and Review: Answers and Discussion   141

PART 4   PEOPLE IN SOCIETY

Chapter 10 *Socialization   143*

Nature and Nurture: Biological and Social
Processes   143

How Socialization Works   145

The Looking-Glass Self: Charles Horton
Cooley   145

The "I" and the "Me": George Herbert
Mead   147

EXCERPT: GEORGE HERBERT MEAD, from *Play and
Games in the Genesis of Self* (1934)   150

Family   150
School   153
Peer Groups   153
The Workplace   154

BOX: Rites of Passage   155

Resocialization and Total Institutions   156

BOX: Ponder   157

Chapter Review   157

Stop and Review: Answers and Discussion   158

Chapter 11 *Deviance and Social Control   159*

The Relativity of Deviance (What We
Already Know)   159

Nonsociological Theories of Deviance   161

Sociological Theories of Deviance: Émile Durkheim and Suicide   162

The Collective Conscience and Structural Strain   163

Egoism and Anomie   164

More Structural Strain: Robert Merton and Anomie   166

Anomie and Modern Social Structure   166

Responses to Anomie   167

Legitimate Versus Illegitimate Means   169

Learning to Be Deviant: Howard Becker's Study of Marijuana Use   170

Learning to Smoke   170

Learning to Perceive the Effects   171

Learning to Enjoy the Effects   172

The Societal Reaction Perspective: Labeling Theory   174

The Functions of Deviance: Maintenance of the Staus Quo and Social Change   177

Box: Ponder   178

Chapter Review   178

Stop and Review: Answers and Discussion   179

PART 5   INEQUALITY

Chapter 12 *Stratification and Inequality   181*

Caste Systems   182

Estate Systems   185

Box: *A Year in the Life of the Peasant   186*

Class Systems   188

Theoretical Conceptions of Class   189

Box: Ponder   190

Some Words About Slavery   193

Social Mobility and Open Versus Closed Systems   194

Chapter Review   196

Stop and Review: Answers and Discussion   197

Chapter 13   *Inequality and Achievement: Social Class   198*

   Box: The Matthew Effect   202

   Explaining Social Stratification   202
    Cultural Explanations   203
    Structural Explanations   204

   The Pygmalion Effect: The Power
   of Expectations   210

   The Fallacy of Hard Work   211

   Box: Ponder   213

   Social Mobility, Social Structure,
   and Social Change   213

   Chapter Review   215

   Stop and Review: Answers and Discussion   215

Chapter 14   *Inequality and Ascription: Race, Ethnicity,
   and Gender   217*

   Why a Dollar Is Not Always a Dollar   218

   Prejudice   222

   Discrimination   223

   Discrimination and "Isms"   225

   The Social Construction of Minority Groups   230

   Gender   233

   Chapter Review   236

   Stop and Review: Answers and Discussion   236

References   239

Glossary/Index   247

Credits   258

Introduction

Have you ever caught yourself thinking about things that people do? Have you ever asked yourself, for example, questions about everyday things like these:

Why do some students always sit in the back of the classroom while others always sit in the front?

Why do African Americans on campus frequently say "hi" to other African Americans, even if they don't know them?

Why do we dress baby girls in pink and baby boys in blue?

Why do people generally not look at one another in elevators—and always face front?

Why do young men, but not young women, spit?

Why do we go to such lengths to pretend we aren't embarrassed when we have to get naked in front of a doctor?

Why do people from small towns tend to act differently from people from big cities?

Why are most people less willing to seek professional help for mental or emotional problems than for physical problems?

Sociologists are trained to find answers to questions about people's behavior. We are especially interested in understanding the effects that people have on one another.

Sociologists are convinced that much of people's behavior is a result of what other people do. A sociologist reviewing the questions just listed would likely say that many of these behaviors result from how people are influenced by others.

This sociological conviction might offend you. Certainly, I like to think of myself as independent-minded; you, too, may like to think that your behaviors are the results of choices you have made out of your own free will. But allow me to persuade you that to understand people's behavior and the choices they make, it is important to take into account the influence of others in their environment.

Even when you think you are making your own choices, often you are only picking from the fairly limited range of options that others allow you. The simple fact is that, depending on your position in society—your age, gender, race, social class, and so on—people expect and allow you to act in various ways. Society places restrictions on your behavior with very little regard for your preferences.

Of course, you can choose not to live up to society's expectations, but if you decide to be contrary, you will pay a price. And, depending on the seriousness of your infraction, that price can range from endless nagging by your parents to a prison sentence and even to death!

Consider marriage. Surely, the decisions whether to get married, whom to marry, and when are very *personal* decisions. Actually, they are not. Examine this matter carefully and you will find that your marital choices are rather restricted. For example, in the United States, you can only be married to one person at a time. And (at least for the time being) you can only marry a person of the opposite sex. Until the late 1960s, many states even had laws requiring people to marry within their own racial group—if you broke these laws, you could be sent to prison or exiled from the state.[1]

Chances are, your family places even more restrictions on your marriage choices. Have you noticed that there are, in effect, family "rules" about whom you can marry? These rules may be unspoken but clear: Your parents may wish you to wed someone of your own race and religion and from the same educational and social-class background. Of course, there is no *law* that says family rules must be followed, but we all know that families have ways of making us suffer.

Even your friends may restrict your marriage (and dating) choices. Consider how they would make you suffer if you started to date some seriously weird geek.

You really have to wonder, why does everyone care so much about whom we marry? Now *that* is a sociological question!

So, What Is Sociology?

Here is a technical definition of sociology: *Sociology is the scientific study of interactions and relations among human beings.*

---

[1]Some states have never rescinded these laws, but because such racial restrictions were ruled unconstitutional by the U.S. Supreme Court in 1967, even where they do exist, they do not have the force of law.

I hope the word *scientific* caught your attention. Including that word in the definition is a reminder that sociologists try to be very careful about how they find answers to their questions. Sociologists do not want their answers to be contaminated by bias or emotion or faulty logic. Therefore, as much as possible, they apply the scientific method to their sociological inquiries.

The Value of Sociology to Students

The goal of this book, and this course, is not so much to introduce you to new worlds as it is to inspire you to take a long hard look at familiar ones. And, I promise you, the reward for doing that will be much greater than the simple gratification of intellectual curiosity. There will be many practical rewards.

The practical value of taking a sociology course is that what you learn, by definition, *never will be irrelevant to your life*—present and future. Each of us lives in the social world; each of us is influenced by others and, to some extent, hopes to influence others. Studying sociology will strengthen your ability to understand how the social world operates and what your place is in it. Moreover, studying sociology will enhance your ability to act effectively in the social world.

Just to whet your appetite, let me share with you one of the most basic sociological truths as it was put into words in 1928 by the sociologist W. I. Thomas: "If people define situations as real, they are real in their consequences." The *Thomas theorem* articulated the sociological finding that had escaped many nonsociological observers. If one truly wants to understand why people do the things they do, one must take into account not only what is *really* going on in a particular situation but what people *think* is going on. For example, if moviegoers believe the theater is on fire, they will react to the threat as if it were real, even if there is no fire. A consequence could be a panic in which people are trampled to death, even though the threat was never "real."

Thomas's insight helps us to understand how people live their everyday lives, too. Suppose the local newspaper runs a series of articles on how people are being victimized by crimes. The reporters pick the most interesting and most gruesome of criminal events on which to focus. Even if the reality is that these are uncommon events and that the actual rate of crime is going down, we would predict that people's fear of crime would increase, which would have important consequences. For example, more people might purchase handguns for protection just at the point when things really are becoming safer. The increase in handgun ownership might result in an increase in handgun deaths—kids playing with guns, panicked homeowners shooting neighbors stumbling around in the middle of the night, and so on.

Certainly, reality is important, because even when people do not define things as real, they can have real consequences. Thus, even if people do not know that the theater is on fire, they will die if they don't escape. But reality is only one factor that we must take into account to understand how people act and interact.

Sociology, then, is the discipline that studies the interactions and relationships among people—the realities and the perceived realities. Even given the seemingly countless variations in people's possible behaviors, sociologists are remarkably successful in shedding light on questions about why people do what they do and how they are influenced by one another.

My goal in this book has been to select the most important concepts that sociologists use and share them with you. My hope is that you, too, might apply these concepts as you work to move about in the social world more effectively and to understand it more thoroughly.

Tips for Studying Sociology— and an Invitation

To get the most out of your study of sociology, you will need to do more than simply read the book. Your goal should be to "own" the concepts—that is, not only to read but to think about the concepts so you can use them to understand social life. To help you achieve this goal, I have scattered Stop and Review questions throughout the book. I urge you to answer these questions. Many of my own students have told me that doing so makes it much easier to understand (and remember) sociological concepts. Several of my students tell me that they learn even more by making a list of the concepts for each chapter along with the definitions given in the book, and then writing their own definitions and examples.

Finally, I enjoy hearing from students (and their teachers, of course). If you have a question, comment, sociological example, or suggestion that you would like to share with me, please do so! I might use your example in the next edition of the book. (If I do that, I will be sure to give you credit—and I will make sure that you receive a copy of the book so you can see your name in print.)

You can contact me via "snail mail" at Department of Sociology, Washington State University, Pullman, WA 99164-4020, or e-mail at ljmcint@wsu.edu. Please include your mail or e-mail address so I can respond.

Responding to Chaos

A Brief History of Sociology

"He who watches a thing grow has the best view of it."

—Heraclitus[1]

I have always suspected that what people choose to study is a result of something other than mere accident. It seems to me that people study what they feel they most need to understand, and frequently, these are things that frighten them.

To the first peoples of the world, nature was overwhelmingly powerful and fear-inspiring; the physical environment dominated the lives of men and women. The time of year dictated daily tasks—planting, reaping, hunting. The available vegetation and game dictated what people ate. Even after plants and animals were domesticated, menus were limited by climate—if you lived in the Northern Hemisphere, probably you would die without ever having tasted a mango or a banana.

It is easy to understand, then, why the earliest people focused their intellectual efforts on gaining an understanding of the physical world. Theirs were pressing questions: Why did the sun rise each morning and set each evening? Would it continue to do so? What made it rain? Why did the wind blow?

Obviously humankind has never "conquered" nature, yet by the beginning of the nineteenth century, humanity had succeeded in making the natural world seem more predictable. But then, just as Westerners seemed to be getting a handle on the natural, their *social* world became frighteningly chaotic. People were accustomed to wars with foreigners, but in the eighteenth century nearly every European nation faced internal war in the form of revolution. By the time the nineteenth century rolled around, the

---

[1] Heraclitus (hera-KLI-tus) was an ancient Greek philosopher (c. 540–480 B.C.E.).

political, economic, and religious foundations of society appeared to be on the verge of crumbling. Things were in chaos. People were frightened.

Inquiries into the Physical World

Although the most dramatic social upheavals occurred in the eighteenth century, rumblings had been heard as far back as the sixteenth century. It was during the sixteenth century that people started to question the validity of long-held beliefs about the fundamental nature of the world.

At first, these questions had to do with the physical world. In the second century of the common era,[2] Greek/Egyptian astronomer Claudius Ptolemy had determined that the earth was the center of the universe. (Actually this idea had been around at least since the fourth century B.C.E., but Ptolemy mathematically "proved" the theory using geometry.) More than a thousand years later, leaders of the Western Church still embraced Ptolemy's view because it meshed with other ideas they held: Of course, the earth is at the center of things—"man" was God's most important creation, and where else would God place man's world but at the center of the universe? Anyway, if things were otherwise—if the earth were not the center of things but revolved around the sun—wouldn't we feel the earth move?

In 1543 a Pole named Mikolaj Kopernik (better known now as Nicolaus Copernicus) in Frauenberg (a town in East Prussia) published a book entitled *On the Revolutions of Heavenly Bodies*. In this book Copernicus suggested that the *sun*, not the earth, was at the center of the universe and that the planets (including the earth)

---

[2] It was once usual to distinguish between B.C. ("before Christ") and A.D. (for *Anno Domini*, or "in the year of our Lord," and not "after death"). This distinction is historically misleading, however, for Jesus of Nazareth was born during the reign of King Herod, and Herod died in 4 B.C. Thus, the birth of Jesus has traditionally been dated at least four years too late.

As an acknowledgment of the arbitrary beginnings of the Western calendar, many contemporary writers have substituted the terms B.C.E. ("before common era") and C.E. ("common era") for the less accurate B.C. and A.D.

Of course, the Christian calendar has never been accepted everywhere in the world. The Islamic calendar, for example, dates the beginning of modern time from *Anno Hegirae* (A.H.), or the year of the Hegira—the year when Mohammed fled from Mecca to Medina (the Arabic word *hijira* means "flight"). The Prophet's flight took place in what the Western calendar calculates to be 622 C.E. (and more specifically, on July 16); that means that the year 2000 C.E. on the Western calendar was 421 A.H. Moving back and forth between the Western/Christian and Islamic calendars is further complicated by the fact that their years are not the same length (the Western calendar is calculated according to solar movement, the Islamic calendar according to lunar movement).

Geocentric

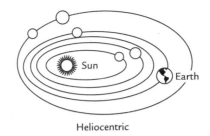

Heliocentric

Figure 1.1 *Competing Views of the Cosmos. Geocentric means "earth-centered"; heliocentric means "sun-centered" (Helios was the sun god of Greek mythology).*

revolved around the sun. In other words, Copernicus properly described the cosmos as heliocentric, not geocentric (see figure 1.1).

The heliocentric perspective did not catch on right away. For one thing, Copernicus was such a timid fellow that he did not publish his theory until he was literally on his deathbed. And even after it was published, many were reluctant to accept the Copernican view. Copernicus's ideas of the universe contradicted those espoused by the Church. Contradicting the Church meant facing possibly serious consequences (even death). Why risk it? At best, Copernicus's theory was a sophisticated guess. There was no way to test it.

Then, along came the Italian astronomer Galileo Galilei, who was born in Pisa in 1564. In 1609 Galileo was visiting in Venice where he learned of the newly invented telescopes. Back home, in 1610, Galileo built his own telescope and was the first to use one to examine the heavens. Galileo found evidence to support the heliocentric theory. In 1632 Galileo presented this evidence in a book entitled *Dialagoi ai due Massimi Sistemi,* or *Dialogue on the Two Great Systems of the World.*

Galileo understood the risk of publicly contradicting the teachings of the Church. In hopes of reducing his risk, Galileo wrote his book as if it were a dialogue between two scholars—one who argued for Ptolemy's (and the Church's) view, the other who propounded Copernicus's theory. At the end of the book, even though he had appeared to be winning the argument, the Copernican supporter suddenly gave up and admitted that the Ptolemaic view was the correct one. Because of this, asserted Galileo, his book *supported* the Church's teaching.

But Galileo had not been clever enough. The final surrender of the Copernican scholar did not make up for the fact that throughout the book the Ptolemaic supporter had been portrayed as an unpersuasive simpleton. Anyone who actually read the book was left with the impression that religious leaders had been proved wrong about the nature of the universe. Because of this, the book was judged to be heresy, and Galileo was summoned to Rome

"The doctrine that the earth is neither the center of the universe, nor immovable, but moves, even with a daily rotation, is absurd, and both philosophically and theologically false, and at the least an error of faith."

—Rome's judgment against Galileo

to face the Inquisition. In other words, the Church leaders put Galileo on trial.[3]

In his defense Galileo argued that there was nothing unholy or irreligious about his theory. After all, as Galileo reminded Church officials, *it was God* who had made the planets revolve around the sun. Galileo even asked the judges to look through his telescope to see the truth for themselves. Some of the judges did look but, stuffed full of Church doctrine, failed or refused to see.

In fact, Galileo's crime (if we must call it that) was to question the authority of the Church. Cardinal Robert Bellarmine, a leading theologian of the Church, as much as told Galileo that it *didn't matter* what proof he had: "Physical reality is not to be explained by mathematics but by the Scriptures and Church fathers." Ultimately, faced with excommunication, Galileo was forced to recant—to take back his theory—and promise to be silent.

Galileo died in 1642, having spent the final eight years of his life in enforced seclusion in Florence, Italy. Some twelve months later in England, Isaac Newton was born. Newton would salvage Galileo's reputation—and bring about the final undoing of the Church's authority over the workings of the natural world.

Newton was a brilliant mathematician—while still a student at Cambridge University, he discovered the binomial theorem—who became a professor at a very young age. His university career was put on hold in 1666, however, when the plague nearly turned London into a ghost town. Newton retreated to his family's farm in Lincolnshire. Farming was of little interest to Newton, so he built himself a laboratory wherein he might continue his research.

At least part of Newton's genius lay in his ability to look at data with a mind free of preconceived notions. He was not like the Church officials, who looked but could not see. Newton studied the works of his predecessors, conducted his own experiments, and saw.

In a book entitled *Philosophiae Naturalis Principia Mathematica* (1687), Newton posited his famous three laws of motion; from these Newton deduced the law of gravitation.[4]

$$v = \sqrt{2gh}$$

$$\sum_{i=1}^{n}$$

$$u = f(x, y)$$

Newton's most famous discovery, gravity, holds up planets. Newton also invented calculus, which often holds up students.

---

[3] The Inquisition was a tribunal or court of the Roman Catholic Church. It had been established in 1233 to deal with heresy, or crimes of unbelief. In 1542 (more than a century before it summoned Galileo), the Inquisition came to be called the Holy Office (though most still called it the Inquisition). In 1965 the Inquisition was replaced by the Roman Congregation for the Doctrine of Faith.

Don't confuse the Roman Inquisition with the much more notorious Spanish Inquisition. The latter had been established by King Ferdinand and Queen Isabella in 1478 to test the faith of converted Jews and, later, of converted Muslims. The Spanish Inquisition made frequent use of torture and capital punishment; the Roman Inquisition made only occasional use of such drastic measures.

[4] The story that Newton's discovery of the law of gravity was inspired when an apple fell on his head was first recounted by the French philosopher Voltaire (1694–1778), who claimed to have been told the tale by Newton's niece.

First Law of Motion—The Law of Inertia

Nothing moves unless and until some force acts upon it.

Second Law of Motion—Law of Acceleration

Force is equal to mass times acceleration ($F = m \times a$).

Third Law of Motion—Law of Action and Reaction

To every action there is always an opposed and equal reaction.

Law of Gravitation

Every particle in the universe attracts every other particle with a force that is proportional to the product of the masses of the two particles, and inversely proportional to the square of the distance between their centers. This force is directed along a line between their centers.

Newton completely undid the traditional view of the cosmos by making it clear that the earth was not the center of the universe. But Newton did more: His simple laws explained the movement of everything visible in the universe. These laws explained not only how planets moved about in the cosmos but why buildings sometimes fell down and bridges sometimes collapsed. Because of Newton, astronomers could calculate the orbits of the planets and engineers could build taller buildings and longer bridges.

> *"Nature and Nature's laws lay hid in Night:*
> *God said, 'Let Newton be!'*
> *And all was light."*
>
> —Alexander Pope

During the next century, religious leaders retreated from their position that their authority was the last word on the natural world. Newton's findings were so compelling that the Church *had* to retreat. But, the Church leaders maintained, it was still God, not gravity, that ordered the individual's place in the *social* world. As was frequently said, "The rich man in his castle, the poor man at his gate, God made them, high and lowly, and ordered their estate." In short, each individual was born into a particular "estate," or rigidly defined social group, and that was the condition in which he or she would die.

It is important to understand that a person's place in the social world was believed to be much more than an accident of birth: The estate or status into which the individual *was* born was the estate into which that person *ought* to have been born. According to religious leaders, God made kingly people kings, generally superior people rich, and generally inferior people poor. Moreover, men were superior to women, and (of course) Europeans were superior to everyone else. If you had been born a woman, or poor, or non-European, you had only gotten what you had deserved.

But people still wondered. Newton had stripped the universe of its great veil of mystery by showing that the planets were governed not by some unknowable cosmic force but by a few simple laws of physics. Surely the mysteries of the more immediate social world could be similarly resolved?

Technology, Urbanization, and Social Upheaval

And so it was that by the end of the eighteenth century, the traditional view of the social world came to be as suspect as the old views of the natural world. Skepticism ran deep. Were the rich really superior to the poor? Were men really superior to women? Were Europeans really superior to everyone else? Some people even had the audacity to propose that kings reigned not by divine right but simply to serve the needs of the people! If that was true, then if a king failed to serve his people, he should be replaced. This very revolutionary idea was reflected in the American Declaration of Independence in 1776 and the French Declaration of the Rights of Man and Citizen in 1789 and was behind the many revolutions that occurred in Europe in the late eighteenth and early-to-mid-nineteenth centuries.

Still, this new world was a fragile one. It lacked political, economic, and social stability. Compounding the problem was the fact that technology kept bringing about even more changes. Richard Arkwright's invention of the water-powered spinning frame, for example, led to the building of giant textile mills. The prospects for employment in the huge mills and other new factories (or *manufactories,* as they were called) lured hordes of people from rural areas to cities. Throughout Europe urban centers grew fast and furiously.

Consider: In 1800, 900,000 people lived in London, 600,000 people in Paris, and 170,000 people in Berlin. By 1900, the population of London was 4.7 million, of Paris 3.6 million, and of Berlin 2.7 million.

Among the new urbanites were millions of desperately poor people. Five-year-old children worked 15-hour days in factories, and countless numbers of unattached men and women could barely earn a living wage. Industry was dangerous, and if the factory didn't kill you, the open sewers and lack of clean water probably would. There was, of course, no health insurance. If you were injured and could not work, or if you lost your job for any reason, you would not eat. Here's how one medical historian has described the scene:

> In the big cities the death rate had reached such levels by the middle of the nineteenth century that there were serious doubts whether sufficient hands would be available for factories, and whether enough able-bodied recruits could be found for the . . . armies. . . . The big city

slums represented reservoirs of infectious diseases and epidemics, menacing not only the poor, but the life and health of the upper classes as well. (Ackernecht 1982, 212)

The new urbanites included many unfortunate souls—people working long hours for tiny wages, insufficient food, and inadequate shelter. These urban poor terrified the urban middle and upper classes—and it was easy to see why. There were obvious and strong links between poverty, riots, and revolutions. In France the urban poor were referred to as the dangerous classes.

The first European countries to experience widespread social upheaval were those countries that had first undergone industrialization: Britain, France, and Germany. It was thus no accident that the first sociologists emerged in those countries—these were the men (and a few women) who offered solutions to the pressing problems of modern industrial society.

One of the first to step forward was Auguste Comte. Born in France in 1798, Comte had witnessed firsthand the social chaos that had followed the French Revolution. Comte urged that some scholars should specialize in studying the problems of modern society and propose solutions. In 1842 Comte named this field of study *sociology*.[5]

As Comte came on the scene, people were saying that the main problem of modern society was that people no longer knew (or were satisfied with) their proper place in society. Instead of focusing on the good of the community and being content with their lot (or estate) in society, people had become selfish, greedy, and uppity. Generally, this sort of individualism was seen to be at the root of social chaos.

Comte's diagnosis was more specific. He argued that his contemporaries—people in this newly modern society—were suffering from "intellectual anarchy" because they no longer shared any beliefs about the way things ought to be.

Auguste Comte called himself the Great Priest of Humanity.

Comte suggested that the history of people's understanding of things (including the social world) followed what he called the Law of Three Stages. In the first stage, which Comte called the theological stage, religious leaders were the major sources of knowledge and intellectual authority. In the second stage, which Comte called the metaphysical, people turned to philosophers for guidance. In the final stage, which Comte called the positive or scientific, knowledge would be based on scientific principles.

Comte believed that social chaos would be overcome when people accepted that it was time to move on to the third stage

---

[5] Comte brought together the Greek word *socius*, or "companion," and the Latin word *logy*, or "study," to create the term *sociology*. In a similar fashion, it was Comte who coined the term *biology*.

The word *scientist* was coined by the English mineralogist and philosopher William Whewell in 1840— about the same time that Comte coined the term *sociology*.

of knowledge. Then, through the science of sociology especially, social harmony would be restored. Scientific sociologists would be the experts on the earthly social world, just as astronomers were the experts on the heavens.

Sociologists would use scientific methods to gain knowledge of the social world. Then they would advise people about how life ought to be lived. Comte went so far as to argue that sociology should take the place of religion as a source of answers to life's important questions: What is right and wrong? What does justice require? Convinced that sociologists should serve as the high priests of the modern world, Comte even wrote to the Roman Catholic pope suggesting that he abdicate and let Comte take his place! Toward the end of his life, Comte began to sign his letters with the title The Founder of Universal Religion, Great Priest of Humanity (see Coser 1971).

Comte's grandiose plans gained him a number of disciples— even the English philosopher John Stuart Mill wrote admiringly of Comte in his *System of Logic*. Some of Comte's followers formed a cult known as Comtism. But eventually he went too far. Comte grew to be more than a tad odd; frankly, he became a quack. By the time Comte died in 1857, sociology was more or less a laughingstock in France.

It would be some time before anyone dared to raise the subject of sociology in France. Eventually, however, the mantle of the discipline was taken up by a scholar named Émile Durkheim.

The Origins of Modern Sociology in France: Émile Durkheim

Like many of his contemporaries, Émile Durkheim[6] was alarmed by the chaos he saw in society. It was important, Durkheim said, to study society and social dynamics to find out what was going on. Yet, whereas many of his contemporaries were repelled by the individualism that had emerged in the late eighteenth and nineteenth centuries, Durkheim wasn't so sure individualism would be the undoing of society. In his first book, *The Division of Labor in Society*, published in 1893, Durkheim explored the sources of order and stability in the modern world. Based on his research, Durkheim argued that even a society filled with selfish individuals would hold together, because even selfish people *need* one another to survive.

---

[6]Émile is a man's name and is pronounced "A-meal," and not, as some mistakenly say, "Emily."

Imagine, for example, a premodern society in which people's livelihoods depended on their herds of sheep and their crops of vegetables. In such a society, most people would spend their time raising sheep and tending crops. Thus, the interests of each individual in the community would coincide—a bad year for sheep or turnips would be a bad year for everyone, and a drought would bring catastrophe for the entire group. In such a society, Durkheim suggested, with a very simple division of labor, people's work would be alike, and so would the people.

This likeness was important, Durkheim claimed, because it was what held people in premodern societies together. Likeness allowed people to experience *solidarity*. Their similar circumstances led them to have shared ideas, values, and goals—or what Durkheim called a *collective conscience*. Durkheim called this sort of solidarity *mechanical* because people in the community functioned together as a simple machine.

One of his professors warned Émile Durkheim (1858–1917) to abandon his plans to become a sociologist because "sociology leads to madness."

Life in modern society is very different, Durkheim said. People's labor is more specialized, and their interests are thus different (and even conflicting). An especially hot summer might be bad for the vegetable farmers but great for the grape growers. A railroad strike might be a disaster for cattle ranchers but a bonanza for chicken farmers, who could easily ship via truck.

Because of this specialized division of labor, said Durkheim, modern society could not be held together by likeness. The collective conscience—people's shared ideas, values, and goals—existed but was a very small part of people's overall consciences. As the division of labor in society became more complex, people became more different (and so, too, did their interests, values, beliefs, and the like).

This brought Durkheim to the point that was terrifying everyone else. If the collective conscience, or what people shared, was so limited, what would hold society together?

Durkheim reasoned that dissimilarity would not mean an end to group solidarity. Indeed, as people became more specialized and different, they grew more dependent on one another. For example, because they worked in specialized occupations, people needed each other as sources of trade. Durkheim called this sort of solidarity *organic solidarity,* because society functioned as a complex entity that depended on the proper functioning of a variety of parts, or organs. In premodern society people had been held together because of likeness; in modern society they were being held together because of their differences.

In *The Division of Labor in Society,* Durkheim thus articulated and resolved a paradox: However much they may want to be free and autonomous, people in modern society have no choice but to

From *Suicide* (1897) and
The Rules of the Sociological Method (1904)
ÉMILE DURKHEIM

What Is a Social Fact?

Sociological method as we practice it rests wholly on the basic principle that social facts must be studied as things, that is, as realities external to the individual.

The system of signs that I employ to express my thoughts, the monetary system I use to pay my debts, the credit instruments I utilize in my commercial relationships, the practices I follow in my profession, etc., all function independently of the use I make of them. Considering in turn each member of society, the foregoing remarks can be repeated for each single one of them. Thus there are ways of acting, thinking, and feeling which possess the remarkable property of existing outside the consciousness of the individual.

Not only are these types of behavior and thinking external to the individual, but they are endued with a compelling and coercive power by virtue of which, whether he wishes it or not, they impose themselves upon him. Undoubtedly when I conform to them of my own free will, this coercion is not felt or felt hardly at all, since it is unnecessary. . . . If I attempt to violate the rules of law they react against me so as to forestall my action, if there is still time. Alternatively, they annul it or make my action conform to the norm if it is already accomplished but capable of being reversed; or they cause me to pay the penalty for it if it is irreparable. . . . In other cases, although it may be indirect, constraint is no less effective. I am not forced to speak French with my compatriots, nor to use the legal currency, but it is impossible for me to do otherwise. . . .

Here, then, is a category of facts which present very special characteristics: [*social facts*] *consist of manners of acting, thinking and feeling external to the individual, which are invested with a coercive power by virtue of which they exercise control over him* [emphasis added].

[Social facts] have a reality *sui generis*.

---

maintain social ties. The structure of society—especially the way labor is divided in modern society—*forces* people to interact and to maintain social relationships with one another.

In that first book Durkheim not only made important discoveries about the relationship between the division of labor and social solidarity but also identified the key to understanding things sociologically. The way to understand society was to focus not on the psychological or biological attributes of individuals but on *the nature of society itself*. This led Durkheim to a fairly startling conclusion: Society and social phenomena actually do exist.

Sui generis is a Latin phrase that means "of its (or her, his, their) own kind." It's pronounced "SOO-ee JEN-air-us" in English. Durkheim stressed that social facts could not be reduced to psychological or biological facts. By this he meant that social facts (e.g., suicide rates) could only be explained by other social facts (e.g., changes in industry or the economy), and not by individual facts.

I call this a startling conclusion because prior to Durkheim, no one had really thought that social phenomena existed. Sure, the word *social* was used, but it meant little more than a group of individuals.

Throughout his life Durkheim continued to explore the social. He claimed that social phenomena have a reality *sui generis*—that is, a unique reality of their own—and that social facts must be distinguished from individual biological or psychological facts.

The discovery of the social provided Durkheim and his followers with a whole arsenal of tools with which to explain important and troubling phenomena. For example, Durkheim discovered that suicide was more than merely a personal thing—suicide *rates*, at least, were strongly influenced by social factors (the economy or political changes, for example).

Likewise, Durkheim would have held that if we want to understand why the rate of divorce increases or decreases, we should look for changes not in the psychological attributes of married people but in the wider society: divorce laws, the availability of child care, the economic pressures on family groups, and so on.

According to Durkheim, *sociology was to be the scientific study of social facts,* or of those things in society that transcend or are bigger than individuals. This is not to say, Durkheim observed, that individuals did not exist or play a role in the modern world. Yet, Durkheim insisted, individuals and individual facts were the domain of psychology and biology. Social facts were the domain of sociology.

1.1 Carefully consider Durkheim's definition of a *social fact*: "manners of acting, thinking, and feeling external to the individual, which are invested with a coercive power by virtue of which they exercise control over him." One category of social facts that interested Durkheim was rules for behavior (what sociologists call *norms*). Are norms truly social facts? Test this for yourself. Does the rule or norm that one must wear clothing to class qualify as a social fact according to Durkheim's definition? Explain why or why not.

STOP & REVIEW

Answers to Stop and Review questions are at the end of the chapter.

The Origins of Modern Sociology in Germany: Ferdinand Tönnies, Max Weber, and Karl Marx

As Durkheim was resolving the paradox of dependency in France, sociology was emerging in Germany under the leadership of Ferdinand Tönnies and Max Weber.[7] Like Durkheim, Tönnies compared premodern and modern societies to see how they differed. But Tönnies followed a different tact: He wished to understand how social relationships between people differed in the two types of societies.

His comparison of the premodern and modern social worlds led Tönnies to conclude that there are two basic categories of social relationships. The first category is made up of those social relationships that people enter into as *ends in and of themselves.* The second category includes social relationships that people enter into as *means to specific ends.*

Ferdinand Tönnies (1855–1936) was one of the first German sociologists.

People enter into relationships that are ends in and of themselves for emotional or affective reasons. An individual's relationship with his or her family is generally an example of this sort of relationship. Ideally we value our families not for what they can buy for us but because of our affection for them. Tönnies called these emotion-based relationships *Gemeinschaft,* or communal, relationships.

People enter into relationships that are a means to an end not out of affection or natural affinity but to achieve some specific goal (for example, financial gain). Tönnies called these goal-driven relationships *Gesellschaft,* or social, relationships.

In your own life, you no doubt experience both sorts of relationships. When you pick someone to be your friend because you enjoy his or her company (and hence think of the relationship itself as the end or benefit you seek), the nature of that friendship relationship is communal, or *Gemeinschaft.*

On the other hand, when you choose to associate with someone because it will help you achieve some goal, the relationship is *Gesellschaft.* For example, if you hire a tutor to help you with chemistry, your specific intention in creating the relationship is to achieve a better grade in chemistry. Of course, you may grow to like your tutor and continue to spend time with him or her even after you pass the final exam. In such a case, then, your relationship has changed from *Gesellschaft* to *Gemeinschaft.* Frequently, a

---

[7]The umlaut (¨) over the *o* in Tönnies' name indicates that the *o* is pronounced differently than one might expect. Generally, an umlaut indicates that the modern version of a word is missing a letter but that the word should be pronounced as if the letter were still present. The proper pronunciation of Tönnies is "TUH-nees."

It is also important to mention that Max Weber is pronounced "Max VAY-ber." (In German, W's are typically pronounced as V's.)

From *Gemeinschaft and Gesellschaft* (1887)

FERDINAND TÖNNIES

Gemeinschaft
(Guh-MINE-shoft)
intimate
association

Gesellschaft
(Guh-ZELL-shoft)
impersonal
association

All intimate, private, and exclusive living together, so we discover, is understood as life in Gemeinschaft (community). Gesellschaft (society) is public life—it is the world itself. In Gemeinschaft with family, one lives from birth on, bound to it in weal and woe. One goes into Gesellschaft as one goes into a strange country.

A young man is warned against bad Gesellschaft, but the expression bad Gemeinschaft violates the meaning of the word. . . .

A bride or groom knows that he or she goes into marriage as a complete Gemeinschaft of life. A Gesellschaft of life would be a contradiction in and of itself. . . .

The Gesellschaft exists in the realm of business, travel, or sciences.

particular relationship will have some elements of *Gemeinschaft* and some elements of *Gesellschaft*—for example, when you and your best friend decide to open a business together or when you join with a few other students to form a study group (which may involve as much socializing as studying).

Tönnies suggested that in modern society more relationships are means to an end, or *Gesellschaft*, than in premodern society, where most human relationships were *Gemeinschaft*, or communal. It is not so much that people themselves have changed. Rather, modern society itself forces people to work and live among others even when they lack emotional attachments. Think about your relationships with your professors. Chances are, these are *Gesellschaft*—means to ends and impersonal. In premodern times students would have been more likely to experience one-on-one, personal relationships with their teachers.

In any particular society one expects to find examples of both *Gemeinschaft* and *Gesellschaft* relationships, as well as relationships that change from one type to the other and relationships that are mixed. The difference between premodern and modern society, according to Tönnies, is that the proportions are different.

One of Tönnies' major contributions to the discipline of sociology was the suggestion that if we wish to understand social life, we have to understand that people enter into relationships for different reasons and that, depending on the type of relationship, we deal with people differently. *The type of the relationship determines the rules of the relationship.* If John believed that he was your best friend (a *Gemeinschaft* relationship), he would take it as a terrible betrayal if you sold him out to gain some benefit for yourself (that is, if you treated your relationship as *Gesellschaft*). On the other hand, the owner of the local supermarket should not be personally offended if you shop at a competitor's store to buy groceries at a cheaper price.

S T O P

&

R E V I E W

1.2 Which of the following types of relationships are most likely to be *Gemeinschaft*? Which are most likely to be *Gesellschaft*?

a. friend–friend
b. wife–husband
c. doctor–patient
d. retailer–customer
e. minister–parishioner
f. parent–child
g. worker–boss

Gemeinschaft
Gesellschaft

1.3 Generally, the banker–client relationship in modern society is *Gesellschaft*. Yet, from watching television advertisements for banks, one might conclude that the banker–client relationship is supposed to be *Gemeinschaft*. For example, many banks seem to make a big deal of claiming to be "friendly bankers" or "good neighbors."

Why would banks promote their services as *Gemeinschaft* rather than *Gesellschaft*? So they can get more buisnes

What, if any, danger is there in thinking of your relationship with your banker as *Gemeinschaft* when it really is *Gesellschaft*? Because you think they care about you

Max Weber was intrigued with Tönnies' idea that people act with a variety of motives and that the type of motive makes a difference in what they do. In Weber's eyes, especially, the fact that people had begun to see one another more and more as means to ends was a part of a larger trend. Weber called this trend the growth of *rational behavior.*

In everyday life we usually compare rational behavior and irrational behavior, as if to suggest that rational behavior is the only behavior that makes sense. But Weber used the term differently: For him *rational* was synonymous with *calculating.* If you have a goal and you sit down to plot how to achieve that goal most efficiently, *that* is being rational.

The opposite of rational for Weber was not *irrational,* but *nonrational* or noncalculating. To Weber nonrational behavior was behavior that was not especially geared to achieving some goal but was simply to be experienced or appreciated for itself.

As he studied history, Weber discovered that people in premodern societies were more likely to engage in nonrational

Max Weber (1864–1920) explored and expanded Tönnies' ideas about people's motivations for acting.

behavior. That is, they were less calculating and less concerned about achieving larger ends; they did things simply because such acts were pleasing. For example, when a premodern person had enough to eat and was living a comfortable life, he or she stopped working. Why not? What was the point of having more stuff than one needed? In premodern society people farmed and produced crafts not merely to earn a living; farming and crafting were *ways of life*, not simply ways to live.

People live a different sort of existence in modern society, said Weber. In the modern world individuals more frequently do things to achieve specific goals efficiently. Most of us work to live; we don't live to work. One way of behaving, for example, might be more fun or pleasing to us, but if there is a more efficient way to behave, we tend to choose efficiency over fun. In modern society, Weber observed, one is considered immature if one does things simply because one enjoys them!

This is not to say that everything that everyone does in modern society is rational (or done as a means to an end); nor is it to say that premodern people were never calculating. In any society, at any time, we can find examples of both kinds of behavior.

Consider art collectors. One sort of art collector, the nonrational, noncalculating kind, might acquire a painting because it evokes a feeling of beauty and awe. Another sort of art collector, the rational, calculating kind, might purchase the same painting but see it merely as a good investment.

Some golfers are nonrational. They play golf because they enjoy the challenge of chasing the little ball around the course so they can whack it. Then there are the rational players—they play golf because it is a good way to soften up customers or clients to make profitable deals.

In the university community I have met both rational and nonrational students. The rational student sees college as a means to an end (for example, a high-paying job); the nonrational student enjoys college because of what he or she learns. (Of course, many students have a mixture of motives.)

Weber wanted to know what it was about modern life that tended to inspire people to choose rational over nonrational behavior. The fact that rationalism seemed to be increasing in the Western world suggested to Weber that something important was happening and that, if we were to understand society and our place in it, we needed to understand the underlying causes and consequences of this trend.[8]

---

[8] Weber's most famous investigation focused on the relationship between religion and the growth of rationality. The result of this investigation, a book entitled *The Protestant Ethic and the Spirit of Capitalism*, first published in 1904–1905, remains one of the most famous works in sociology.

S T O P
&
R E V I E W

1.4 Think about two things you do for what Weber would call rational reasons. In what respect are your motives rational?

1.5 Think about two things you do for what Weber would call nonrational reasons. In what respect are your motives nonrational?

Karl Marx

Although many sociologists rank Karl Marx among the most important founders of sociology (along with Durkheim and Weber), it is curious that they do so. As one of his biographers wrote, "To write about Marx as a sociologist is to be hedged in with perils." Marx did not think of himself as a sociologist, and indeed, he was contemptuous of the sociologists whom he knew. As far as Marx was concerned, their focus on the social was entirely misdirected; only economics counted.

Marx was born in Germany in 1818 and studied philosophy and law. His early political activities made it impossible for him to achieve an academic position and, ultimately, even to stay in Germany. When he fled to France and continued to criticize the German government, Germany prevailed upon France to expel Marx. After a short stint in Brussels, he found himself in England, where he would stay almost continuously until his death in 1883. With Friedrich Engels, he wrote and published *The Communist Manifesto* in 1848. This brief document helped shape the revolutions that re-created much of the world over the course of the next century.

Karl Marx (1818–1883) is perhaps best known as the "father" of communism.

Marx's conception of the world was a singular one. In his mind, the most crucial thing about a society was its primary mode of production and distribution of goods—that is, its economic system. Given this, Marx argued, the people of any society could be divided into two distinct classes: the bourgeoisie and the proletariat. The bourgeoisie consisted of the people who owned the means of production—specifically, the owners of the factories that produced the goods sold and distributed throughout society. The proletariat consisted of the workers—the people who survived by selling their labor to the bourgeoisie. As far as Marx was concerned, everything else—ideas, values, social conventions, art, literature, morals, law, and even religion—was "epiphenomenal," or secondary to and in the service of the economic realities of society.

Thus, for example, Marx argued that religion was the "opium of the people" and existed only to mask the inequalities and injuries of the economic system. Religion had no real importance in the overall scheme of things because once the people woke up and realized the real injustices of the economic system, there would be no need for religion, and it would disappear.

To say that Marx was not a sociologist is not to say that he did not have a great influence on sociology. He did. His influence was of two sorts. First, many "Marxist" sociologists have made important contributions to modern sociology. As you will read in chapter 3, a major school of sociologists is a proponent of what some call the *conflict tradition* or the *Marxist tradition*. As you will learn later in this text, some Marxist concepts (for example, ideology and alienation) have even been adopted by mainstream sociologists.

Second, Marx's work had a tremendous impact on sociology because of its influence on Max Weber. Weber was still in school when Marx died, but he came of age in an era when Marx's ideas were hotly debated in Germany. Indeed, it has been said that much of Weber's sociology was a *debate with the ghost of Karl Marx*. More specifically, much of what Weber wrote was a rejection of Marx's "monocausal" theory that the economic system was the driving force behind all things social. There are, Weber said, no *ultimate* causes—we must look not only at the influence of economic or material things but also at the influence of ideas and values.

The Origins of Modern Sociology in England: Herbert Spencer

The pioneering English sociologist Herbert Spencer believed that society was governed by laws in much the same way that the physical world was. His interest lay in understanding how societies evolve; his belief was that societies evolve just as animal species do.

Spencer's work on evolution was first published in 1852.[9] Six years later, Charles Darwin published his theory of evolution in *On the Origin of Species by Means of Natural Selection, or the Preservation of Favored Races in the Struggle for Life.* After Darwin's work was published, Spencer's ideas came to be known as social Darwinism.[10]

---

[9]"A Theory of Population, Deduced from the General Law of Animal Fertility," *Westminster Review* LVII (1852). It was in this work that Spencer introduced the phrase "survival of the fittest."

[10]Charles Darwin, the English naturalist, published *On the Origins of Species* in 1859. Given the timing, it is curious that Darwin's theory was not labeled "natural Spencerism" instead of Spencer's theory being labeled "social Darwinism."

Darwin's theory would have been published even later had it not been for what must have seemed (to Darwin, at least) the most appalling coincidence. Fourteen years after returning home from his famous trip on the HMS *Beagle*, Darwin was still gathering evidence for his theory (knowing it would be very controversial). Then, in 1857, another English scientist, Alfred Russel Wallace, fell ill in Borneo. According to the story, Wallace passed his three days in bed by working up a theory of evolution that was in many respects identical to Darwin's. Wallace sent his paper to Darwin for comments. Darwin was dumbfounded. Not wanting to become a historical also-ran, Darwin rushed his *On the Origin of Species* into print even though he believed it to be incomplete. For the rest of his life, Darwin referred to his work as a mere abstract.

Herbert Spencer (1820–1903) promoted the theory of social Darwinism (sort of looked like Ebenezer Scrooge, didn't he?).

Spencer's theories were very popular in some circles. Those who adhered to social Darwinism saw the world as a jungle in which only the superior ought to prosper. Especially popular was the principle that Spencer referred to as *survival of the fittest*. This principle summed up Spencer's basic thesis that if we simply leave people alone to compete, the best will survive and the inferior will perish. The overall result of natural social evolution, according to Spencer, is that society gets better over time. However, social improvement will continue only so long as people do not interfere with the natural course of things. Consequently, Spencer and his followers opposed any kind of state assistance to the poor; they even opposed public schools.

In the wrong hands this principle can be deadly. For example, it was used to justify the superior positions in society of whites over blacks and rich over poor. In this respect Spencer's theory was hardly an improvement on the premodern theories of social status, which had held that God placed people in the estates they deserved. Baldly stated, according to Spencerian doctrine, if someone was rich, it was because he or she was superior; if blacks had a difficult time thriving in white society, it was because they were inferior.

In the United States and Germany, especially, there were many who found Spencer's ideas compelling. With social Darwinism they could justify the enslavement of Africans and the near genocide of Native Americans. Later, in Germany, principles of social Darwinism were invoked by the Nazis to justify their decision to exterminate the Jews.

Charles Loring Brace (1826–1890), who founded the Children's Aid Society in the United States, had this to say about Spencer's ideas:

"Would not mankind take chloroform if they had no future but Spencer's?"

Spencer viewed social competition as a kind of purifying process in which the weak were weeded out. Spencer cautioned his readers not to feel pity for the losers—the poor, weak, or otherwise disadvantaged. Social competition, Spencer claimed, is a "stern discipline, which is a little cruel that it may be very kind." He wrote about the pain and suffering (and deaths) of "inferior" people. These deaths only *seemed* to be tragic, said Spencer. They are not tragic, but beneficial to society!

> When regarded not separately but in connection with the interests of universal humanity, these harsh fatalities are seen to be full of beneficence—the same beneficence which brings to early graves the children of diseased parents and singles out [some but not others to be] victims of epidemics. (1852)

The bottom line, said Spencer, is we must face facts: The competition to survive will be won by the best because those who survive and thrive, by definition, are the "best." Showing pity for social losers only leads to "spurious philanthropy" and is a waste of time, effort, and money. As one of Spencer's students warned, if we do not like survival of the fittest, we have only one possible alternative, and that is the survival of the unfittest. The former is the law of civilization; the latter is the law of anticivilization. We have our choice between the two, or we can go on, as in the past, vacillating between the two, but a third plan [offering help to the poor and helpless] for nourishing the unfittest and yet advancing civilization, no man will ever find. (Sumner 1934, II)

Sociology in the United States

Sociology came to prominence in the United States later than it had in Europe, possibly because the United States experienced the social chaos of the Industrial Revolution later than France, England, or Germany. Whereas the process of industrialization was virtually completed in the European nations by 1850, the United States did not experience full-fledged industrialization until after it fought its civil war in the 1860s.

The first sociology course was taught by William Graham Sumner, a professor at Yale University. The first sociology department in the United States was organized in 1892, at the University of Chicago. In 1905 sociologists organized the American Sociological Society (soon changed to the American Sociological Association for reasons that might seem obvious). The goal of the ASA was and is to promote the scientific study of society.

Early U.S. sociologists differed from their European counterparts in that they did not focus all their efforts on building sweeping theories of society. In addition to theory building, the U.S. sociologists concentrated on solving the specific social problems—poverty, crime—that had arisen (or so it was thought) as a consequence of the large immigrant population. In other words, while European sociologists were attempting to build sociology into a *basic* science like physics or chemistry, many of the early U.S. sociologists treated sociology as an *applied* science, like engineering. Indeed, some of these sociologists called themselves social engineers.

Out of this initial enthusiasm for social engineering came the first sociologist to win the Nobel Prize: Jane Addams. In 1889 Addams and a colleague, Ellen Gates Starr, founded Hull House, a settlement house that served the needs of the poor in Chicago. Hull House was also the base from which Addams conducted her research into the causes and consequences of poverty. Other Chicago sociologists specialized in studying specific manifestations of modernity—hobos, dance hall girls, prostitution, gambling, and the like. In general, the focus of early sociology in the United States was as much on social reform as on theory building.

Jane Addams (1860–1935) was the first sociologist to win a Nobel Prize.

*W. E. B. Du Bois
(1868–1963) was
highly critical of the
race system in the
United States.*

Born in Great Barrington, MA, William Edward Burghardt (W. E. B.) Du Bois was the first person of African descent to receive a Ph.D. from Harvard University. After a short stint as an instructor at the University of Pennsylvania, he took a job at Atlanta University in 1897. From 1933 to 1944, Du Bois chaired the department of sociology at the university.

Like Marx, Du Bois saw society as conflict-ridden; but Du Bois argued that Marx had overlooked the importance of race and ethnicity in modern society. According to Du Bois, it was not enough to focus on economic differences in society—racial differences were even more important. Convinced that once the injustice of the race system in the United States had been exposed, it would be remedied, Du Bois published more than seventy books on race and race relations, including *The Philadelphia Negro* (1899), *The Souls of Black Folk* (1903), *Darkwater* (1920), and *Color and Democracy* (1945). Turning to direct political activism, in 1909 Du Bois helped found the National Negro Committee, which soon came to be known as the National Association for the Advancement of Colored People (NAACP). Du Bois was a vocal critic of other black leaders—like Booker T. Washington—whom he saw as too willing to compromise the position of blacks in American society. Du Bois, it has been said, "took the lead in making the United States and the World recognize that racial prejudice was not a mere matter of Negroes being persecuted but was a cancer which poisoned the whole civilization of the United States" (James 1967, 365). Many members of the NAACP found his ideas too radical—especially after he gave up on the idea of integration and began to promote the idea of segregation—and eventually he was dismissed from the NAACP. In 1961 Du Bois renounced his U.S. citizenship and moved to Ghana, where he lived until his death.

The Place of Sociology in Modern Society

The founders of sociology in Europe—Durkheim, Tönnies, Weber, and Spencer, as well as Americans like Sumner and Addams who followed them—brought sociology from laughingstock to prominence by the end of the nineteenth century. Although (fortunately) the more dangerous ideas of Spencer have been largely discredited, the works of the others are still held up as models of good sociological work. The articles and books by Durkheim and Weber, especially, continue to have a tremendous impact on sociologists. In spite of their many differences, each of these scholars insisted that the social world was worthy of study. Each believed that by bringing to bear the tools of science on the social world, he or she could help make sense of it. Like Copernicus, who was skeptical of the traditional view of the natural world, these sociologists were skeptical of traditional views of the social world. As we will explore in the following chapters, the tradition of skepticism continues.

Chapter Review

1. Make a list of the sociological concepts that you learned in this chapter. Define each term. (*Hint:* You will learn the most from this exercise if, in addition to defining each concept, you create an example of it in your own words.)

2. What sorts of social changes helped to lead people to question the nature of social reality (and thereby helped to spur the creation of sociology)?

3. List two of your relationships that are *Gemeinschaft* and two that are *Gesellschaft*. Explain why you have categorized each relationship as either *Gemeinschaft* or *Gesellschaft*. Then assume that you had to leave some of your relationships. Which would be easier to replace—those that are *Gemeinschaft* or those that are *Gesellschaft*? Why?

4. Weber distinguished between rational and nonrational behavior but said that many actual behaviors contain elements of both rationality and nonrationality. What is a behavior that you do that contains elements of both rationality and nonrationality? Explain what is rational and what is nonrational about this behavior.

Answers and Discussion

1.1 Durkheim said that social facts were "manners of acting, thinking and feeling external to the individual, which are vested with a coercive power by virtue of which they exercise control over him."

The norm that one must wear clothes is a social fact. It is external to the individual (it exists outside of him or her and would still exist even if the individual claimed it did not exist). Does this norm have coercive power? Yes. Imagine that you wanted to go to class in the nude. Wouldn't there be some coercion used against you either to prevent you from doing this or to punish you after the fact?

1.2 The types of relationships that are mostly likely to be *Gemeinschaft* (that is, personal and close) are friend–friend, wife–husband, minister-parishioner, and parent–child. The types of relationships most likely to be *Gesellschaft* are doctor–patient, retailer–customer, and worker–boss.

STOP
&
REVIEW

1.3 Why would banks advertise as if they had *Gemeinschaft* relations with their customers? Probably because they know that people would choose to interact with friends rather than cold and impersonal bankers. The thing is, however, a bank cannot be your friend. The law requires banks, for example, to treat people equally and to do such things as foreclose on mortgages when people don't pay on time. Those are certainly not behaviors one would expect from one's friends! The tension between *Gemeinschaft* and *Gesellschaft* relations also explains why many wise people advise against lending money to friends and family members.

1.4 and 1.5 These two questions could be answered in a number of ways. By way of example, here are my answers:

1.4 Two things I do for what Weber would call rational reasons:
   a. Pay my bills each month. Paying my bills is a clear example of doing something as a means to an end (keeping a decent credit rating).
   b. Show up for class on time. This is a means to a couple of practical ends: keeping my students calm (of course, they get upset if I'm late and they don't get to spend the entire class period with me) and keeping my chairperson happy.

1.5 Two things I do for what Weber would call nonrational reasons:
   a. Build furniture. Building things is a pleasurable activity. It is not a rational activity because it always costs me more to make something than it would to buy it. Moreover, although I have sold a few pieces of my furniture, I never have made more than I paid for the materials.
   b. Do graphics on my computer—it's fun.

My insight: As I was answering these questions, I stumbled onto an important insight: Question 1.5 was really hard to answer. I spent 10 minutes not being able to think of a single thing that I do for nonrational reasons.

Did you have the same problem? Of course, I do nonrational things; it's just that I "rationalize" these activities. Consider one of my answers—building furniture. I was tempted to say that I build furniture as a means to an end—carpentry helps me reduce stress, and reducing stress is important if I am going to be a productive worker. But, really, carpentry is an end in and of itself; it's something I do because I enjoy it.

Similarly, I was tempted to claim that I do computer graphics because they help me teach. But it is simply not rational to spend 45 minutes designing the perfect graphic to illustrate one sociological concept. Again, I do it because I enjoy it. It is a happy coincidence that I can use graphics in the classroom.

It is almost as if I am reluctant to admit to spending time in nonrational ways, as if nonrational behavior is wasteful. The fact that I rationalize my behavior this way suggests that Weber was on to something important when he observed that life was becoming more rational. I feel almost guilty when I do stuff for enjoyment and tend not to do fun stuff unless I can rationalize it—and thereby make it seem rational.

The Sociological Eye

M odern sociologists continue to be inspired by two important qualities stressed by early sociologists: (1) the focus on the social and (2) skepticism.

The Focus on the Social

It is this focus on the social that makes the sociological perspective unique. Because of this social focus, the sociological perspective allows sociologists to see much that escapes the notice of other observers.

The American sociologist C. Wright Mills sharpened the sociological perspective with his concept of the *sociological imagination*. The defining quality of the sociological imagination, Mills said, is the ability to look beyond what he called the *personal troubles* of individuals to see the *social issues* operating in the larger society.

> The sociological imagination enables its possessor to understand the larger historical scene in terms of its meaning for the inner life and the external career of a variety of individuals. . . .
>
> The first fruit of this imagination—and the lesson of the social science that embodies it—is the idea that the individual can understand his own experience and gauge his own fate only by locating himself within his period, that he can know his own chances in life only by becoming aware of those of all individuals in his circumstances. (1959, 5)

For American sociologist C. Wright Mills (1916–1962), the key to the sociological imagination was the ability to distinguish between personal troubles and social issues.

Mills argued that most individuals feel trapped by the problems they encounter—and that their sense of entrapment comes from believing that their personal troubles are necessarily of their own making. Mills believed that sociologists can help rescue people from such traps.

Without guidance from the sociological imagination, we are tempted to attack all problems by treating individuals. This is because people have trouble seeing beyond their personal and immediate circumstances. With such limited vision or imagination, people cannot discover that some of their worst problems are a result of *social* forces.

The advantage of the sociological imagination or perspective, then, as Mills discovered, is that it opens up new resources for problem solving. Many of the most serious problems experienced by individuals, such as unemployment, have *social* causes, so it is futile to try to remedy or fix them at the individual level.

> When, in a city of 100,000, only one man is unemployed, that is his personal trouble, and for its relief we properly look to the character of the man, his skills, and his immediate opportunities. But when in a nation of 50 million employees, 15 million men are unemployed, that is a [social] issue, and we may not hope to find its solution within the range of opportunities open to any one individual. . . . Both the correct statement of the problem and the range of possible solutions require us to consider the economic and political institutions of society, and not merely the personal situation and character of a scatter of individuals. (Mills 1959, 9)

Or, Mills says, consider marriage:

> Inside a marriage a man and a woman may experience personal troubles, but when the divorce rate during the first four years of marriage is 250 out of every 1,000 attempts, this is an indication of a structural [social] issue having to do with the institutions of marriage and the family and other institutions that bear upon them. (1959, 9)

As mentioned briefly in chapter 1, the French sociologist Émile Durkheim applied the sociological perspective to the problem of suicide. To most of Durkheim's colleagues, the decision to kill oneself seemed to be the most personal and individual of decisions. But, said Durkheim, *suicide is also a social issue.* From studying the differences in suicide statistics across different European countries, Durkheim found that the rate of suicide tended to vary with the degree of *social integration* in a particular society. In other words, *the rate of suicide varies with the degree to which people have strong ties to their social groups.*

More specifically, Durkheim found that people with weaker or fewer ties to their social groups were more likely to commit suicide. This finding helped to explain the fact that single people had higher rates of suicide than married people. Likewise, understanding the relationship between suicide and social integration helped to explain why Protestants (who are encouraged by their religion to be independent) had higher suicide rates than Catholics.

The sociological perspective of Durkheim, or what Mills later called the sociological imagination, suggested that suicide is not simply an individual problem, or personal trouble. Durkheim himself argued that the rate of suicide would decrease if more emphasis were placed on integrating people into society. To put it another way, according to Durkheim, the rate of suicide would drop if people were given more opportunities to bond with one another.

It is easy to find examples of situations in which the sociological imagination or perspective adds to our understanding. Sociologists who study organizations, for example, have discovered that working in a bureaucracy can have a tremendous impact on people's behavior. Regardless of how warm and caring people are *off* the job, their "on-the-job personalities" can be rigid, authoritarian, and uncaring—because that is how the structure of the organization forces them to be. People who work in bureaucracies have to follow the rules and act without regard for differences among individual clients. (Just remember this the next time you visit the registrar's office! If you want to make the system work for you, you need to take into account the ways in which the person across the counter is constrained by his or her position.)

Likewise, sociologists who study social inequality have examined the fact that people of different races are treated differently in most societies. This inequity should come as no surprise to you. But what may surprise you is that racial discrimination is not merely a matter of individuals being nasty to one another. Frequently, racism is a result of factors built into social systems. Because of this *institutional racism*, individuals may get locked into a larger pattern of racist behavior, perhaps without even being aware of it, let alone being able to resist it. The admissions officer at the exclusive private university who is told to give preference to the children of alumni is perpetuating racist admissions policies (because most of the alumni are white), even though he or she may personally abhor racism. The loan officer at the bank who is told not to approve loans for homes in certain parts of the city (populated mainly by African Americans) may not be racist, but her institution forces her to act as if she is. This does not, of course, excuse racist activities, but it does suggest that the fight against racism has to involve more than educating individuals. We have to treat this problem (or, as Mills would say, this *social issue*) at a higher level.

2.1 Describe the difference between crime as a personal trouble and crime as a social issue.

Skepticism

Like their nineteenth-century predecessors, contemporary sociologists are skeptical of commonly accepted explanations of things. Indeed, skepticism is an important foundation of scientific curiosity. If one accepts everyday explanations for things, there is no reason to inquire further. For example, in years past, only those who were skeptical of the commonly accepted "fact" that humans could not fly attempted to build "aeroplanes." Similarly, in the early nineteenth century, engineers believed that buildings could not be constructed more than a few stories high. But the skeptics among them, working with technology and the laws of physics, designed the immense structures that dominate the skylines of modern cities.

Sociologists are especially skeptical about the impact of social things. As an outgrowth of his skepticism, American sociologist Robert K. Merton provided us with an important research technique. Merton said that really understanding social things involves identifying both their *manifest* (intended and obvious) and *latent* (unintended and frequently hidden) consequences. Merton called these consequences functions.

One of the most obvious examples of the importance of latent consequences involves the modern experience with prisons. The manifest function of the prison system is to protect society by locking up dangerous criminals. As many researchers have found, however, one of the latent functions of the prison system is the production of more knowledgeable criminals—that is, convicts learn from one another in prison about how to commit crimes!

Here are two more examples of manifest versus latent functions. The first has to do with medicine.

In the nineteenth century there were hundreds of medical schools throughout the United States. The quality of these schools was uneven: Some offered hands-on training while others stressed only theory. Some required three years of study after four years of college, while others required three years of medical study but no college degree. Some taught traditional ("allopathic") medicine, while others pursued more novel approaches (such as homeopathy, osteopathy, chiropractic, and botanical medicine). Some had well-endowed laboratories and libraries, while others did not.

In the early twentieth century, some members of the American medical profession believed that society would be better off if its physicians were trained in a more scientific manner. In 1910 the American Medical Association (AMA) commissioned one of its members, Abraham Flexner, to conduct a study of medical schools throughout the country. As he would report to the AMA, Flexner was appalled at the variety of training methods he encountered. Citing the Flexner Report as evidence, the AMA lobbied government

---

Nail Down That Distinction
Between Manifest and Latent Functions!

University Education

Manifest function: educate young adults

Latent function: keep young adults out of the job market, thereby easing competition for older adults

Mother's Day and Father's Day

Manifest function: provide an opportunity to express gratitude to one's parents

Latent function: help greeting card companies boost sales in the spring and summer months

Carrying a Briefcase

Manifest function: carry one's stuff

Latent function: indicate one's occupational status (for example, demonstrate that one is employed doing nonmanual labor)

---

officials to clamp down on schools that did not offer a specific sort of training. As a result, hundreds of medical schools were forced to close their doors.

The manifest, or intended, consequence of tightening regulations for medical schools was to produce better-trained physicians. But this change in regulations had several latent consequences as well. One latent consequence was that practitioners who could not afford the more expensive training offered by traditional schools or who did not agree with traditional notions of medicine were forced out of the profession.[1] Tightened regulations also forced medical schools that trained women and African Americans to close their doors because they could not afford the expensive laboratory equipment and libraries that the AMA rules required. (Note that Flexner presented

---

[1] It is important to point out that even in the early twentieth century, regular (allopathic) medical practitioners could not successfully treat diseases like tuberculosis, syphilis, and polio. Nor were such things as the importance of wearing rubber gloves universally accepted among medical personnel (many hospitals did not provide gloves for surgeons, and most surgeons did not want the added expense of purchasing their own). Furthermore, regular medical treatments frequently did more harm than good. For example, during the nineteenth century, many people died from being "bled" by their physicians, who had hoped to drain out "bad humors" from the body. Some treatments even called for the letting of more blood than we now know exists in the entire body (George Washington was said to have met his death this way). In contrast, alternative medical approaches generally took a less invasive, more supportive approach. Thus, ironically, one was generally safer *not* being treated by regular medical personnel.

no evidence that the patients of physicians trained in alternative schools without laboratories and libraries were worse off than the patients of physicians who had trained at, say, Harvard.) And finally, doctors trained in the traditional manner no longer had to compete with the oftentimes more popular nontraditional practitioners.

Here is an example of how unintended or latent functions may have an impact on one aspect of *your* life.

New college professors generally must endure a six-year probationary period. At the end of this time, the quality of the professor's teaching, research, and service work is evaluated by senior colleagues. If the accomplishments of the probationary professor are deemed acceptable, they will grant him or her *tenure.* But if he or she has not lived up to expectations, the professor is denied tenure and forced to leave the university.

In the past few decades, most universities and colleges have tightened up their tenure requirements. Fifty years ago, tenure was practically a given. Today, things are different; most junior professors[2] spend their first years working like crazy to fulfill tenure requirements. One of the most important requirements is to conduct research and publish the results. As a rule of thumb, if you don't publish a fair amount, you will be denied tenure (hence the so-called publish-or-perish rule).

The manifest function, or intended consequence, of emphasizing the importance of research for tenure is to produce more knowledge of the natural and social world. Universities do not want professors who simply sit around doing nothing. Professors should be out there, studying and making scholarly contributions. The latent function or consequence, however, is that some professors neglect their teaching responsibilities to do their research.[3]

This is not to say that all latent functions or consequences have a negative impact on society's usual functioning or, as sociologists would put it, are *dysfunctional.*[4] The unintended consequence of an action can be positive, or *functional.* For example, the manifest function of a neighborhood party is to have fun; a latent function

---

[2]Untenured professors typically are called assistant professors. Among the senior professors who have tenure, there are two ranks: associate professor and full professor.

[3]Fortunately, as we begin the twenty-first century, university officials seem to be backtracking a bit and are once again beginning to emphasize the importance of teaching. At my own university, for example, candidates for tenure and promotion are required to show a measure of success in both teaching and research.

[4]Notice the spelling of *dysfunctional.* The *dys* prefix, which has its roots in the Greek language, suggests that something is defective, difficult, or painful. This prefix is frequently encountered in medicine—for example, *dysentery* ("painful intestine"), *dyspeptic* ("painful digestion"), or *dystrophy* ("abnormal growth"). On the other hand, the *dis* prefix, which is derived from Latin, tends to mean "apart," "asunder," or "deprived of"—for example, *dissemble, disable,* or *disrespect.* So, although the two prefixes are pronounced the same in English, they carry different meanings.

can be to bring neighbors together or promote crime fighting. The manifest function of riding bicycles to work is to increase riders' fitness; a latent function can be fewer cars on the road or less air pollution.

Merton's distinction between manifest and latent functions is important. It reminds us to look beyond the obvious—frequently, the least obvious consequences are the most important ones.

2.2 For each of these common social events, list as many manifest and latent functions as you can:

    a. college athletics

    b. attending church

    c. attending sociology class

Chapter Review

1. Make a list of the sociological concepts that you learned in this chapter. Define each term. (*Hint:* You will learn the most from this exercise if, in addition to defining each concept, you create an example of it in your own words.)

2. Sociologists often have a difficult time persuading lay people that there is something to be gained by looking at divorce, racism, poverty (or anything else, for that matter) as a social issue rather than just a personal trouble. In your considered judgment, why might this be so?

3. What is a possible benefit of looking for latent as well as manifest functions of things in the social world?

Answers and Discussion

2.1 According to Mills's perspective, crime as a personal trouble involves the circumstances and problems of the people who are directly touched by the crime. For example, Joe Student was arrested for breaking and entering. Why on earth did Joe do such a thing (seeking the cause of the crime in Joe's personal circumstances)?

Crime as a social issue involves looking at the larger aspects of crime and the ways these are affected by historical and social circumstances. For example, the rate of burglaries is on the increase. What is happening in the rest of society (perhaps in the economic arena) that might be influencing this?

2.2

    a. Manifest functions of college athletics include enhancing school spirit, helping students develop physical as well as mental skills, and increasing the fame of the college or university. Latent functions include helping students who otherwise would not be able to attend college (because of poverty, for example) to do so by winning athletic scholarships, acting as a training ground for future professional athletes, and exploiting the talents of athletes from underprivileged backgrounds without actually having to provide a real education for them. (That's pretty cynical, isn't it? That last one might be a dysfunction of college athletics.)

b. Manifest functions of church attendance include worshiping and joining with others to celebrate important beliefs. Latent functions include having an opportunity to dress up and see what other people are wearing and how their children behave.

c. Manifest functions of attending class regularly include learning the assigned material more thoroughly and having the opportunity to hear brilliant lectures by your professors. Latent functions include impressing your professors with the sincerity of your quest for knowledge and having more opportunities to make friends with other students, or even having a quiet time to write a letter.

Science and Fuzzy Objects

Specialization in Sociology

"It is difficult to paint a clear picture of a fuzzy object."

—Ludwig Josef Wittgenstein (1959)

The first time I read Wittgenstein's statement,[1] I was struck by how profoundly it applied to sociology. As far as I was concerned, there was hardly anything more fuzzy than sociological phenomena. Many of my colleagues would probably not want to admit that what they do is study fuzzy stuff, but Wittgenstein's observation does help to explain why sociologists rarely make statements like "this causes that" or "if you do that, then this definitely will happen." Generally, sociologists do not like to commit themselves that far; they are more likely to say something to the effect that "if that happens, then it is likely that this will happen."

This really bugs some sociology students—the ones who like things cut and dried, who want their knowledge to be clear, definite, and certain. Unfortunately for these students, there is not much of that sort of knowledge in sociology.

I hasten to point out that the fact that many of sociologists' predictions about what will happen are probabilistic rather than certain is in no way the fault of sociology! That's where Wittgenstein's point that it is hard to paint a clear picture of a fuzzy object comes in. The stuff that sociologists study is some of the fuzziest in the universe.

Most sociologists long ago accepted that to understand a particular social event or interaction, they must take a multitude of factors into account. They also accepted that generally it is

---

[1] The philosopher Wittgenstein (VIT-gen-stine) was born in Vienna in 1889 but became a naturalized British subject in 1938. Before turning to philosophy, Wittgenstein had studied engineering.

35

impossible to make predictions with absolute assurance. We can frequently predict what *most* people will *likely* do under particular sets of circumstances, but we can offer no guarantees.

Of course, sociology is not the only science that studies fuzzy objects. But many of those working in other disciplines have demonstrated a tremendous ability to ignore the fuzzy qualities of the subjects that they study.

There have been important exceptions, however. In 1927 physicist Werner Heisenberg published his account of what he called the *uncertainty principle*. Heisenberg argued that there are important limits on science's ability to measure and predict the behavior of physical objects. To support his argument, Heisenberg demonstrated that *"it is impossible to measure, predict, or know both the position and momentum simultaneously of a particle, with unlimited precision in both quantities."* (For example, to measure a particle's position, one must interfere with its momentum.) Heisenberg's point stunned many physical scientists:

Albert Einstein rejected Heisenberg's uncertainty principle on the grounds that "God does not play dice with the universe." One suspects, then, that, his hair notwithstanding, Einstein was not comfortable with fuzzy objects.

> [Many physicists believed] that if the positions and velocities of all the bits of matter in the universe were known at one time, and if all the various force laws were known, the positions and velocities of all these bits of matter could be calculated and predicted for any future time. All future effects would be the result of earlier causes. Even if the task of measuring all these positions and velocities were humanly impossible, and even if the discovery of all appropriate laws were impossible, nevertheless the positions and velocities did exist at a previous time and the laws do exist; therefore the future is predetermined.

> But Heisenberg's uncertainty principle says this is not so. It is, in principle, impossible to make the measurements with sufficient precision or even to calculate them from the future positions and velocities because we cannot know the future positions and velocities. (Speilberg and Anderson 1987, 218–219)

This was unsettling news to many physicists who wanted to believe that if they kept working at it, they would someday (at least theoretically) be able to measure and predict everything in the cosmos.

How have scientists learned to cope with the fuzziness or indeterminacy of the physical world? Some physical scientists seem simply to ignore it. And, in point of fact, a great deal of scientific progress can be made by treating phenomena as if they are predictable. Recently, however, some scientists have become more receptive to the unpredictable or chaotic nature of the world. And, once they open their eyes,

> chaos seems to be everywhere. A rising column of cigarette smoke breaks into wild swirls. A flag snaps back and forth in the wind. A

dripping faucet goes from a steady pattern to a random one. Chaos appears in the behavior of the weather, the behavior of an airplane in flight, the behavior of cars clustering on an expressway, the behavior of oil flowing in underground pipes. . . . That realization has begun to change the way business executives make decisions about insurance, the way astronomers look at the solar system, the way political theorists talk about the stresses leading to armed conflict. (Gleick 1987, 5)

Chaos theorists work forward from the principle they call *sensitive dependence on initial conditions*—that is, the idea that a very small initial difference may lead to an enormous change to the outcome. In meteorological studies (studies of the weather), this principle is sometimes called the Butterfly Effect, based on the notion that a butterfly stirring the air today in Seattle can transform storm systems next month in Singapore.

You might be wondering why I have taken us so far afield from sociology. Why discuss physics? I do have a point: We must not dismiss scientific explanations and predictions merely because they do not pan out in all instances. The inability of physicists to predict both the position and momentum of particles with absolute accuracy does not undermine physics' claim to being a science. Likewise, the fact that sociologists cannot offer predictions with absolute certainty does not make their work less scientific. As many scientists in all disciplines are now learning, one must learn to accept the existence of fuzzy objects.

Dividing Up the Task

In addition to being fuzzy, society is big—so big that it is impossible to look at the whole of it at once. Therefore, most sociologists specialize by taking chunks of society and making these their particular concerns. Sociologists also tend to specialize in how they approach the study of their chunks. Understanding how sociologists divide things up will help you to understand how sociologists approach their work.

There are three sorts of divisions. The first has to do with what chunk of society a sociologist chooses to study; the second and third are a bit more complex and have to do with how particular sociologists approach their research.

What Sociologists Study

1. Topic area or subject matter

How Sociologists Study

2. Theoretical perspectives (paradigms)
3. Levels of analysis

Table 3.1 Popular Topic Areas Within Sociology

Age	Family and sex	Religion
Art	Formal organizations	Science and technology
Collective behavior	Gender	Small groups
Culture	Health care	Social change
Demography	Law	Social movements
Deviance	Mass media	Socialization
Economy	Military	Sports
Education	Political institutions	Stratification
Environment	Race and ethnicity	Work and occupations

Topic Area or Subject Matter

There are many topic areas within sociology—indeed, some sociologist, somewhere, probably is studying every social thing that exists. Table 3.1 lists some of the more popular subjects that are of interest to sociologists. Some sociologists focus their attention on only one area; others may divide their attention between two, three, or more areas. For example, my own major area of research is law, but I also study the family and work.

Theoretical Perspectives (Paradigms): Functionalist, Conflict, and Symbolic Interactionist

A more abstract way to divide up the discipline or field of sociology is in terms of theoretical perspectives, or paradigms (pronounced "PAIR-a-dimes"). A paradigm is akin to a framework or model of the world.

There are three major theoretical perspectives, or paradigms: functionalist, conflict, and symbolic interactionist. The differences between these perspectives mostly have to do with the sets of assumptions about the nature of the social world on which each paradigm is based.

THE FUNCTIONALIST PARADIGM

Sociologists who work from a functionalist paradigm tend to share three major assumptions about the nature of the social world:

1. Within a particular society, there is a great deal of consensus about what values and norms are important. In a particular society, for example, there may be consensus that working hard is important, that murder is bad, that obtaining a lot of wealth is good, and so on. Regardless of the nature of the

values and norms, functional perspectives assume that there is a general consensus about them in society.

2. Society is an entity or whole that is made up of many integrated parts. Because all the parts are integrated, or tied together, when one part of society changes, then other parts will change in response. For example, if the industrial system changes, then the education and family systems will change as well.

3. Society tends to seek stability and avoid conflict. Conflict is not normal, but is dysfunctional or pathological.

THE CONFLICT PARADIGM

Theories that emerge from the conflict paradigm tend to be based on assumptions that seem opposite to theories that grow out of the functionalist paradigm:

1. Within any particular society, there are subgroups of people who cherish different beliefs and have conflicting values and goals.

2. Society is made up of subgroups that are in ruthless competition for scarce resources.

3. Society is never harmonious; conflict is normal in a society.

THE SYMBOLIC INTERACTIONIST PARADIGM

Symbolic interactionists are sometimes called *social constructionists* because of their interest in how people construct their own social worlds. The kinds of questions that symbolic interactionists ask have to do with such issues as how people use symbols to make sense of their environments. Most symbolic interactionists share four basic assumptions about the nature of the social world:

1. How people act depends on how they see and evaluate reality.

2. People learn from others how to see and evaluate reality.

3. People constantly work to interpret their own behavior and the behavior of others to determine what these behaviors "mean."

4. When people do not attach the same meanings to behaviors or perceive reality in the same way, there will be misunderstanding and conflict.

3.1 In your own words, summarize the three major theoretical perspectives/paradigms used in sociology.

Which Paradigm Is Correct?

Many students are confused especially by the differences between the conflict and functionalist paradigms. They seem so opposite to one another—how can both be valid? That's a good question. A few sociologists would answer by stating that one of the two perspectives is wrong. But others (including me) would say that both are right—that there is both consensus and dissent in society, and that both consensus and conflict need to be studied. In my experience, the paradigm adopted depends on which of these aspects of society one judges to be the more interesting and important.

As you might guess, sociologists tend to ask different kinds of questions about their subject matter depending on the paradigm or perspective they hold. Those who have adopted the functionalist or consensus perspective tend to focus on what holds society together and on how changes in one part of society lead to changes in other parts. Those who have adopted the conflict perspective tend to focus on the kinds of things that create tension and conflict between people and groups and on the ways people from one group may exploit people from another group. Those who adopt the symbolic interactionist paradigm tend to look at how ideas emerge from social interaction and then affect that interaction.

Let me offer an example from my own favorite subject area: law. Here are some questions that sociologists working from the different paradigms might ask:

Functionalists

As societies move from agricultural to industrial-based economies, how does this affect the functioning of their legal systems? How does the legal system function to help the economic system run smoothly? How does law function to help build consensus and preserve order in society?

"But your honor—I'm so broke I don't even have a paradigm."

Conflict Theorists

How do people with power use the law to maintain their power? For example, how do rich people use property laws to keep poor people from making financial gains? How do powerful people use the law to force less powerful people to share the values of the rich (even when those values might have negative consequences for poor people)?

Symbolic Interactionists

How do the rules of evidence affect the way people can tell their stories in court? How do attorneys learn to plea bargain how much prison time a particular defendant should get? How are these bargains negotiated?

Sociologists can become very attached—sometimes *too* attached—to one of these theoretical perspectives. Becoming too attached means forgetting that there is value in each of the three paradigms. Truth be told, understanding any complex phenomenon may require the sociologist to make use of the insights offered by all three paradigms. It is probably impossible, for example, to have a society in which there is no consensus or no dissent. Furthermore, in all societies, people have to work to communicate and negotiate the meaning of things. Therefore, because each paradigm offers a different window on the social world, each paradigm enhances our understanding.

Levels of Analysis:
Microsociology and Macrosociology

The third and most abstract way that sociologists divide up their discipline is to distinguish between different *levels* of analysis. Roughly speaking, depending on the level of analysis one uses, one might be doing *microsociology* or *macrosociology*. Microsociologists generally focus on the interactions of individuals and the context of those interactions. Macrosociologists, on the other hand, focus on broader social phenomena, such as whole social structures, systems, and institutions.

A sociologist who studies the family from a microsociological perspective might ask questions about the relationships between family members. For example, what kind of *division of labor* exists in the average American family? In other words, who does the dishes? Who makes the financial decisions? Who has primary responsibility for child care?

A sociologist who studies the family from a macrosociological perspective might look at the impact of economic change on divorce and birth rates in a particular society. Are advances in technology, for example, related to lower birth rates? Do changes in the occupational structure of a society have an impact on the divorce rate?

Although most sociologists tend to do either macrosociological or microsociological research (rather than combine the two), nearly everyone realizes that both kinds of work are important. If we want to gain an understanding of the family, or crime, or religion, or whatever, it is important to study the phenomenon from *both* perspectives.

3.2 In your own words, explain the difference between microsociology and macrosociology.

Chapter Review

1. Make a list of the sociological concepts that you learned in this chapter. Define each term. (*Hint:* You will learn the most from this exercise if, in addition to defining each concept, you create an example of it in your own words.)

2. Assume you were interested in gaining an understanding of the relationship between teachers and students in your college or university. What two or three questions would you ask if you were guided by a functionalist perspective? If you were guided by a conflict perspective? How about the symbolic interactionist perspective?

3. Look back over the questions you constructed in response to question 2. Do these tend to be the kinds of questions that a microsociologist would ask or a macrosociologist? Explain how you reached your conclusion.

Answers and Discussion

3.1

   a. *Functionalist* (also known as the consensus perspective): Sociologists who operate from this perspective assume that there is a lot of consensus about values, goals, and so on in society. They focus on the kinds of things that help to maintain this consensus. For example, if a functionalist studied the American family, he or she might examine the ways in which the family helps out the larger society (such as by teaching children the right values and goals). Functionalists see conflict as pathological; if it exists, then something is wrong with the society.

   b. *Conflict:* These sociologists assume that many groups with different values compete in society. Conflict is thus a normal part of social interaction. Conflict theorists focus on the nature of this

conflict and the way it works. For example, how do men maintain
their superior place in the labor market over women? In what ways
do social institutions—like the criminal justice system—serve the
needs of the powerful over the powerless?

c. *Symbolic interactionist:* These sociologists assume that people construct their own worlds and ask how this process takes place. How
do people come to agree on what symbols mean? Symbolic interactionists assume that the process is one of negotiation. How does
this work?

3.2 Microsociologists always include individuals somewhere in their
focus; macrosociologists don't. For example, many sociologists study
work. A microsociologist would be interested in how individuals select
and learn their jobs, how they get along with their bosses, and how men
and women relate in the workplace. A macrosociologist, on the other
hand, would rather look at how, for example, changes in the political
system affect the labor market or how technological changes affect the
unemployment rate.

Who's Afraid of Sociology?

Once, on about the third day of the semester, a student in my introductory sociology class walked up to me and said, "Sociology is the work of the devil." Then he left.

I never saw that student again. But had he given me the chance, I would have told him that I disagreed with his assessment. In fact, I am sure that the devil hates sociology more than most things.

It is true that sociology emerged at a time in history when many individuals (including some sociologists) were questioning the authority of religious leaders. It is likewise true that a few of those early sociologists even thought that sociology might some-day replace religion. But there is nothing inherently antireligious about sociology. Of course, the skepticism and questioning attitude of sociologists does threaten some people in authority. (Whether that is a bad thing is for you to judge. In any case, as I will discuss shortly, whether something is good or bad is *not* a proper sociological question.)

As much as sociology may threaten religious leaders, it is not really a threat to the social institution of religion—and certainly it is no threat to God (just imagine!). Sociologists are concerned with issues of *observable facts.* In other words, sociologists (like other scientists) tend to be preoccupied with the *empirical* world.

The Empirical World and Inconvenient Facts

This concept of empirical is an important one in science. *Empirical* refers to things that can be observed through the use of one's physical senses—sight, hearing, touch, taste, and smell. If a thing cannot be seen, heard, touched, tasted, or smelled—or, more specifically, if it is not *observable*—it is of little interest to sociologists.

For example, a sociologist doing research might well ask, "Do people in a particular society believe in God?" or, "What impact

44

do religious beliefs have on a person's behavior?" or, "What are the manifest and latent functions of religion in society?" But no working sociologist would ask, "Is there a God?" or, "Is God more fond of Buddhists, Catholics, Muslims, Jews, or Protestants?" or, "Is religion X more correct in its beliefs and practices than religion Y?" These are *not* sociological questions.

Admittedly, anyone who preaches unquestioned obedience to authority will be troubled by sociology. This is well evidenced by the fact that in the twentieth century, whenever a dictator came into power, one of his first acts was to reassign or fire all the sociologists—anything to keep them from making trouble by asking questions. Obviously, you cannot have a successful dictatorship as long as people are questioning authority and being skeptical about its claims. Sociology can flourish only in a free society.

I remember that *my* first sociology course was quite an awakening. Like my classmates, I frequently was appalled to learn some of the stuff that sociologists have uncovered about society. Still, that was in 1972, and in those days we were just learning not to be shocked when we found out that there is a dysfunctional underside to society.

As a sociology professor, I have observed that some students become uncomfortable when they encounter the results of sociological research. I guess that even now it can be shocking to discover that many of the things you always accepted as true are, in fact, false.

Max Weber had a term for those pieces of evidence that contradict what you have always believed and/or want to believe about the social world; he called them *inconvenient facts*. As far as Weber was concerned, it was the sociologist's duty to deal with inconvenient facts. Indeed, Weber argued that one of the best things a sociology teacher could do

> is to teach his students to recognize inconvenient facts—I mean facts that are inconvenient for their party [that is, political] opinions. And for every party opinion there are facts that are extremely inconvenient, for my own opinion no less than for others. I believe the teacher accomplishes more than a mere intellectual task if he compels his audience to accustom itself to the existence of such facts. (Weber 1918/1958, 147)

Here are some empirical facts that have upset some beginning sociology students; in the Weberian sense, these are examples of inconvenient facts. Keep in mind that each of these facts about life in the United States has been validated by a great deal of research.

> Even when they do the exact same jobs and have the exact same educational background, men tend to earn more money

than women, and whites tend to earn more than African Americans. (See, for example, chapter 14 of this book.)

The majority of adults who sexually abuse children are heterosexual. (See Greenberg 1988; Sullivan 1995.)

Whether students get into college has more to do with their parents' socioeconomic standing than with their own intelligence or high school grades. (See chapters 12 and 13 of this book.)

Friendships between people of different races are as stable as friendships between people of the same race. (See Hallinan and Williams 1987.)

When they hear such things in lectures or read them in articles or books assigned in sociology classes, some students react as if the professor (me) is trying to pull a fast one: How can it be true that there is still salary discrimination based on gender and race? How can it be true that most child molesters are heterosexual? How can it be that money and status will get you into college over brains and knowledge? How can such things happen in a society that promotes equality, or in which the supposed corrupting influence of homosexuals is so feared, or in which people are supposed to succeed on their own merit?

Our society, like all societies, aspires to many things. But, as with all societies, there can be discrepancies between the ideal world and the real world. It may be disturbing to learn of these discrepancies, but hiding from them will not make the world a better place.

It is important to remember that the goal of sociology is not to undermine society or people's beliefs. Still, I can assure you of one thing: Any belief that can't stand up to objective scrutiny is hardly worth having. Sociologists cultivate the skill of examining beliefs about the nature of the social world and seeing which ones stand up to the evidence.

4.1 What did Weber mean by the term *inconvenient fact*?

Ethnocentrism

The most difficult thing about doing sociology is examining people whose customs and traditions differ from our own. Each of us likes to believe that his or her own people's customs and traditions are best. And when we encounter people whose ways of life are different, our tendency is to make a value judgment. More specifically, we generally do not see difference as merely difference but as an indication of inferiority.

The human tendency to judge others as inferior is very much evident in the written records of those who were the first to explore other countries and to encounter "foreigners." When Europeans first met Africans, for example, they found African customs so different from European ones that they doubted that the Africans were even human. It seems likely that the Africans' first responses to the Europeans were similar.

To the ancient Greeks, the language of foreigners sounded like nonsensical stammering, like "bar-bar-bar." Because of this, the ancient Greeks came to call all foreigners "barbarians." Similarly, the Aztec peoples called their own language *nahuatl*, meaning "pleasant sounding," but called other people's languages *nonotl*, meaning "stammering." Modern languages reflect a similarly near-universal disdain for foreign peoples:

> In Japanese, the word for foreigner means "stinking of foreign hair."[1] To the Czechs a Hungarian is "a pimple." Germans call cockroaches "Frenchmen," while the French call lice "Spaniards." We in the English-speaking world take French leave, but Italians and Norwegians talk about departing like an Englishman, and Germans talk of running like a Dutchman. Italians call syphilis "the French disease," while both French and Italians call con games "American swindle." Belgian taxi drivers call a poor tipper "un Anglais." (Bryson 1990, 17)

This process of judging other peoples and their customs and norms as inferior to one's own people, customs, and norms is called *ethnocentrism*. Table 4.1 lists common ethnocentric attitudes toward one's own group and toward outsiders.

The positive side of ethnocentrism is that it brings together people and builds solidarity within a particular society. It is similar to believing that your team is the best team. Much as believing that one's team is the best helps to unite students and boost school spirit, believing that one's culture is the best helps to unite people in society. To use Durkheim's phrasing, ethnocentrism promotes social solidarity.

The negative (or dysfunctional) side of ethnocentrism is that it can lead to nasty consequences: prejudice, discrimination, even genocide or "ethnic cleansing."[2] For example, in 1619, a group of

"[Ethnocentrism is the view] of things in which one's own group is the center of everything and all others are scaled and rated with references to it. . . . Each group nourishes its own pride and vanity, boasts itself superior, exalts its own divinities, and looks with contempt on outsiders."

—William G. Sumner (1906)

---

[1]A close reader of the first edition of this book told me that the Japanese word for foreigner is *gaikokujin*, or more frequently *gaigin*, "which translates to 'foreigner' or 'outsider.'" But, according to my reader, either word is "pejorative, and no one would use it in public except children who haven't been socialized not to repeat in public what their parents say in the home." I confess that my knowledge of Japanese is very limited; but I did quiz more than a dozen of my students who are from Japan. When I asked, "What word do the Japanese people use to refer to people from other countries?" each one told me *gaigin*. I am still investigating this matter!

[2]The term *genocide* was introduced by Raphael Lemkin. In 1944, in his study of the Axis (German–Italian) rule of occupied Europe during World War II, Lemkin proposed the term to denote the destruction of a nation or an ethnic group. He coined the word by joining the ancient Greek word *genos* ("race, tribe") with the Latin term *cide* ("killing").

Table 4.1 Ethnocentric Attitudes—Toward One's Own Group and Toward Outsiders

Toward Own Group	Toward Outsiders
See members as virtuous and superior	See outsiders as contemptible, immoral, and inferior
See own values as universal and intrinsically true	See outsiders' values as false (where they differ from own group's values)
See own customs as original and centrally human, as reflecting true "human nature"	See outsiders' customs as suspicious, ignorant, and lacking in humanity

For an excellent introduction to the issue of ethnocentrism, see Levine and Campbell 1972.

religious dissidents in England sought a place where they could have religious freedom. These Pilgrims chose North America. Why? Because no "people" lived there! Here's how one of their leaders, William Bradford, explained the Pilgrims' rationale:

> The place [the Pilgrims] had their thoughts on was some of those vast and unpeopled countries of America, which are fruitful and fit for habitation, being devoid of all civil inhabitants, where there are only savage and brutish men which range up and down, little otherwise than the wild beasts of the same. (Quoted in Holmes 1891, 36)

Because the native inhabitants of North America had different customs and lifestyles, they were seen by these English as less than human and more like "wild beasts." This sort of reasoning allowed many European settlers (and their descendants) to believe that they were as justified in killing Native Americans as they were in killing any dangerous animal.

In my own experience, many people who live in the United States are ethnocentric about being ethnocentric! What I mean is that people in our society seem to think that we are the only ones who are ethnocentric—implying, perhaps, that we are the only ones who have any right to feel superior.

It comes as a shock to many North Americans to find, for example, that we smell bad to many Asians (it's because of all the dairy products we consume). Likewise, when the Thonga people of Africa first saw visiting Europeans kissing, they reacted with horror and disgust: What sort of people would engage in "eating each other's saliva and dirt" (Hyde 1979, 18)?

For sociologists, ethnocentrism is especially dangerous because it gets in the way of understanding. If we really want to understand why people in society X act the way they do, how their institutions work, and what their customs are, we have to see them in the context of *their* society. Ethnocentrism hinders such understanding because it means we are viewing society X in terms of our own society.

Avoiding Ethnocentrism Can Be Difficult

Even when we tell ourselves sternly that we must be objective, that we must examine the people of other cultures in terms of their cultures, it is difficult. Anthropologist Napoleon Chagnon gives a startling example of how difficult it can be to avoid being ethnocentric. Chagnon studied the Yanomamö Indians of South America by living among them for more than a year. Here's part of what he wrote about his first day in the field. Imagine yourself in his shoes: Could you have remained "objective"?

My first day in the field illustrated to me what my teachers meant when they spoke of "culture shock.". . .

We arrived at the village, Biaasi-teri, about 2:00 P.M. and docked the boat along the muddy bank at the terminus of the path used by the Indians to fetch their drinking water. It was hot and muggy, and my clothing was soaked with perspiration. . . .

I looked up and gasped when I saw a dozen burly, naked, filthy, hideous men staring at us down the shafts of their drawn arrows! Immense wads of green tobacco were stuck between their lower teeth and lips making them look even more hideous, and strands of dark-green slime dripped or hung from their noses. We arrived at the village while the men were blowing a hallucinogenic drug up their noses. One of the side effects of the drug is a runny nose. The mucus is always saturated with green powder and the Indians usually let it run freely from their nostrils. My next discovery was that there were a dozen or so vicious, underfed dogs snapping at my legs, circling me as if I were going to be their next meal. I just stood there holding my notebook, helpless and pathetic. Then the stench of the decaying vegetation and filth struck me and I almost got sick. I was horrified. . . .

The whole situation was depressing, and I wondered why I ever decided to switch from civil engineering to anthropology in the first place. I had not eaten all day, I was soaking wet from perspiration, the gnats were biting me, and I was covered with red pigment, the result of a dozen or so complete examinations I had been given by as many burly Indians. These examinations capped an otherwise grim day. The Indians would blow their noses into their hands, flick as much of the mucus off that would separate in a snap of the wrist, wipe the residue into their hair, and then carefully examine my face, arms, legs, hair, and the contents of my pockets. I asked Mr. Barker [a local missionary and Chagnon's temporary guide] how to say "Your hands are dirty"; my comments were met by the Indians in the following way: They would "clean" their hands by spitting a quantity of slimy tobacco juice into them, rub them together, and then proceed with the examination. (Chagnon 1977, 4–7)

Encounters with different cultures challenge one's taken-for-granted assumptions about the way things are and ought to be. Social scientists refer to the resulting feeling of disorientation as culture shock.

Our initial reaction to the Yanomamö likely would be one of horror and disgust—just as it was Chagnon's reaction. In time, however, if we tried to keep an open mind, we too could become accustomed to the Yanomamö's ways—once we saw these in the context of their entire living situation.

> Mr. Barker and I crossed the river and slung our hammocks. When he pulled his hammock out of a rubber bag, a heavy, disagreeable odor of mildewed cotton came with it. "Even the missionaries are filthy," I thought to myself. Within two weeks everything I owned smelled the same way, and I lived with the odor for the remainder of the field work. My own habits of personal cleanliness reached such levels that I didn't even mind being examined by the Indians, as I was not much cleaner than they were after I had adjusted to the circumstances. . . .
>
> I discovered that it was an enormously time-consuming task to maintain my own body in the manner to which it had grown accustomed in the relatively antiseptic environment of the northern United States. Either I could be relatively well fed and relatively comfortable in a fresh change of clothes and do very little fieldwork, or, I could do considerably more fieldwork and be less well fed and less comfortable. (Chagnon 1977, 4–7)

It could certainly be argued that Chagnon's experiences were extreme, that most social scientists do not venture into such exotic locales. But one does not have to go very far to experience the shock of cultural differences. Probably, even in your own city or town, there are groups of people who live their lives very differently than you do. Quite possibly, you experienced a bit of culture shock when you first arrived at college!

When one encounters cultural strangers, one's first reaction is likely to be the same as Chagnon's when he met the Yanomamö. Ethnocentrism is normal. However, because it gets in the way of understanding, social scientists work to overcome it.

"Culture shock refers to the whole set of feelings about being in an alien setting, and the resulting reactions. It is a chilly, creepy feeling of alienation, of being without some of the most ordinary, trivial—and therefore basic—cues of one's culture of origin."

—Conrad P. Kottak (1992)

4.2 What does it mean to be ethnocentric? What's an example of ethnocentrism?

4.3 What is culture shock? What's an example of culture shock?

Cultural Relativism

Sociologists work to overcome their ethnocentrism by practicing something called *cultural relativism*. Cultural relativism is *the belief that other people and their ways of doing things can be understood only in terms of the cultural context of those people.* This is based on the assumption that if our goal is to truly understand people's behavior, we have to look for clues in *their* culture.

Some people have misunderstood this notion of cultural relativity. They suspect that it implies that any one way of doing things is as good as any other way. As far as sociologists are concerned, however, cultural relativity has nothing to do with assessing which ways of doing things are better or worse. Remember, "Which way is better or worse?" is *not* a legitimate sociological question.

For sociologists, cultural relativity means being objective enough to understand people's behaviors in terms of their culture and social situation. Sociology does not agree or disagree with, or approve or disapprove of, behavior; sociology seeks to understand and explain behavior. And understanding and explaining is difficult to do unless one is willing to look at things in their own context.

Ethnocentrism can lead to shocking cases of ignorance. During a debate over the merits of bilingual education, for example, one congressman quite seriously said to Dr. David Edwards (head of the Joint National Committee on Languages):

"If English was good enough for Jesus Christ, it's good enough for me."

—Quoted by Bill Bryson (1990)

Chapter Review

1. Make a list of the sociological concepts that you learned in this chapter. Define each term. (*Hint:* You will learn the most from this exercise if, in addition to defining each concept, you create an example of it in your own words.)

2. What is cultural relativism? Why is it considered crucial for sociologists?

Answers and Discussion

4.1 Weber used the term *inconvenient facts* to refer to facts or data that go against one's social and political beliefs. For example, suppose you are very much in favor of imposing the death penalty on convicted murderers. If that were the case, the following facts might be inconvenient for you:
   a. There is no evidence that the threat of the death penalty has any appreciable effect on a country's murder rate.
   b. In the United States, it costs more to put a person to death than to keep him or her in prison for life.

By the way, it is amazingly difficult to think of examples of inconvenient facts. That is not because they aren't there, but because it is easier to try to ignore them.

4.2 Your definition of ethnocentrism should include the ideas that it occurs when we judge other people's customs and behaviors against the standards of our own culture. Asking a kilted Scotsman why he is dressed like a woman is ethnocentric.

4.3 Culture shock is that feeling of disorientation and even squeamishness that one feels when plunked down into a different culture. Chagnon felt this as he stood there and let the Yanomamö examine him.

5

The Vocabulary of Science

During the past century, science has revolutionized the way we live and die. Yet those of us who do science follow a relatively simple method. First, we specify some concepts of interest to us. Second, we posit, or suggest, some relationship between those concepts. Third, we test whether the posited relationship reflects what happens in the real world. If our testing shows that our posited relationship does reflect what goes on in the real world, we conclude that we have succeeded in understanding something about the nature of things in the world.

Simple, right? Well, you might well ask: If science is so simple, why is it that scientific reports seem so complex and that reading and untangling them is so daunting? The answer is that the simplicity of the scientific method only becomes clear once one has conquered the basic vocabulary used by scientists.

The good news is that science uses a language that crosses many academic disciplines. Therefore, learning this language not only is crucial for your sociology course work but will help you in other sorts of classes as well.

Variables

The first step in doing science involves picking the concepts of interest to us. We call these concepts *variables*. When sociologists speak or write about their research, they tend to use the term *variable* a lot. To call a concept a variable means, in the first place, that it is a thing of interest in a particular piece of research.

Variables are special because they have two important characteristics. First, a variable is something that is thought to influence or be influenced by another thing. For example, suppose I were to assert that "income is thought to influence voting behavior." That assertion makes reference to two variables: income and voting behavior. The first, income, is a variable because it is thought to

52

influence voting behavior. The second, voting behavior, is a variable because it is thought to be influenced by income.

Here are a few more examples. In each case I have italicized the variables.

Gender is thought to influence *occupation*.

Religious affiliation is thought to be influenced by *income*.

Educational attainment is thought to influence *income*.

Age is thought to influence *attitudes toward using computers*.

Income is thought to be influenced by *race*.

The second important characteristic of a variable has to do with the idea of variation or difference: A variable is a thing that has varying *attributes* (an attribute is a characteristic or a quality that describes a thing).

For example, the attributes of the variable gender vary from, or include, female and male. The attributes of religious affiliation vary from, or include, Catholic, Jewish, Protestant, other, and no religion. The attributes of the variable educational attainment vary from zero years of schooling to twelve or more years of schooling (with a number of steps in between those two extremes). The attributes of the variable income vary from zero dollars earned a year to $1 million or more earned a year, again with a number of steps in between.

Depending on the circumstances, the attributes of a particular variable will be defined in different ways. Table 5.1 illustrates two ways of listing the attributes of the variable religious affiliation.

How you define your list of attributes depends on the nature of the group you are studying. If the group is known or expected to be very diverse, then something like list 1 is appropriate. If the group is known not to be very diverse (that is, if it is made up of people from only a few religions), then list 2 is more appropriate,

Table 5.1 Attributes of Religious Affiliation

List 1		List 2
Baha'i	Protestant	Catholic
Buddhist	Roman Catholic	Jewish
Confucian	Rosicrucian	Protestant
Eastern Orthodox	Shinto	Other
Hindu	Tao	None
Islamic	Other	
Jewish	None	

as long as it includes the names of the religions to which most of the people you are studying are likely to be affiliated.

You will see right away that list 1 is quite a bit longer than list 2. But there is one crucial thing that is common to both lists: Each is totally inclusive—every person in the world has one of these attributes.

STOP & REVIEW

5.1

a. Identify the variables in each assertion.

Example
Marital status *is thought to influence a person's* happiness.
  i. Number of beers consumed per week is thought to influence a student's GPA.
  ii. Frequency of tooth brushing is thought to influence the number of cavities gotten each year.

b. Now go back and list the attributes of each variable.

Examples
Marital status: *never married, married, separated, divorced, widowed, other*
Happiness: *extremely happy, somewhat happy, somewhat unhappy, extremely unhappy*

c. "Thought question": One way sociologists define the term *variable* is as "a logical grouping of attributes." Explain what this definition means.

Hypotheses

Ultimately, scientists are interested in the relationships among different variables. So, after we identify the variables of interest to us, we posit a relationship between them. The result is called a *hypothesis*. Here are some simple hypotheses:

H_1: Gender affects occupation.
H_2: Age affects income.
H_3: Social class affects voting behavior.
H_4: Religious affiliation affects attitudes toward abortion.
H_5: Occupation affects income.

When we create a hypothesis, we are not asserting that it reflects something true. Hypotheses can be either true or false. We create them to test whether the posited relationships between the variables are true or false.

Each of the five hypotheses just given follows the same basic form: Variable X influences variable Y. This format is really a form of shorthand. The more precise way of stating the hypothesis is this: *Different attributes of variable X are related to different attributes of variable Y.*

Let's reexamine the first three of our five hypotheses for their more precise meaning.

Shorthand Version

   H_1: Gender affects occupation.

Longhand Version

   H_1: Differences in gender are related to differences in occupation. [That is, men and women tend to be employed in different occupations.]

Shorthand Version

   H_2: Age affects income.

Longhand Version

   H_2: Differences in age are related to differences in income. [That is, people in different age groups tend to earn different amounts of income.]

Shorthand Version

   H_3: Social class affects voting behavior.

Longhand Version

   H_3: Differences in social class are related to differences in voting behavior. [That is, people from higher social classes tend to vote differently than people from lower social classes.]

5.2 Now *you* translate the fourth and fifth hypotheses into their longer versions on a separate piece of paper.

STOP & REVIEW

   Shorthand Version
   H_4: *Religious affiliation affects attitudes toward abortion.*

   Longhand Version
   H_4: *Differences in* _____ *are related to* _____.
   [That is, _____.*]*

   Shorthand Version
   H_5: *Occupation affects income.*

   Longhand Version
   H_5: *Differences in* _____ *are related to* _____.
   [That is, _____.*]*

In the examples I have used thus far, it has been fairly easy to identify the variables. Sometimes, however, you might have to ponder a particular hypothesis for a while before you can identify the variables.

Here I have listed four sets of hypotheses. You should be able to confirm that the variables are the same for each hypothesis in a particular set. (Do not assume that the hypotheses in a particular set mean the same thing, however.)

Set A

H_{6A}: Gender influences occupation.
H_{6B}: Men and women tend to have different occupations.

Set B

H_{7A}: Age affects income.
H_{7B}: The very young and the very old tend to have less income than middle-aged workers.
H_{7C}: Younger workers are more likely to earn a minimum wage than older workers.

Set C

H_{8A}: Social class affects voting behavior.
H_{8B}: The higher one's social class standing, the more likely one is to vote Republican in national elections.
H_{8C}: The lower one's social class standing, the more likely one is to vote Democrat in national elections.

Set D

H_{9A}: Religion influences attitudes toward abortion.
H_{9B}: Catholics are more likely to oppose abortion than Protestants are.

STOP & REVIEW

5.3 Read the following hypotheses and identify the variables.

H_{10}: Poor people tend to commit street crimes, while rich people tend to commit white-collar crimes.
H_{11}: Catholics are more likely to oppose the death penalty than are Protestants and Jews.
H_{12}: Married people are more likely to own pets than single people are.
H_{13}: The hotter the weather, the more ice cream people will buy.
H_{14}: Students who earn good grades tend to study more than do students who earn poor grades.

Kinds of Variables:
Independent Versus Dependent

Remember the first defining characteristic of a variable? (It's a thing that is thought to influence or be influenced by another thing.) The distinction between *influence* and *influenced by* is a clue to the fact that there are two kinds of variables: There are variables that influence other things and variables that are influenced by other things.

When a variable influences another thing, it is called a *cause;* when a variable is influenced by another thing, it is called an *effect.* So,

Variables that influence or affect other things = causes
Variables that are influenced or affected by other things = effects

With this new knowledge about variables as causes and as effects, let's look back at our original five hypotheses. Each hypothesis posits or suggests a cause-effect relationship.

H_1: Gender affects occupation.
H_2: Age affects income.
H_3: Social class affects voting behavior.
H_4: Religious affiliation affects attitudes toward abortion.
H_5: Occupation affects income.

Hypothesis 1, for example, posited that being a man or a woman causes individuals to choose different occupations. To make these cause-effect relationships more obvious, we could rephrase our hypotheses this way:

H_1: Gender differences (cause) occupational differences (effect).
H_2: Age differences (cause) income differences (effect).
H_3: Social class differences (cause) voting behavior differences (effect).
H_4: Differences in religious affiliation (cause) differences in attitudes toward abortion (effect).
H_5: Occupational differences (cause) income differences (effect).

As you might suspect, there are special names for these two types of variables. A variable that is believed to influence another variable (that is, to be a cause) is called an *independent variable.* A variable that is thought to be influenced by the independent variable (that is, to be an effect) is called a *dependent variable.* Therefore,

Independent variable/cause	affects	dependent variable/effect
H_1: gender	→	occupation
H_2: age	→	income
H_3: social class	→	voting behavior differences
H_5: occupation	→	income

This distinction between independent and dependent variables is really an important one. If you confuse them, you will make a big mess out of your analysis of the social world.

How can you remember that the independent variable is the cause and the dependent variable is the effect? One way is to recall that the effect depends on the cause just as *the dependent variable depends on the independent variable.* Another way to remember the difference is to think of the word *INCA:* the *IN*dependent variable is the *CA*use.

It might help to remember that the cause of something always happens before the effect. So, if one variable obviously comes before another variable, it will be the cause (INCA = independent variable). (Be careful, however; not all variables that come before another variable are causes of the variable. For example, one generally attends kindergarten before attending college, but we would not say that attending kindergarten is the cause of attending college!)

S T O P
&
R E V I E W

5.4 Identify the *independent variable* (the cause) in each of the following hypotheses:

H_{15}: Education affects income.
H_{16}: Income affects vacation choices.
H_{17}: Marital status affects vacation choices.
H_{18}: Mental health is affected by marital status.
H_{19}: Regularity of church attendance is influenced by marital status.
H_{20}: People with more education tend to have higher-paying jobs.
H_{21}: People with higher-paying jobs tend to own more computers.
H_{22}: People with light skin tones tend to sunburn more easily.

Kinds of Relationships: Directionality

Often you will discover that the relationships between two variables may be one of two types: positive or negative. The difference is fairly simple: *Variables that vary in the same direction have a positive relationship; variables that vary in the opposite direction have a negative relationship.*

How does this work? Consider the following hypothesis, which posits a *positive* relationship between eating and weight:

H_{23}: Increased eating causes increased weight.

The relationship between eating and weight is a positive one because these two variables vary in the same direction. That is, the *more* you eat, the *more* you weigh; and the *less* you eat, the *less* you weigh.

Now consider this hypothesis, which posits a *negative* relationship between exercise and weight:

H_{24}: Increased exercise causes decreased weight.

The relationship between exercise and weight is a negative one because these two variables vary in opposite directions. That is, the *more* you exercise, the *less* you weigh; and the *less* you exercise, the *more* you weigh.

So, in the abstract, *positive* relationships look like this:

↑ independent variable → ↑ dependent variable

That is, as the independent variable goes faster, or gets bigger, or becomes more important, the dependent variable goes faster, or gets bigger, or becomes more important. Or, as the independent variable goes slower, or gets smaller, or becomes less important, the dependent variable does too:

↓ independent variable → ↓ dependent variable

On the other hand, *negative* relationships look like this:

↑ independent variable → ↓ dependent variable

That is, as the independent variable goes faster, or gets bigger, or becomes more important, the dependent variable goes slower, or gets smaller, or becomes less important. Or, as the independent variable goes slower, or gets smaller, or becomes less important, the dependent variable varies in the opposite way.

↓ independent variable → ↑ dependent variable

5.5 Identify the variables in each hypothesis, and then indicate whether the posited relationship is positive or negative:

> H_{25}: The longer you live, the more money you will earn.
> H_{26}: The higher your social class, the more education you are likely to have.
> H_{27}: The higher your social class, the less likely you are to be arrested for committing a crime.
> H_{28}: Children are more likely than adults to take naps.
> H_{29}: The more frequently an individual attends services at a church, temple, synagogue, or mosque, the more likely that person is to donate money to religious causes.
> H_{30}: The more education one has, the less likely one is to be prejudiced against those of different races.
> H_{31}: Older people tend to be less fearful of dying than younger people.

S T O P
&
R E V I E W

Operational Definitions

After we select the variables of interest and formulate hypotheses, we need to arrange things so that we can test our hypotheses. Recall our very first hypothesis: Gender affects occupation. When we set up that hypothesis, we posited a relationship between gender and occupation. To put it another way, we posited that men and women are likely to have different sorts of occupations. Testing this hypothesis will mean determining whether there is indeed a relationship between gender and occupation in the real world.

Before we can test our hypothesis, however, we must create something called an *operational definition* for each of our variables. Many people call this *operationalizing* the variables. Creating an operational definition essentially involves *transforming the variables into things that can be observed and measured.*

Generally, operationalizing a variable simply means listing its attributes so that you can count the presence or absence of those attributes in the real world. For example, in operationalizing gender, we can easily identify two attributes:

Gender

> woman
> man

Operationalizing occupation is a bit trickier, but we can still do it in a fairly straightforward manner. Here is one way we might operationalize occupation:

Occupation

> professional
> manager or owner of business
> skilled laborer
> unskilled laborer
> not employed
> other

Suppose I am interested in looking at the relationship between a student's major in college and how many hours per week that student studies. My hypothesis is that students who major in the sciences study more hours per week than do students who major in the humanities or social sciences. So, I have two basic variables: major field of study and hours per week spent studying. Here's how I might operationalize the variables of interest to me:

Primary Major

> social sciences
> humanities
> physical sciences
> other
> not yet declared

Hours Studied per Week

> none
> fewer than 5 hours per week
> 5–15 hours per week
> 16–25 hours per week
> more than 25 hours per week

There are two rules to keep in mind when operationalizing variables. First, the list of attributes must be *exhaustive;* that is, every thing or person being observed must fit into one category. Second, the list of attributes must be *mutually exclusive;* that is, no one person or thing should be able to fit into more than a single category.

Suppose we wanted to operationalize the variable type of car. Consider the following list of attributes:

two-door
four-door
station wagon

Is this a good way to operationalize type of car? No. The attributes on this list are not mutually exclusive because a particular car could fit into two categories (for example, a two-door station wagon).

5.6 Operationalize the following variables.

STOP
&
REVIEW

Example
Year in college: Freshman, sophomore, junior, senior, other
    or
Year in college: First, second, third, fourth, other

a. age
b. race
c. political party affiliation
d. amount of television watched per week
e. attitude toward capital punishment

Tables and Figures

The point of putting data (pieces of information) into a table or figure (such as a bar chart, pie chart, or graph) is to present those data clearly.[1] Still, until you get some experience, tables and figures can be quite confusing. When you come across a table or figure in an article, you might even be tempted to rely on the author's explanation of what that table or figure shows rather than take the time to study the data for yourself. But this can be dangerous, because the author may not have interpreted the data correctly or may have written a misleading account of those data. Remember—be skeptical.

---

[1] Perhaps you've never noticed it before, but the word *data* is plural, so you should read plural verbs with it (for example, "the data are . . ."). The word that is used to refer to a single piece of information is *datum* (so, "this datum is . . .").

Usually, no matter how many pieces of information are packed into a figure or table, you can figure out what it means by following a few steps:

1. *Begin by reading the title of the table or figure carefully.* A proper title will, for example, tell you the name of each of the *variables* that are described in the table or depicted in the figure. (When people misinterpret a table or a figure, it is generally because they skipped this step! The title is so important!) Examine table 5.2. The title tells you that the table shows the variable median annual incomes of people in the United States. The title also tells you that the table shows the differences in median income for people in different (variable) categories of gender, race, and educational background.

2. *Determine the source of the data.* Is it trustworthy? Data in table 5.2 are drawn from the U.S. Bureau of the Census, which is considered to be a fairly reliable source. Would you be as likely to trust data gathered from a call-in talk show? Why or why not?

3. *Read any "notes" that accompany the table or graph.* Not all tables or figures have notes, but when they are included, notes give additional information about the data. The note in table 5.2, for example, explains that the data refer to the total money income of full-time and part-time workers, ages 25 and over. Thus, we know that these data are pretty complete: They cover adults who work both full- and part-time.

4. *Examine any footnotes.* Footnote *a* in table 5.2 tells you that these data are categorized by the highest grade completed. This information is included to avoid confusing the reader.

Table 5.2 U.S. Median Annual Income by Gender, Race, and Education

Demographic Group	Overall Median Income	Years of Schooling[a]				
		Fewer Than 9	9–11	12	13–15	16 or More
White males	$35,747	$16,648	$21,159	$30,655	$35,529	$52,329
African American males	$27,253	$15,653	$17,901	$24,710	$30,027	$40,400
White females	$21,482	$10,793	$11,507	$17,244	$21,235	$33,359
African American females	$20,742	$ 7,740	$10,829	$16,571	$22,737	$33,955

Note: These figures include the total money income of full-time and part-time workers, ages 25 and over, as of March 1998.
[a] In terms of highest grade completed.
SOURCE: U.S. Bureau of the Census, *Money Income of Households, Families, and Persons in the United States: 1988, Current Population Reports,* Series P-60, No. 162 (Washington, DC: U.S. Government Printing Office, 1999).

Without this additional information, you might have concluded, for example, that the variable years of schooling had to do with the actual number of years the individual spent in school. This footnote alerts you to the fact that people listed under 12 years of school did not spend 12 years in the first grade, but actually graduated from high school.

5. *Look for trends in the data.* Be sure to look both *horizontally* and *vertically.* What does the table tell you about the relationship between the variables?

   a. *Vertically.* For example, in the first two columns, check out the relationship between demographic group and overall median income: This table shows that, overall, men tend to earn more than women, and whites tend to earn more than African Americans.

   b. *Horizontally.* For example, check the relationship between each of the demographic categories and level of income. For example, this table shows that, generally, the more years of schooling an individual has, the more income he or she has. In other words, *there is a positive relationship between income and years of education.* If you don't see this, keep looking!

Figure 5.1 illustrates the same data as table 5.2 (except that "overall median income" is missing). To read figure 5.1, follow the same

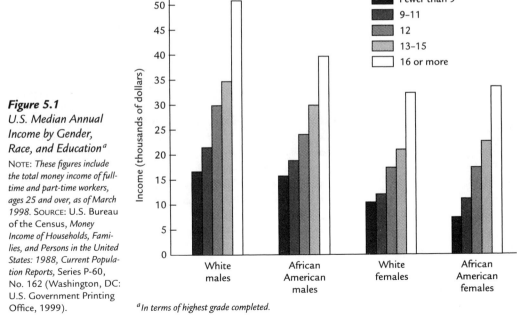

Figure 5.1
U.S. Median Annual Income by Gender, Race, and Education[a]

NOTE: *These figures include the total money income of full-time and part-time workers, ages 25 and over, as of March 1998.* SOURCE: U.S. Bureau of the Census, *Money Income of Households, Families, and Persons in the United States: 1988, Current Population Reports,* Series P-60, No. 162 (Washington, DC: U.S. Government Printing Office, 1999).

[a] *In terms of highest grade completed.*

Figure 5.2 *Average Weekly Salary of Male and Female Workers in Clerical and Managerial Positions, 1991*

SOURCE: U.S. Bureau of the Census, *Current Population Reports, 1992* (Washington, DC: U.S. Government Printing Office, 1992).

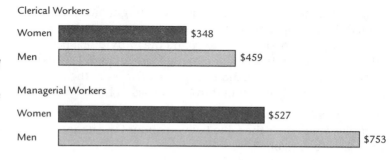

Clerical Workers

Women $348

Men $459

Managerial Workers

Women $527

Men $753

steps as for reading table 5.2: Read the title, check the source, and look for trends. The primary difference between tables and figures is that with figures, although the data are less precise, overall trends are easier to spot.

STOP & REVIEW

5.7 Use the data given in table 5.2 to determine whether each of the following statements is true or false:

    a. Income tends to rise with educational level regardless of race or gender.

    b. The benefit of (proportion of income gained by) going to college is the same for men and women.

    c. White male high school graduates have incomes as high as African American males with some college experience.

    d. African American women appear to improve their earning power through college education to a greater extent than do white women.

5.8 Given the data in figure 5.2, what conclusions can you draw about the differences between men's and women's salaries?

5.9

    a. A friend mentions to you that a lot of "strangers" have moved into her town recently. This is making her nervous. She says to you: "You're studying sociology. What are the *facts*? Aren't I more likely to be murdered by a stranger than by someone I know?" Then she says, "Anyway, I always feel safest when I'm surrounded by family and friends."

       Based on your analysis of the data shown in table 5.3 (page 65), how would you respond to your friend's statements?

    b. Who is more likely to be the victim of a crime committed by a stranger—a woman or a man? What factors might account for this difference? (See table 5.4, page 65.)

Table 5.3 Total Murders and Nonnegligent Manslaughters Known to Police, by Victim–Offender Relationship, United States, 1991[a]

Relationship of Victim to Offender	Number
Spouse	1,200
Parent	328
Offspring	552
Sibling	215
Other family	388
Acquaintance	5,598
Friend	764
Boyfriend	269
Girlfriend	483
Neighbor	229
Stranger	3,235
Unknown relationship	8,247
Total	21,508

[a]Murder is premeditated killing. Nonnegligent manslaughter includes all killings that were not accidental but also not premeditated.

SOURCE: *National Institute of Justice Sourcebook, 1993* (Washington, DC: U.S. Government Printing Office, 1993).

Table 5.4 Victim and Offender Relationships in Violent Crime, by Sex, 1999, in Percent

Relationship of Victim to Offender	Gender of Victim	
	Female	Male
Nonstranger		
Intimate partner	20%	3%
Other relative	6%	4%
Friend/acquaintance	42%	37%
Stranger	32%	55%
Relationship unknown	1%	2%
Total	101%	101%

SOURCE: Bureau of Justice Statistics, *Criminal Victimization, 1999,* National Crime Victimization Survey (Washington, DC: U.S. Government Printing Office, August 2000).

Table 5.5 Violence and Theft by Victim's Gender, Race, Age, and Income in the United States[a]

Victim's Race and Gender[b]	Type of Crime		
	Violent[c]	Murder	Theft
White males	35	9	73
White females	20	3	64
Nonwhite males	49	51	71
Nonwhite females	32	11	56

Victim's Age	All Violent Crime	Theft
12–15	57	112
16–19	72	121
20–24	59	123
25–34	35	82
35–49	22	65
50–64	10	39
65 and older	4	18

Victim's Household Income	All Violent Crime	Theft
Less than $7,500	50	74
$7,500–$9,999	45	65
$10,000–$14,999	31	59
$15,000–$24,999	29	64
$25,000–$29,999	27	73
$30,000–$49,999	22	72
$50,000 or more	21	83

[a] Rates per year per 1000 population.
[b] In the case of sexual violence, almost all victims are women; more specifically, most victims of sexual violence are young women between the ages of 16 and 24.
[c] Violent crimes except homicide.
SOURCE: U.S. Department of Justice 1989, 1990.

5.10 Use the data given in table 5.5 to determine whether each of the following statements is true or false:

  a. Overall, men are more likely than women to be victimized by crime.
  b. Overall, whites are more likely to be victims of violent crime than are nonwhites.
  c. The very rich and the very poor are more likely to be victims of theft than are people in middle-income categories.

d. Younger people are more likely to be victims of violent crime than older people are.

5.11 Assume your professor is a white female who is 45 years old. Based on the data presented in table 5.5, what are her approximate chances of being a victim of a violent crime? (And do not answer, "It depends on how hard the midterm exam is.")

a. very likely
b. somewhat likely
c. somewhat unlikely
d. not likely at all
e. cannot determine

Chapter Review

1. Make a list of the sociological concepts that you learned in this chapter. Define each term. (*Hint:* You will learn the most from this exercise if, in addition to defining each concept, you create an example of it in your own words.)

2. Go to chapter 14 and examine table 14.3.
   a. What is/are the dependent variable(s) in this table?
   b. What is/are the independent variable(s)?
   c. What do the data suggest? (In other words, what are the relationships between the independent and dependent variables?)

3. Convert the data from table 14.3 into a figure (see figures 5.1 and 5.2 for examples). Which makes the relationships between the independent and dependent variables more clear? Why?

Answers and Discussion

5.1

a.
   i. *Number of beers consumed per week* is thought to influence a *student's GPA.*
   ii. *Frequency of tooth brushing* is thought to influence the *number of cavities gotten each year.*

b. *Number of beers per week:*

   This variable could be operationalized by creating categories or by the exact number:

   none
   1–2

3–4
5–8
9–12
more than 12   or 0, 1, 2, 3, 4, 5, 6, 7, 8, 9, 10, 11, 12, 13 . . .

Student's GPA
   0.0–2.0
   2.1–2.5
   2.6–3.0
   3.1–3.5
   3.6–4.0   or 0.0, 0.1, 0.2, 0.3, 0.4, 0.5, 0.6 . . .

Frequency of tooth brushing
   never
   less than once a day
   1 or 2 times a day
   3 times a day or more

Number of cavities gotten each year
   0
   1
   2–3
   4 or more   or 0, 1, 2, 3, 4, 5, 6, 7 . . .

Hint: When you use categories, make sure that they are relevant ones. If every one of your respondents gets more than five cavities a year, they will all check the same category. This won't help you. It may be that those who brush more frequently do get fewer cavities, but ten as opposed to twenty cavities. How do you tell what categories are important? Ask around! Find out what the range is.

   c. Attributes are characteristics of a variable. The variable sex, for example, has two attributes: male and female. If we knew only the attributes and applied some logic, we could name the variable. For example, consider these three attributes: felony, gross misdemeanor, misdemeanor. What's the variable? (Levels of seriousness in crime.) Likewise, consider these attributes: private, corporal, sergeant, lieutenant, captain, major, colonel, general. What's the variable? If you apply logic, you can figure it out (military rank).

5.2
   H_4: Differences in religious affiliation are related to differences in attitudes toward abortion. That is, people who belong to different religions tend to have different attitudes toward the issue of abortion.
   H_5: Differences in occupation are related to differences in income. That is, people in certain occupations tend to earn less than people in other occupations.

5.3
   H_{10}: level of wealth or poverty, type of crime committed
   H_{11}: religious affiliation, attitude toward the death penalty
   H_{12}: marital status, pet ownership
   H_{13}: temperature, sales of ice cream
   H_{14}: amount of time spent studying, grades

5.4 *Hint:* When faced with a choice between variables, logically the cause has to come before the effect.

H_{15}: *Education* affects income.

H_{16}: *Income* affects vacation choices.

H_{17}: *Marital status* affects vacation choices.

H_{18}: Mental health is affected by *marital status*.

H_{19}: Regularity of church attendance is influenced by *marital status*.

H_{20}: People with more *education* tend to have higher-paying jobs.

H_{21}: People with *higher-paying jobs* tend to own more computers.

H_{22}: People with *light skin tones* tend to sunburn more easily.

S T O P
&
R E V I E W

5.5

H_{25}:
variables: age, income
direction: positive (that is, as your age increases, your income increases)

H_{26}:
variables: social class, education
direction: positive (the higher the social class, the higher the education)

H_{27}:
variables: social class, likelihood of being arrested
direction: negative (the higher the social class, the less likely you are to be arrested)

H_{28}:
variables: age, likelihood of taking naps
direction: negative (the older a person is, the less likely he or she is to nap)

H_{29}:
variables: frequency of attendance at religious services, amount donated to religious causes
direction: positive (the more one attends, the more one gives)

H_{30}:
variables: education, prejudice
direction: negative (the more the education, the less the prejudice)

H_{31}:
variables: age, fear of dying
direction: negative (as age increases, fear decreases)

5.6 (Remember, *operationalizing* simply means turning a variable into something that can be observed and measured, which generally involves coming up with a list of the variable's attributes. Each list of attributes must be exhaustive, and the attributes must be mutually exclusive.)

a. Age (either in categories or as straight numbers)
less than 5 years old
5–8 years old
9–15 years old
16–21 years old
more than 21 years old   or 0, 1, 2, 3, 4, 5, 6, 7, 8, 9, 10, . . .

b. Race
black
white

Asian
Hispanic
other

c. Political party affiliation

Democrat   (You could add to your list the name of any
Independent   political party you know of. But always remem-
Republican   ber to add the "other" and "none" categories.
other   That's really the only way to be sure of being
none   exhaustive (or inclusive of every possible person).

d. Amount of television watched per week
none
no more than 2 hours
2–5 hours
6–10 hours
more than 10 hours   or 0, 1, 2, 3, 4, 5, . . .

e. Attitude toward capital punishment
strongly oppose   or: On a scale of 1 to 10, with 1 being
somewhat oppose   strongly opposed and 10 being strongly
somewhat in favor   in favor, rate your attitude toward
strongly in favor   capital punishment.

5.7

a. This is true. Income tends to rise with educational level regardless of race or gender. For each row (for example, white males, African American males, and so on), you can look across from left to right. As you move from "Fewer than 9" to "16 or more" years of education, in each row the amount of income increases.

b. This is false. The benefit of (proportion of income gained by) going to college is *not* the same for men and women. To figure out how this is so, first compare the incomes of high school graduates (12 years of education) to those of college graduates (16 or more years). To clarify the matter, make a new table that focuses only on this information.

	12 Years	16 or More Years	Difference
White males	$30,655	$52,329	$21,674
African American males	$24,710	$40,400	$15,690
White females	$17,244	$33,359	$16,115
African American females	$16,571	$33,955	$17,384

Clearly, males earn more than females of the same race at either level of education. And, in terms of absolute dollars gained by graduating from college, males gain more by getting a college degree.

STOP
&
REVIEW

	Difference Between Median Incomes of High School and College Graduates
White males	$21,674
African American males	$15,690
White females	$16,115
African American females	$17,384

However, these raw numbers can be misleading. You might notice as well that, proportionately, women gain more by getting a college degree. Female college graduates tend to earn more than twice as much as their counterparts with only a high school degree. Men do not double their salaries by getting a college degree.

c. This is true. White male high school dropouts have a median income of $30,655, while African American males with some college experience have a median income of $30,027.

d. This is true. African American women do improve their earning power by obtaining a college degree more so than white women. Indeed, African American women seem to gain more from having a college degree (as opposed to just a high school degree) than do men of either race.

	Difference	Percentage Gain from a College Degree over a High School Degree
White males	$21,674	70%
African American males	$15,690	63%
White females	$16,115	93%
African American females	$17,384	104%

You can calculate the percentage increase this way: Divide the difference between high school and college salaries by the high school salary and multiply by 100.

For white males—$21,674 divided by $30,655 = .70 × 100 = 70%

For African American males—$15,690 divided by $24,710 = .63 × 100 = 63%

For white females—$16,155 divided by $17,244 = .93 × 100 = 93%

For African American females—$17,384 divided by $16,571 = 1.04 × 100 = 104%

5.8 The data in this figure are pretty clear. Men tend to earn more than women regardless of the nature of the job. A sociologically naive person might say that men tend to earn more than women because men are more likely to be managers and women are more likely to be clerical workers.

But these data make that naive statement seem really suspect. Even if we only compare the salaries of men and women who do clerical work, it turns out that men's salaries tend to be more than 30 percent higher than women's salaries.

The difference between men's and women's salaries at the managerial level is even bigger. Men tend to earn 40 percent more than women in managerial positions.

5.9

a. The easiest way to analyze these data is to add the different categories into groups. Because your friend seems to think that she is more in danger from strangers than from family and other groups, let's compare those. I am going to create a new table to highlight those differences—table 5.3a.

Table 5.3a Total Murders and Nonnegligent Manslaughters Known to Police, by Victim–Offender Relationship, United States, 1991

Relationship of Victim to Offender	Number	Percent
Family[a]	2,683	12.5%
Nonfamily, nonstranger[b]	7,343	34.1%
Stranger	3,235	15.0%
Unknown relationship	8,247	38.3%
Total	21,508	99.9%

[a] Includes spouse, parent, offspring, sibling, other family.
[b] Includes acquaintance, friend, boyfriend, girlfriend, neighbor.

This new table upsets conventional wisdom. The data suggest that you should be more fearful of people you know (family, friends, neighbors) than of strangers!

b. Men are much more likely than women to be victimized by strangers (and less likely to be victimized by intimate partners or relatives). I will leave it to you to decide why this might be so.

5.10

a. True—overall, men are more likely than women to be victimized by crime. First, notice that the data in this table represent rates of criminal victimization per 1000 people. Thus, the first row of data translates this way: 35 out of 1000 white males were victims of violent crime (short of murder), 9 out of 1000 white males were victims of murder, and 73 out of 1000 white males were victims of theft.

Keep looking at that top section of the table. If you look carefully, you will see that the trend is that males, overall, are more likely to be victims of crime. It might help to re-array the data this way:

	Violent	Murder	Theft
Nonwhite males	49	51	71
White males	35	9	73
Nonwhite females	32	11	56
White females	20	3	64

b. False—overall, whites are *not* more likely to be victims of violent crime than are nonwhites. Look at the data this way:

	Violent	Murder	Theft
Nonwhite males	49	51	71
Nonwhite females	32	11	56
White males	35	9	73
White females	20	3	64

c. True—the very rich and the very poor are more likely to be victims of theft than are people in middle-income categories. (Notice, too, that the more money you make, the less likely it is that you will be a victim of a violent crime.)
d. True—younger people are more likely to be victims of violent crimes than older people are.

Here the general trend seems to be that the older one gets, the safer one becomes from violent crime.

5.11 The answer is d, "not likely at all." White females are the least likely of people in any category to be victims of violent crimes (3 per 1000 population). Also, this professor is in an age group that has a relatively low rate of victimization.

STOP
&
REVIEW

Doing Social Research

A ny sociologist worth her (or his) salt has a broad repertoire of techniques or methods for finding answers to questions. This must be so because finding good answers to different kinds of questions requires different kinds of techniques. So, it will be the nature of the questions to which you want to find answers that determines your choice of method.

Two Traditions: Quantitative and Qualitative Research

There are two major approaches to or traditions of sociological inquiry. One tradition can be traced back to the work of the French sociologist Émile Durkheim. As you will recall from chapter 1, Durkheim saw sociology as the study of social facts. Sociologists, he said, should study social facts in much the same way that chemists study chemical facts and biologists study biological facts. Durkheim was proposing, in other words, that sociology follow the research model established by natural scientists. As scientists, sociologists should observe and measure the actions of social facts. For Durkheim, the goal of sociology was to discover the laws that govern social behavior—just as Newton had discovered the laws that govern planetary behavior. Because research done according to the natural sciences model gathers data that is easily expressed in numbers, this research tradition is often referred to as *quantitative research*.

The second sociological research tradition can be traced back to the work of the German sociologist Max Weber. Weber, too, saw sociology as a science, but he argued that because the subject matter of sociology differs from that of the natural sciences, its research techniques should also differ. According to Weber, following the natural sciences model would leave sociological work incomplete. Human beings have important qualities that set them apart from the objects of natural sciences investigation—that is, human beings think and feel, and they frequently do things for reasons. Thus, said Weber, sociology must go beyond the natural sciences model and be an *interpretative science*—it must take into account the social meanings/reasons attached to behaviors. Weber proposed that sociologists adopt two goals: predicting and understanding social behavior. This sort of research is frequently called *qualitative research* because it focuses not only on the objective nature of behavior but on its meaning (or quality). Although qualitative researchers often use numbers to quantify certain kinds of data, they are more focused on obtaining data that are difficult to quantify. Qualitative research reports generally devote more space to people's descriptive accounts of their own experiences than to numbers that quantify these experiences.

In this chapter, I will describe a variety of methods used by sociologists. Whether they practice in the quantitative or qualitative research tradition, sociologists typically follow one of four basic methods for obtaining data: surveys, experiments, observation, and unobtrusive methods. As you read through the description of each method, be aware each method has its own strengths and weaknesses and is best suited for answering particular sorts of research questions.

First Things First: The Lit Review

No matter which research method sociologists ultimately choose, the first stage is always the same: a review of existing literature on the topic. Many call this phase of research the *lit review*. Now, when you are anxious to actually do some research, spending time in the library doing a lit review may seem a wearisome prospect. But it is never a waste of time!

In the first place, someone may have already found an answer to your question—possibly even a good answer. If that's the case, wouldn't you want to know before wasting your time and energy? Of course, you may indeed find a better answer, but your task will be much easier if you start by determining what is already known.

American sociologist Pitirim Sorokin once compared the researcher seeking sociological knowledge to the explorer seeking out new lands. How tragic for the researcher, Sorokin suggested, to arrive at his or her destination only to hear, "Been there, done that."

> Not knowing that a certain theory has been developed long ago, or that a certain problem has been carefully studied by many predecessors, a sociologist may easily devote his time and energy to the discovery of a new sociological America after it was discovered long

ago. Instead of a comfortable crossing of the scientific Atlantic in the short period of time necessary for the study of what has been done before, such a sociologist has to undergo all the hardships of Columbus to find, only after his time and energy are wasted, that his discovery has been made long ago, and that his hardships have been useless. Such a finding is a tragedy for the scholar, and a waste of valuable ability for sociology and society. (1928, xviii–xix)

Personally, I think Sorokin missed the most important point: How embarrassing to arrive back from sailing the theoretical Atlantic and announce, "The world is flat!" In other words, even worse than reinventing the wheel is inventing *a wheel that will not roll!*

Even if your search of the literature reveals no answer to your particular question, inevitably you will find important clues. Studying what other people have already done, for example, may suggest ways of phrasing your questions or focusing your research in more interesting ways.

The importance of the literature review first really struck me as I was doing research for my Ph.D. dissertation. My topic was public defense attorneys—those attorneys who are paid by the state to defend people who cannot afford a lawyer of their own. When I began my research, my question was fairly simple: How could these attorneys defend clients whom they knew to be guilty of horrible crimes?

So, I did what every good researcher does—I went to the library and started looking for what other social scientists had already found out. The time I spent in the library was enlightening, but in an unexpected way: I found *no* answers to my research question because, according to my predecessors, public defense attorneys *really do not defend their clients!* What? The sociological point of view was that because public defenders are paid by the same agency that pays the prosecutors (the state), they are really just fake lawyers. Even many of the public defenders' clients said that! I particularly recall reading an interview of Eldridge Cleaver in *Playboy* magazine in which he stated that PD stands not for public defender but for "penitentiary dispatcher."[1]

What I personally observed during the first few days in the courtrooms watching these attorneys work made me very skeptical of the conventional wisdom about public defenders. Indeed, I would discover a great deal of evidence that public defenders did about as well for their clients as private attorneys do for theirs. To put it baldly, the information I obtained seriously undermined the

---

[1] It's interesting what one gets to read in the course of doing research, isn't it? A friend of mine did her dissertation on romantic love in American society. Parts of her data were gleaned from so-called romance magazines (such as *True Romance*) and tabloids (like the *National Enquirer*)—all in the name of science.

work of my predecessors. They, not me, were the flat-earthers who had fallen for the conventional wisdom.

Does this mean that I regard my time in the library reading the existing literature as a waste of my time? No way! What I learned from my lit review forced me to phrase my questions about public defenders in much more interesting ways. The issue was not simply how public defenders defend their clients but also why no one thinks they do!

Moreover, what would have happened had I published my findings without taking the time to discuss previous studies and to explain why their conclusions were wrong and mine were right? My readers likely would have thought that I was terribly naive (at best) or an idiot (at worst).

So, the time spent reviewing the work of others is time well spent. The more you know about your predecessors' work, the better you will be prepared to make your own contribution!

The Survey

The idea of the survey is pretty straightforward: If you want to get answers to your questions, simply ask! More specifically, if your research question requires knowing who people are and/or what they think about something, the survey is a good method.

More technically, a *survey* is a series of questions asked of a number of people. Sometimes we ask these questions orally, either face-to-face or over the phone. Other times we give people the list of questions on paper and ask them to write their own answers. The first method is generally referred to as an *interview*; the second method is generally called a *self-administered questionnaire*.

The survey method is popular in sociology because surveys are particularly suited to obtaining information from large numbers of people. Indeed, this ability to obtain data from large numbers of people is the main strength of the survey method. Frequently, survey researchers can obtain information from hundreds, or even thousands, of people in their research.

Surveys are especially appropriate for discovering basic "demographic information" (such as age, gender, income, education, and religious affiliation).[2]

---

[2] The term *demography* is derived from the Greek *demos* ("people") and *graphein* ("to draw or describe"). It was first used, as near as we can tell, by Achille Guillard in his 1855 book *The Elements of Human Statistics*. Demographers study such things as the size of populations and the factors that affect population growth and composition—for example, the rates of marriage, birth, death, and immigration.

Another strength of the survey method is that it allows researchers to obtain information about things that cannot be observed directly, such as attitudes. Using survey techniques allows researchers to tap into people's attitudes on a large variety of issues (for example, "Do you think the president is doing a good job?" or "Do you approve or disapprove of same-sex marriage?").

The weakness of the survey method is that while it can get at people's attitudes, it is not a good way to measure people's actual behavior. If you wish to know about what people *do*, a survey might provide you with misleading information.

Information about people's behavior that is obtained from surveys can be misleading for a number of reasons. For one thing, people might not want to admit (even to themselves) certain behaviors. But more important, many people cannot give an accurate account of their behaviors even when they want to. People may remember, for example, which candidate they voted for in the last election, but they will probably not be able to remember how much campaign literature they read and whether it influenced their decision to vote.

TYPES OF SURVEY QUESTIONS

When you ask questions in a survey, it is important to phrase them in ways that make it possible for respondents to answer. Survey researchers ask two types of questions: *closed-ended* and *open-ended*.

Using the closed-ended format requires that you not only ask the question but also provide answer categories. The respondent answers the question by picking a particular category. Here are some examples of closed-ended questions:

1. Are you: _____ male _____ female?

2. What is your present marital status?
    _____ never married
    _____ married
    _____ separated
    _____ divorced
    _____ widowed

Closed-ended questions can be quite complex:

1. Do any children under the age of 18 live with you full time?
    _____ no _____ yes
        If yes, how many?
            _____ 1–2
            _____ 3–4
            _____ 5 or more

2. Are you presently employed?

     ____ no   ____ yes

          If yes, is your work:

             ____ full time

             ____ part time

             ____ other

A particular kind of closed-ended question is frequently used to ask people about their attitudes on sets of issues. This sort of question is sometimes called a *matrix* question because the answer categories look like a matrix, or array of numbers:

Here are some statements that have been made by students from your college. Please indicate the degree to which you agree or disagree with each by circling the appropriate number to the right of the statement.

	Agree strongly	Agree somewhat	Disagree somewhat	Disagree strongly
1. No student should be allowed to consume alcohol on campus.	1	2	3	4
2. Students should be required to study a minimum of 6 hours each school night.	1	2	3	4
3. Students who miss a class more than once a term should be suspended.	1	2	3	4
4. Faculty should be subject to a dress code.	1	2	3	4

To ask a closed-ended question, you have to know what the appropriate answer categories might be. Sometimes you might not be able to determine these categories in advance. Or you might want to hear or read respondents' answers in their own words. In such cases, open-ended questions should be used:

1. What is the most important thing you have learned so far in this sociology class? Why does that seem important to you? (Please explain.)

2. What is the thing that you like most about your sociology class? Why?

3. What is the thing that you like *least* about your sociology class? Why?

THE ART OF ASKING QUESTIONS

In his book *The Art of Asking Questions*, Stanley L. Payne pointed out that it is pretty cheeky to expect people to answer survey questions:

> People are being exceedingly gracious when they consent to be interviewed. We may ask them to give us anywhere from a few minutes to many hours of their time in a single interview. We may ask them to expose their ignorance with no promise of enlightenment. We may try to probe their innermost thinking on untold subjects. We may sometimes request their cooperation before telling them who the sponsor is and before indicating the nature of our questions—for fear of prejudicing their answers. (1951, 114)

Payne argued that researchers must work hard not to annoy their respondents but rather to treat respondents graciously.

Six Guidelines for Crafting Survey Questions

1. *Adapt the phrasing of questions to the educational level of respondents, but do not be insulting.* "What is your GPA—that is, your grade point average?" sounds patronizing, because it seems to presume that people do not know what GPA stands for. Yet, we do have to deal with the fact that some people may not know what a GPA is. To explain the meaning of your question without sounding patronizing, try rephrasing: "What is your grade point average, that is, your GPA?"

2. *Avoid double negatives in a question.* Here's an example: "Do you oppose denying students access to their files or not?" What!?

3. *Avoid "marathon" questions.* Consider this example: "What do you think we should do about cheating on campus— should we abolish take-home exams, even if this means that students only get tested on writing that they have rushed through, as in in-class exams, or should we allow take-home exams even if this means a number of students will cheat?" Whew!

4. *Don't ask "double-barreled" questions.* That is, ask only one question at a time. Here's a double-barreled question: "Do you favor or oppose giving medical care to small babies and bums?" Well, gee, how can I answer that?

5. *Don't ask "leading" or "loaded" questions.* That is, avoid wording questions in ways that will lead respondents to answer one way over another in spite of their true opinions. Here's a loaded or leading question: "Do you agree with the Democrats that we ought to keep religion and the state separate?" As soon as your respondent sees the word *Democrat*, it will influence his or her answer. ("What, me agree with Democrats? No way; I don't care what the subject is!")

6. *Don't ask questions that your respondents cannot answer.* Unanswerable questions range from ones that ask for inaccessible information ("How many ice cubes did you use last year?" or "Do you believe that the chaos theory poses a serious threat to quantum physics?") to illogical ones ("Have you stopped beating your wife?" or "Quick, is Mickey Mouse a cat or a dog?").

6.1 Here are five poorly constructed survey questions. Indicate what is wrong with each of them.

    a. Do you agree that pulchritude possesses exclusively cutaneous profundity?

    b. Do you agree that colleges ought to do away with homework and drinking alcoholic beverages on campus?

    c. How old were you when you learned to spell *president*?

    d. At what point will you stop lying to me about your answers to these questions?

    e. Do you approve of the practice of bogarting?

The Experiment

Experimentation is the time-honored method for examining causal relationships between variables. I call experiments *time-honored* because I am sure that the first ones were done way back in the earliest days of humanity—perhaps when a cave dweller looked at a hunk of saber-toothed tiger and wondered what would happen if she roasted it over the fire before eating it. Technically, an *experiment* involves manipulating the independent variable (the heat of the meat) and observing (tasting) the effect on the dependent variable (the taste of the meat).

The strength of the experimental method is that it is really the only means by which we can explore causal relationships among variables. In other words, it is the only way to determine for sure that changes in the independent variable cause changes in the dependent variable. But we can only test and be sure about causal relationships if we follow the rules of experimentation *exactly*. Later, I will lay out these rules explicitly. First, work your way through the following example.

The Experiment: An Illustration

My lifelong dream is to think of ways that will help students to do better in their college courses. Toward that end, I have discovered a new technique: If students write the word *sociology* on the hand with which they write, their grades will improve. So, my hypothesis is that students with *sociology* written on their hands will get better grades than students without *sociology* written on their hands. To test my hypothesis, I am going to do an experiment.

In year 1 of my experiment, I let things proceed as normal—I don't tell students the secret of writing *sociology* on their hands. I record the grades they received on an objective test that was graded by another instructor who had no knowledge of the nature of the experiment. In year 2 of the experiment, I tell students to write *sociology* on their hands. At the end of this course, I record the grades they received on an objective test that was graded by another instructor who had no knowledge of the nature of the experiment. It turns out that students in year 2 had better grades than the students in year 1. Does this mean that I should accept my hypothesis as true?

Not so fast! The design of my experiment is flawed because it does not rule out other causes for the differences between group 1 and group 2. Group 2, for example, had a more experienced teacher (me, after a year of practice) than group 1, and perhaps that explains the difference. Who knows? Given the design of my experiment, I can't rule out the possibility that group 2 did better not because they knew the secret, but because of an improved teaching performance from me, but because of the text.

What I need to do is to have two groups at once. Students in one group will be told to write *sociology* on their hands. In other words, students in the first group will experience the manipulation of the independent variable. We will call these students the *experimental group*. Students in the other group will not be exposed to the secret, but everything else will be the same. We will call this second group the *control group* because its presence will help us to determine whether the outcome is due to the secret or to something else. If the students in the experimental group have better grades than the students in the control group, given that the only difference between them is that the students in the experimental group knew the secret, then we can conclude that the secret is what makes the difference in the dependent variable (grades).

Of course, to make this work, I have to be sure at the outset that there are no significant differences between the students in the experimental group and the students in the control group. Suppose I divided the class in half, with students in the front as the experimental group and students in the back as the control group. This would be a foolish way to assign students to groups because there might be some differences between students who choose to sit in the front and those who choose to sit in the back. (In fact, I am fairly sure that there are such differences!)

If I assigned people to groups based on where they sit, this could affect the outcome of my experiment. For example, it's possible that students who choose to sit in the front tend to be more motivated and to get better grades than students who sit in the back of the classroom.

What I need to do is assign each of the students *randomly* to each group. To accomplish this, I might put all the students' names into a hat and draw them out one at a time. The first name out will go in the control group, the second in the experimental group, the third in the control group, the fourth in the experimental group, and so on.

What I have illustrated here is what is known as a *true* or *classic experiment*. In this sort of experiment, the researcher manipulates the independent variable (knowing the secret) and observes the outcome (grades). To really know whether the independent variable is the cause of the difference, the researcher needs at least two groups: (1) an experimental group, which receives the treatment or experiences the manipulation of the independent variable, and (2) a control group, which the researcher pretty much leaves alone. Finally, it is crucial that subjects be assigned randomly to the control and experimental groups.

If I have faithfully followed the rules of experimentation, and it turns out that members of the experimental group receive better grades than the members of the control group, then I can be reasonably confident that the independent variable (writing *sociology* on one's hand) is what caused the difference.

This example highlights the strength of the experimental method of research. That is, it is really the *only* method that allows us to test the causal relationship between variables. When we can assign people randomly to experimental or control groups and then test the effect of the independent variable on the experimental group, we usually can rule out that something besides change in the independent variable is causing change in the dependent variable.

Yet this example also highlights the weakness of the experimental method. In real life, only rarely is one variable actually a cause of another. A student's grades may be affected by a whole series of things—interest in the subject matter, the student's intelligence, the way the professor deals with students of a particular sex, race, or age. It is very difficult to test very complex hypotheses in an experiment because it is difficult to manipulate and control more than one or two variables at a time.

For this reason, many people believe that experiments are not really all that valid, because in real life more than one variable is operating. Of course, experimenters can structure the

---

Five Rules for Doing True Experiments

1. Have at least two groups (control and experimental).
2. Randomly assign people to groups.
3. Treat the experimental group by manipulating the independent variable.
4. Observe the effect of the treatment on the dependent variable in the experimental group.
5. Compare the dependent variable differences (the outcome of treatment) in the experimental and control groups.

---

circumstances so as to make them more like real life. However, this then increases the problem of controlling what is really going on in the experiment.

Experiments can be done only when the researcher knows exactly which variables he or she wishes to test. Therefore, experiments are not helpful unless the researcher already knows a lot about a topic—enough to know which variables are probably causing an effect.

Observation

Of course, all forms of research—even lit reviews—involve some sort of observation. But when sociologists talk about *observational research*, they generally mean a particular research technique in which the researcher directly observes the behavior of individuals in their usual social environments, not in a laboratory. Some sociologists refer to observational research as *field research*, because the normal social world is the field in which sociologists conduct their research.

Different strategies are used in observational or field research. In one strategy, the researcher acts as a *complete participant*. The complete participant essentially goes "undercover" and does not tell the people being observed that he or she is doing research. At the other extreme is the *complete observer*, who views things from a distance (or from behind a one-way mirror) or somehow blends into the social scenery. The complete observer is generally unknown to the people being observed. Finally, midway between these two extremes, is the *participant observer*, who admits to being a researcher so that people know they are being studied.

The particular strength of observing people in the field is that this technique enables researchers not only to observe behavior (that can be done in a laboratory!) but to observe behavior *in its natural context.* When we observe behavior in its natural context, we glean important clues about the impact of context on behavior. Moreover, observational research enables the researcher to get information about individuals who are not able to fill out questionnaires or respond to oral survey questions, such as small children.

The weakness of observational methods includes the fact that only relatively small groups can be observed at once. Moreover, observational research is probably the most labor-intensive kind of research. Finally, the very fact of researcher participation in field research can influence subjects, and therefore findings, in what is known as the *Hawthorne effect.*

Beware the Hawthorne Effect

Back in the 1920s, a group of social scientists wanted to investigate the sorts of things that could influence worker productivity. They chose to study this issue in a factory that made electrical parts: the Western Electric Hawthorne Works in Chicago.

A number of workers agreed to go along with the study—even though they were not told the exact nature and goals of the research. These workers were divided into control and experimental subjects and were placed in special rooms in the factory where they could be easily observed and where the working conditions could be controlled by the scientists.

The researchers believed that worker productivity could be improved by introducing better working conditions (for example, more light, rest breaks, earlier quitting times, meals). So, they provided the workers in the experimental group with these benefits. As expected, worker productivity increased.

What was not expected was the increase in productivity that workers in the control group demonstrated. What was going on here? Even though these workers received none of the benefits enjoyed by the workers in the experimental group, their productivity increased.

As it turned out, what was going on was that the real independent variable was the increased attention that the workers were receiving from the researchers! The increase in productivity in both cases was caused simply by participation in an experiment!

The Hawthorne effect (as it is now called) is an example of what social researchers call the *reactive* effects of research. We know now that reactive effects are not limited to experiments but can take place when there is contact between researcher and subject or when subjects know they are the objects of research.

Unobtrusive (Nonreactive) Research

Most research methods have an impact of some sort on the people being studied. People may respond to surveys in ways they think the interviewer wants them to respond or in ways they think make them seem to be better people. As the idea of the Hawthorne effect suggests, simply knowing that one is being studied can have an impact on one's behavior. Unobtrusive methods are strategies for studying people's behavior in ways that do not have an impact on the subjects.

ARTIFACTS

Archeologists use unobtrusive measures. They dig up the sites of ancient settlements and look for the artifacts that inhabitants left behind. From these artifacts, they can tell a great deal about a people's culture. This sort of unobtrusive research uses what sociologists call *accretion measures*. Similar techniques can be used to build an understanding of contemporary social processes.

> On a particular college campus, the dean of students receives phone calls from parents who are concerned that students might be drinking too much alcohol. The dean decides to do some research to determine just how much drinking is taking place on campus. Her first thought might be, "If I want to know something, why not simply ask?" So, she designs a questionnaire that asks about drinking behaviors and sends a copy to each student on campus. The dean tabulates the responses with a sigh of relief: 99.99 percent of the students say that they rarely drink more than one beer a week.
>
> The assistant dean (who majored in sociology) warns his boss that the data from the questionnaire might be biased. It's possible, he says, that the students did not wish to reveal the true amount of drinking because they were afraid of the consequences. It is also possible that some of the students were so drunk when they filled out the questionnaire that they had no idea of how much they had been drinking.
>
> The assistant dean (who got an A in his introductory sociology class) suggests an alternative: What about taking an unobtrusive approach to the question? He sketches out a research design and carries it out. What he finds is that there probably is a drinking problem on campus and that something ought to be done about it.
>
> So what was the research design? The assistant dean used a kind of trace measure to determine the amount of drinking. More specifically, he got up early one Saturday morning, visited each residence hall, and counted the beer bottles and cans that had been left in the recycling bins and garbage cans. There are 600 students in the school, yet he found 7200 empty beer cans and bottles! Because he knows that the garbage cans and recycling bins are emptied each Friday morning, he is fairly confident that the average student in the college drank 12 cans or bottles of beer sometime between Friday morning and Saturday morning.

As you might guess, a great deal of information can be obtained from what people throw away! Next time you think of it, check your own garbage—I'm betting that you will find clues to your social class origins, your student status, and possibly even your grade point average.

USE OF EXISTING STATISTICS

The U.S. government gathers and publishes incredible amounts of data on everything from how many bedrooms people have in their houses to how many people are arrested for robbery. These data are readily available in libraries and are great starting places for researchers. If you are interested in the differences between men's and women's salaries, for example, the data have already been collected! If you are interested in prisons—their size, their rate of growth, their population—the data are in the library. Businesses and other organizations gather and publish data, too.

CONTENT ANALYSIS

Content analysis involves subjecting some text to careful scrutiny to see what it reveals about its author, the times in which it was written, and so on. The texts that may be studied with content analysis include personal diaries, literature, television shows, radio commercials, magazines and newspapers, and even rock and roll music.

Children's books have frequently been subjected to content analysis, and the results are quite revealing:

> Throughout the 1970s, parents and educators conducted studies to document objectively how men and women were portrayed in the curriculum. . . . It was easy to investigate, there was no need to use time-lapse photography to stop the action. The messages were already frozen on the textbook pages.
>
> [One group of researchers] studied 134 elementary school readers from sixteen different publishers and found the following ratios:

Boy-centered stories to girl-centered stories	5:2
Adult male characters to adult female characters	3:1
Male biographies to female biographies	6:1
Male fairy tale stories to female fairy tale stories	4:1

In a study of award-winning children's books, the results were similar:

> When girls and women were included, they were typecast. They looked in mirrors, watched boys, cried, needed help, served others, gave up, betrayed secrets, acted selfishly, and waited to be rescued. While men were involved in 150 different jobs, women were housewives. When they took off their aprons and discarded their dishtowels, they worked outside the home only as teachers and nurses.

Children's literature and school texts routinely included derogatory comments about being female. For example,

"Women's advice is never worth two pennies. Yours isn't worth even a penny."

"Look at her, Mothers, just look at her. She is just like a girl. She gives up."

"We are willing to share our great thoughts with mankind. However, you happen to be a girl." (Sadker and Sadker 1994, 69–70)

The strength of unobtrusive methods is that they do not require the cooperation of the people being studied. Moreover, the research process itself does not in any way affect the behavior being studied. Unobtrusive researchers study social things after they have occurred. The weakness is that unobtrusive research can only study things that leave traces. Moreover, these traces must be solid enough to last until they can be observed.

The Importance of Triangulation

Triangulation is a term that social researchers borrowed from geodetic surveying—a discipline that has developed techniques for determining the size and shape of the earth and the location of specific landmarks. In geodetics, one uses knowledge of trigonometry to locate a third point by taking bearings from two fixed points that are a known distance apart.

In sociology, we use the term *triangulation* to refer to a research strategy that helps us zero in on social phenomena. Because each research method has both weaknesses and strengths (in other words, because there are advantages and disadvantages to every method), whenever possible researchers use more than one method to obtain data. More specifically, researchers try to use methods whose strengths and weaknesses balance out. When methods are combined so that the strengths of one method overcome the weaknesses of another method, we speak of triangulating research methods.

For example, my interviews with public defenders (of all ranks) suggested that they were paid less than prosecutors. Even the prosecutors agreed. But I was suspicious about the validity of this notion because how much people earn tends to be a closely held secret. I triangulated by checking the official budgets for the public defenders' and prosecutors' offices. What I found was that there was no appreciable difference between how much public defenders and prosecutors were paid. However, I did find some important clues to why the lawyers might feel differently rewarded for their work. The budget for the prosecutors' office included a lot more money for amenities (phones, photocopying, law journals, investigators, secretaries, and the like). No doubt, the sense that public defenders were being paid less was tied to their perception that they received fewer perks and resources for actually doing the job.

Here my triangulation (even though it was really only "biangulation") was successful. The advantage of using existing statistics (for example, budgets) is that they lay out the facts in a fairly reliable manner while data from interviews may not be so reliable. However, the facts of the budget did not speak for themselves; it was only through my interviews that I discovered the sense of deprivation that one set of lawyers had when compared to the others. They were right about being relatively deprived, just not right about the source of this feeling.

Sampling

Once you have selected your method (or, whenever possible, your methods), you have some decisions to make about whom you will interview, observe, or experiment on. In other words, you have to make some decisions about your sample. The *sample* is that portion of the larger population that you will study to make inferences about the larger population.

Why not simply study the entire population? Generally, the cost of studying an entire population is beyond the financial resources of researchers. Anyway, if one's sample is selected properly, the results can be as valid as results obtained from the entire population.

Drawing a sample is both a science and an art. In fact, some social researchers make their livings simply by helping others draw good representative samples. I will not go into much detail here, but I will share the basics of this process with you.

How big your sample should be depends on one thing especially: how diverse the population is. If the population is very diverse (*heterogeneous*), then you will have to draw a large sample to get representativeness. Imagine two jars filled with gum balls. The first one contains fifty gum balls—ten each of five different flavors. The second one contains fifty gum balls of the same flavor. If I drew only one gum ball from the second jar, my sample would be absolutely representative. But if I drew only one gum ball from the first jar, I would miss four of the flavors. I would need at least five different gum balls to accurately reflect the contents of the first jar. So, as a general rule of thumb, we can say that *the more diverse a population is, the larger the sample needs to be.*

When you hear about surveys done before elections, for example, you will frequently hear about two sorts: scientific and nonscientific. The difference usually has to do with the sort of sampling technique used. Scientific surveys use samples that are drawn according to the rules of random sampling; unscientific surveys use nonrandom sampling techniques.

Don't be confused about this. In science, the word *random* has a specific technical meaning—*every element in the population has the same probability of being in the sample.* To be able to say that one has obtained a true random sample of, say, students at Home Town U requires that every college student who attends HTU have the same probability of being picked to be in the sample. Thus, for example, if I wanted to pick a random sample of students, I would not use the dean's list, because students with low GPAs would not have the same probability of being included. I would also not draw my sample only from students who lived in residence halls, because students who lived off-campus would have no chance of being in the sample.

To get a random sample of students at HTU, I would have to obtain a list of every student taking college courses and pick from that.

Standing on the street corner with a clipboard and asking questions of people passing by is not using random sampling! (This sort of sample is called a *convenience sample.*)

6.2 For each of the following research questions, indicate which would be your first choice of research methods and why.

a. How will people vote in the upcoming municipal elections?

b. How do preschool boys and girls interact with each other compared to how sixth-grade boys and girls interact?

c. How does a particular secret organization socialize its new members?

d. What are the effects of increasing wages on employee productivity?

e. Are women or men more likely to have their personal space invaded when waiting in line (for example, at the grocery store or bank machine)?

f. To what degree do people who live in the United States believe that people from other countries are honest?

g. Has the number of children in the average family increased or decreased since the 1950s?

h. The Ajax company has instituted a program for recycling paper. Are employees actually recycling paper?

i. Do patients recover from surgery faster when taken care of by physicians specially trained to have a sympathetic bedside manner?

Ethics and Social Research

When researchers make decisions about how to do their research, they are guided by two important concerns. One concern is, Which method is best, given the nature of my research problem? But the second, and more important, concern is, What is the risk that my research might harm someone—one of the research participants or even other people in the community?

This is not to say that research that involves risk cannot be done. But today's researcher is required to reduce the risk as much as possible. And, where risk is necessary and the benefits of the research are great, the researcher is required to obtain *informed consent* from any person who participates in the research. What is informed consent? It is consent that is obtained after the potential research participant has been told what he or she will be asked to do, what the benefits will be, and what the possible harms are.

To help researchers make ethical decisions (and to help ensure that they do), most universities and colleges have established Institutional Review Boards (IRBs). These review boards are made up of members of the faculty as well as members of the community. Their job is to examine each research plan to ensure that the researchers who designed it have given the appropriate amount of thought to the possible risks and benefits of the research.

j. Are professors in the humanities more or less likely to publish articles and books than professors in the social sciences?

Chapter Review

1. Make a list of the sociological concepts that you learned in this chapter. Define each term. (*Hint:* You will learn the most from this exercise if, in addition to defining each concept, you create an example of it in your own words.)

2. Describe the essential difference between unobstrusive and obtrusive research strategies.

3. Why is triangulation important in social research?

4. Suppose you wanted to test the following hypothesis (in your location): College men drink more beer than college women.
   a. Which research strategy would be your first choice to test this hypothesis? Why?
   b. Explain how you would triangulate your research and why.

STOP
&
REVIEW

Answers and Discussion

6.1

a. The high-falutin' phrasing of the question makes it unclear. Simplify the phrasing: "Do you agree that beauty is only skin deep?"

b. This is a double-barreled question; it asks two questions. It is very likely that most people would have different opinions on the two things being asked about and so they would have trouble answering this question. If you really want to know people's views on these matters, ask two separate questions.

c. This is a good example of a question that asks for information that will probably not be accessible to the subject. So, you would probably receive a lot of "I don't knows" in response—or people would make some wild guesses.

d. This is not a question that all people could answer. A person who has been lying to the interviewer could answer this question, but a person who has not been lying would have trouble answering, because it's illogical.

e. This question may be unclear to many respondents because it uses a slang term ("bogarting" was a term used years ago to refer to anyone who hogged a marijuana cigarette for too long before passing it along to the next person in the group).

6.2

a. The best way would be to ask people how they intend to vote. There really is no other way (that I can think of).

b. A survey probably would not work because the children are so young that they wouldn't be able to articulate their interaction patterns. Observation of boys and girls interacting would be best.

c. This could be tricky. On the one hand, you could ask members of secret organizations how they socialize their new members. It is likely, however, that members of such organizations would be reluctant to tell an interviewer their secrets. It is possible, though not likely, that you could find some documentation on this, perhaps a booklet entitled "How to Socialize New Members of Our Secret Organization." Ordinarily, such documents published by organizations are great sources of information, but secret organizations probably don't publish much stuff. Of course, many secret organizations might publish their secrets to help out their members, and you might steal such a document. However, the ethics of this are questionable (at best). The most obvious method would be covert observation, also ethically questionable.

d. Experimentation.

e. Observation.

f. Probably a survey (either self-administered or interview format). The survey is a good way of getting at people's attitudes.

g. The use of existing statistics, such as census data, would be the most straightforward and reliable method. Why pay to do a survey when the government has already collected the data?

h. You could ask the employees whether they are following through, but the best way would be to look in the garbage: Are there recyclable materials there?

i. This would make a lovely experiment!

j. Again, you could survey a number of professors. However, many likely would be "mistaken" about how much they have published or might exaggerate to look better. It would be better to look at lists of publications and count for yourself. Or you could ask professors for copies of their resumes (called curriculum vitae in academia). Generally, professors are pretty diligent about recording their publications on their vitae.

S T O P

&

R E V I E W

Culture

As I sit down to write about culture, I feel like an ant trying to describe an elephant. The first thing that must be said about culture is that it's *big*. But my task is more difficult than the ant's— an ant can turn away from the elephant and not see it. I cannot escape from culture; it surrounds me, it's inside of me, and I take it wherever I go. In short, culture is ubiquitous.[1]

Not only is it always and everywhere, but culture makes a difference in how I live my life. My culture influences what I eat, how I speak, what I believe, how I behave, and what I value. Clearly an understanding of culture is essential for anyone who wishes to understand people's behaviors and interactions with others.

Two eminent anthropologists defined culture this way:

> Culture consists of patterns, explicit and implicit, of and for behavior acquired and transmitted by symbols, constituting the distinctive achievements of human groups, including their embodiments in artifacts; the essential core of culture consists of traditional (i.e., historically derived and selected) ideas [beliefs] and especially their attached values; culture systems may, on the one hand, be considered as products of action, on the other, as conditioning elements of further action. (Kroeber and Kluckhohn 1952, 181)

That's a pretty tough introduction to culture, so in this chapter I am going to make understanding culture easier by separating out its various parts.

---

[1] If you don't know this word, look it up—it's everywhere!

Material and Nonmaterial Culture

Culture has both material and nonmaterial attributes. *Material culture* includes all those things that humans make or adapt from the raw stuff of nature: computers, houses, forks, bulldozers, jewelry, telephones, socks, bologna sandwiches, oil paintings, and so on.

As this list suggests, material culture includes some very sophisticated and complex objects. But to create a piece of material culture, one does not have to bring a thing very far from its natural state. Suppose I pick up a stick in the forest and use it to help me keep my balance. This walking stick becomes as much a part of material culture as my personal computer.

There is a difference, however, between my walking stick and the sticks that I ignored: The sticks that remain on the floor of the forest are merely sticks. They have no other meaning and are not, therefore, pieces of material culture.

To put it more technically, I can say that *material culture is made up of artifacts.* Artifacts are by-products of human behavior.[2]

NONMATERIAL CULTURE

Nonmaterial culture is different first of all because it is made up of intangible things—and these intangible things also vary from simple to complex. Our ideas about truth and beauty, about happiness and boredom, about what is funny and what is not, about right and wrong—all these are part of nonmaterial culture. So, too, are the words with which we express these ideas. We can divide up nonmaterial culture into five basic categories: symbols, language, norms, values, and beliefs.

SYMBOLS

A symbol is anything that represents something else to more than one person. The symbols on my computer keyboard include $ (dollar), % (percent), & (and), £ (English pound), § (section), ¶ (paragraph), © (copyright), and ™ (trademark). Each of these marks is a symbol because it stands for something other than itself—a ¶ is not a paragraph, but merely symbolizes a paragraph.

Some objects are symbols in that they mean something other than themselves. In the English language of flowers, if you give someone a red rose it means something different than if you give someone a lily.

Humans Are to Culture as Fish Are to Water

"The last thing which a dweller in the deep sea would be likely to discover would be water. He would become conscious of its existence only if some accident brought him to the surface and introduced him to air. Man, throughout most of his history, has been only vaguely conscious of the existence of culture and has owed even this consciousness to contrast between the customs of his own society and those of some other with which he happened to be brought into contact."

—Ralph Linton (1945)

---

[2] The linguistic root of *artifact* is similar to the Latin root for *artificial*, which means "made by humans."

By definition, symbols are social things—if an object has meaning only to one individual, it is not a symbol. So, let's say that a symbol is anything that at least two people agree represents something other than itself.

Ugh. That sounds so dry. I want to convey the fact that symbols are worthy of study by sociologists because in the interaction between human beings, symbols are powerful things. *They are powerful because we react to them as if they were the real thing.* For example, if someone gives me a rose, I am apt to feel pleasure; if someone paints a swastika (the symbol of Nazi Germany) on my synagogue, I will get very angry. Symbols do not simply convey information—they are powerful enough to invoke emotions!

LANGUAGE

Language is an organized set of symbols, but language is such an essential part of nonmaterial culture that I think it deserves its own section. Many sociologists argue, in fact, that without language, there can be no culture at all. After all, to have symbols, we need some means of learning what these objects stand for—and the best way of conveying such meanings between people is through the use of language. It would be difficult to sustain nonmaterial culture without language. Certainly any activity that requires cooperation between individuals (from hunting game to building rockets) is facilitated by language.

Language is made up of certain kinds of symbols (spoken or written words and gestures) and rules (such as grammar and syntax[3]) for using these. Language-use rules are important because words in and of themselves cannot convey complex meanings very clearly. Although sometimes it might seem as if having to fol-

---

Different parts of a culture system tend to reinforce one another. Notice how these children's jumping rhymes tend to reinforce traditional gender-role expectations.

"John and Mary sitting in a tree,
K-I-S-S-I-N-G.
First comes love, then comes marriage,
then comes Mary with a baby carriage.
How many babies did she have?
1, 2, 3, 4..."

"I'm a little Dutch girl, dressed in blue.
Here are the things that I like to do:
Salute to the captain, curtsy to the queen,
and hit them both with a rotten tangerine."

"Johnny on the ocean, Johnny on the sea,
Johnny broke a bottle, and he blamed it on me.
I told Ma, Ma told Pa,
and Johnny got a lickin', ha-ha-ha.
How many lickin's did he get?"

"Cinderella dressed in yella,
went upstairs to meet her fella.
On the way her girdle busted.
How many people were disgusted?
1, 2, 3, 4..."

---

[3] Rules of syntax have to do with proper word ordering.

low the rules of grammar gets in the way of being able to express ourselves, without such rules we would be hard-pressed to understand one another. Examine the following pairs of statements; they demonstrate how syntax can make all the difference:

"Man shot in head accidentally dies"
    versus
"Man accidentally shot in head dies"

"Congressman sat informally on the carpet and discussed food prices and the cost of living with several women"
    versus
"Congressman sat informally on the carpet with several women and discussed food prices and the cost of living"

Or how about this headline: "Missouri Pacific to drop passengers from three trains" (Lederer 1987, 83).

Gestures are part of language as well. Nodding your head up and down, for example, communicates a different message than shaking your head back and forth does.

NORMS

In sociology we call rules about behavior *norms*. Norms also are part of nonmaterial culture. Some norms, of course, are more important than others. Consider these four norms about how women should dress when they attend a church or temple in the United States:

Women must not wear white shoes after Labor Day (early September).

Women must not wear jeans.

Women must not wear clothing that exposes their navels.

Women must not wear clothing that exposes their breasts.

Compared to the others, the first norm seems pretty trivial. Someone who violated it would probably only be punished by a quick glance of disapproval. Depending on the church, someone who violated the second norm might get anything from a long nasty stare to a request to leave. The same can be said for the third norm—but many would see a violation of the "no navel" norm as possibly more offensive than a violation of the "no jeans" norm. However, the woman who arrives at church with bare breasts will not be able to ignore her punishment. She will not only receive disapproving looks from other members of the church but might even be arrested.

This brings us to an important point: The way to judge the importance of a norm (and even whether it exists) is to observe how people respond to behavior. Based on the church members'

Sociologist Ian Robertson illustrated the difference between *folkways* and *mores* this way:

"A man who walks down a street wearing nothing on the upper half of his body is violating a folkway; a man who walks down the street wearing nothing on the lower half of his body is violating one of our most important mores, the requirement that people cover their genitals and buttocks in public." (1987, 62)

responses, we can not only identify the norms but get a sense of how important they are.

TYPES OF NORMS

Having observed lots of norm violations and responses to norm violators in many societies, social scientists realized that there were different categories of norms.

In his book *Folkways* (1906), sociologist William G. Sumner divided norms into two categories:

1. *Folkways.* These represent casual norms; violations are not taken very seriously. Eating cereal for breakfast and pizza for dinner are examples of folkways. At worst, the punishment for violating a folkway might be a dirty look, rolled eyes, or disapproving comment ("You eat pizza for *breakfast!?*").

2. *Mores.* These are anything but casual. Mores reflect important rules, such as the norms against unjustified assaults on other persons.[4]

Later, sociologists added a third category:

3. *Taboos.* There are norms that are so deeply held that even the *thought* of violating them upsets people. For example, in the United States, there is a taboo against eating human flesh.

7.1 Think of at least one example of each of the following norms: folkway, mos, and taboo. Explain why your example fits the definition of each norm.

SANCTIONS

If you violate a norm, you can expect a certain type of response from others—what sociologists call a *negative sanction*. The seriousness of this negative sanction depends on the importance of the norm. Violations of folkways might be sanctioned by a comment or a nasty look. Violations of taboos, on the other hand, might be sanctioned by expulsion from the social group, imprisonment, or even death.

The form of the negative sanction can vary as well. Sociologists distinguish between formal and informal negative sanctions.

Formal sanctions are official responses from specific organizations within society, such as the government, universities, or

---

[4]*Mores* (pronounced "MORE-rays") is the plural of *mos*. Technically one would write that "the rule against murder is an important mos, and one of the most important mores." For some reason, hardly anyone ever refers to a particular mos; generally, the issue is discussed in terms of the plural—*mores*.

churches. Formal negative sanctions meted out by the government include prison sentences and fines. Formal negative sanctions doled out by a university range from library fines to expulsion. Formal negative sanctions given by a church range from having to do penance to excommunication.

Informal sanctions come from the individuals in social groups. Informal negative sanctions can range from being laughed at and made to feel humiliated to being given the cold shoulder by everyone in the group.

There is no cut-and-dried correspondence between the form of a negative sanction and its effect or consequences. The formal negative sanction of a parking ticket is less painful to many than the informal sanction of being laughed at or ignored by one's friends or family.

Note, too, that someone who violates a norm can (and frequently does) receive both a formal and an informal sanction. Students caught cheating in a sociology course, for example, may receive the formal negative sanction of a failing grade and the informal negative sanction of expressions of disgust from friends and family.

Of course, it is not simply norm *violating* that evokes responses from others. If your behavior is in keeping with a norm or, especially, if it goes beyond what is expected, you may be rewarded with a *positive sanction*. Positive sanctions also range from small to large and can be either formal or informal. Formal positive sanctions are those given out officially by some organization and can range from receiving an A in a sociology course to winning the Nobel Peace Prize. Informal positive sanctions range from a smile to a standing ovation.

The Power of Informal Sanctions

As I suggest in the text, there is no necessary correspondence between the type of a negative sanction (formal or informal) and its effect or consequences. Nonetheless, many of my students seem to presume that being at the receiving end of a formal sanction must be worse than being the victim of an informal sanction. William James, an early psychologist, knew that informal sanctions can be much more powerful:

> If no one turned round when we entered, answered when we spoke, or minded what we did, but if every person "cut us dead," and acted as if we were nonexisting things, a kind of rage and impotent despair would ere long well up in us, from which the cruellest bodily tortures would be a relief; for these [tortures] would make us feel that, however bad might be our plight, we had not sunk to such a depth as to be unworthy of attention at all. (1890)

7.2 Using the diagram below as a model, write appropriate examples of each type of sanction.

Types of Sanctions

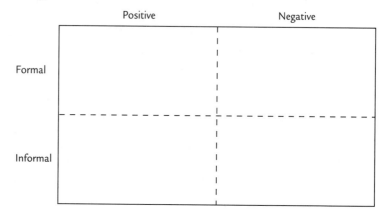

VALUES

In important respects, norms are one way that people in society have of expressing their values. So, once you have identified a group's norms, you can begin to see its values. For example, when you observe a negative sanction being given to someone who

---

What Do Americans Value?
(Williams 1970)

Achievement and success
Hard work
Efficiency and practicality
Science and rationality
Progress
Material comfort
Equality
Freedom
Democracy
The superiority of their own group

Ponder

Think of some instances of values in conflict. For example, in what ways might the values of *achievement* and *success* conflict with the value of *equality*? How about *democracy* and *freedom*?

Ideology

The concept of ideology generally refers to knowledge that has been distorted by social, economic, or political interests. The term was invented at the beginning of the nineteenth century by the French philosopher Antoine Louis Claude Destutt de Tracy, who used it to distinguish his new science of ideas from both the old study of philosophy and the study of empirical facts. But the concept of ideology gained currency only when it was taken up by Karl Marx and Friedrich Engels in their book *The German Ideology*. Marx and Engels used ideology to refer specifically to the set of ideas found in law, religion, literature, and art that the upper classes use to maintain their economic superiority:

> The ideas of the ruling class are in every epoch the ruling ideas: i.e., the class, which is the ruling material [economic] force of society, is at the same time its ruling intellectual force. The class which has the means of material production at its disposal, has control at the same time over the means of mental production, so that thereby, generally speaking, the ideas of those who lack the means of mental production are subject to it. The ruling ideas are nothing more than the ideal expression of the dominant material relationships . . . ; hence, of the relationships which make the one class the ruling one, therefore the ideas of its dominance. (1845–46/1963, 39)

In 1929 Karl Mannheim (a Hungarian sociologist who established the sociology of knowledge as an important field of study) published a work entitled *Ideology and Utopia*. In that book Mannheim expanded on Marx and Engel's use of the concept. As Mannheim pointed out, it is not only the ruling or upper class that has a particular worldview (or, to use the German term, *Weltanschauung*). The *Weltanschauung*—or the beliefs, worldviews, and ideas of people in all sorts of groups (ethnic and racial as well as economic)—can likewise be distorted by their social, political, and economic interests.

cheated, you might suspect that honesty is a value. (Or perhaps not getting caught is the thing that is valued.)

Values are general or abstract ideas about what is good and desirable, as opposed to what is bad and undesirable, in a society. For example, in a particular society, honesty might be valued over dishonesty, loyalty over disloyalty, liberty over restraint, and order over disorder.

The abstractness of values sometimes creates problems of conflict. The values themselves might not necessarily conflict, but the real-world implications might. A group of people might accept the same values in principle but find that they cannot agree on how to put these values into practice. For example, if your best friend asks to copy your test answers, does your loyalty to your friend win out over your commitment to honesty?[5]

Similarly, in our society we value freedom, but we also value safety and security. For example, should we pass laws that take away from people's liberty to preserve order in society? Since its founding, the U.S. legal system has struggled to balance laws that protect freedom with laws that protect people's safety.

IDEAS AND BELIEFS

Social scientists use the term *belief* to refer to *people's ideas about what is real and what is not real*. Beliefs, then, have to do with what people accept as factual. For example, as I mentioned in chapter 1, people once believed that the earth was the center of the universe.

Beliefs and values are frequently related. Church leaders were reluctant to let go of their beliefs about the geocentric nature of the cosmos because it was in keeping with their values. But beliefs and values are different, too. Most people in society regard the preservation of human life as an important value, but many disagree with respect to their beliefs about who qualifies as a human being.

How It Adds Up

Having separated out the different elements of culture, it is time to reexamine that definition of culture. Read it through again—this time, it should make more sense.

Statements of Belief

Men are stronger than women.
God exists.
Hard work leads to personal success.
The earth is round.
Women are smarter than men.
The heart is the seat of emotion.
Germs cause disease.
Two plus two equals four.

---

[5] Allow me to interject a personal observation by suggesting that this is no real dilemma—what *friend* would ask you to cheat and thereby place you in jeopardy of failing the course?

Culture consists of patterns [norms], explicit and implicit, of and for behavior acquired and transmitted by symbols, constituting the distinctive achievements of human groups, including their embodiments in artifacts; the essential core of culture consists of traditional (i.e., historically derived and selected) ideas [beliefs] and especially their attached values;

As you may recall, there was a final part of the definition:

culture systems may, on the one hand, be considered as products of action, on the other, as conditioning elements of further action. [emphasis added]

Let's explore this final part of the definition by distinguishing between culture as a product of action and as a conditioning element of further action.

Culture as a Product of Action

This part is fairly simple: Culture systems (the total package of material and nonmaterial cultural things) are created by humans and in this sense are products of action. Because culture is a product of human action and interaction, we would expect different groups of humans to have different cultures. And thus it is that the content of culture systems varies widely across societies.

That being the case, any examination of a culture system can reveal a great deal about the people who share in that culture. Think of how much archeologists have learned merely by examining the remains of material culture, such as a clay bowl or hammered piece of metal, left behind by peoples long dead. These artifacts can tell us a great deal about the level of technology in a society, as well as its members' norms, values, and beliefs.

The *content* of language itself reveals a great deal about a culture. What can you deduce from the fact that the Masai of Africa have seventeen terms for *cattle*? That the Ifugeos of the Philippines have twenty terms for *rice*? That the residents of the Trobriand islands of Papua, New Guinea, have a hundred words for *yams*? That the people of the Solomon Islands have nine words for *coconut*? For that matter, what can you deduce from the fact that college students may have upward of two dozen words for *vomit*?

Even parts of our language that we assume mimic natural sounds are cultural. A dog may say "bow-wow" in English, but Spanish dogs say "gua-gua," Russian dogs say "af-af," and Japanese dogs say "wan-wan."

It is not just the spoken word that varies across societies. Gestures have different meanings to different peoples as well. Nodding your head up and down means you agree—right? (Nod

In Great Britain and in other countries, these gestures have distinctly different meanings.

"Up yours!"   *"Victory!"*

In the United States, thumbs-up means "good job" or "A-OK." In Australia, Nigeria, and other places, this is a very rude gesture.

your head.) But if you were visiting Bulgaria, parts of Greece, the former Yugoslavia, Turkey, Iran, or Bengal and you nodded your head up and down, it would be read as disagreement (Axtell 1991, 60).

So much of what we take for granted as "natural," as instinctual or genetic, is really a product of culture. For example, linguist Ray L. Birdwhistell observed that "we have found no gesture or body motion which has the same social meaning in all societies" (1970, 35). In his book *Word Play*, Peter Farb adds that "human beings everywhere rotate their heads upon their necks, blink and open wide their eyes, move their arms and hands—but the significance of these nonverbal signals varies from society to society" (1993, 204).

Norms, values, and beliefs vary from culture to culture, just as language does. These differences can often result in travelers feeling a sense of "culture shock."[6]

Culture as a Conditioning Element of Further Action

The easiest way to explain how culture conditions our actions or behaviors is to say that culture puts us all in the same rut. For the most part, it is a reasonably comfortable rut, but it is a rut nonetheless.

Every society has problems that must be solved, such as providing shelter, food, and clothing. Once a particular problem has been solved in a satisfactory way, people tend to stick with that solution. And their children repeat these solutions, as do their children. Along the way, of course, the solutions are likely to become more elaborate, but they do tend to follow the established path. In other words, once a track through the problems of life is established, people tend to stay on that track.

This rut, or the influence of culture, is so comfortable to most of us (after all, most of us have never experienced anything else) that it is difficult to see until you really look. But it can be seen! Consider the following examples.

As you drive through town, you will notice (if you look) that most people have solved the problem of shelter in the same basic ways. The houses and apartment buildings themselves look remarkably alike. They all have doors and windows. And in spite of the fact that there are many colors from which to choose,

---

[6] Recall Chagnon's response to the Yanomamö (described in chapter 4). That was a great illustration of culture shock.

Problems Identified and Resolved in All Known Cultures
(Murdock 1945)

Beliefs about death	Numerals
Bodily adornment	Personal names
Calendar	Population policy
Cleanliness training	Property rights
Cooking	Puberty customs
Cosmology	Religious rituals
Courtship	Sexual restrictions
Dance	Soul concepts
Decorative art	Sports
Divination	Superstition
Dream interpretation	Surgery
Education	Toolmaking
Ethics	Trade
Etiquette	Weaning
Faith healing	Weather control

---

most people paint their houses white, gray, light blue, or some "earth tone."

The next time you go out to dinner, watch the people around you to see how they have solved the problem of *how* to eat. In the United States people tend not to eat Jell-O with their fingers; they use a spoon. Most people will lick an ice cream cone but not a bowl of ice cream (even when the bowl is made of edible material). Tomatoes are served in a green (vegetable) salad but not in a fruit salad—even though a tomato is really a fruit. And most people eat the main course before the dessert.

The next time you go to class, look around at your classmates and see how they have solved the problem of clothing themselves. How many of the women are wearing fancy dresses? You know that a woman is likely to have at least one such dress in her closet, but even if it is her favorite dress, she won't wear it to class. How many of the men are wearing lipstick? Why are several people wearing baseball caps, but not a single one is wearing a football helmet?

The similarities in our solutions to the everyday problems of shelter, food, and clothing are more than coincidental. The ways in which we construct our dwellings, eat our food (and even what we consider to be food), and cover our bodies are not the only possible solutions to the problems of shelter, food, and clothing. But they are the solutions chosen by those who have gone before us, and though we have elaborated on them, these traditions or customs influence how we live our lives.

Varieties of Cultural Wisdom

Proverbs are one repository of cultural wisdom. Every culture has them—for example, Haitians caution, "Do not insult the mother alligator until after you have crossed the river"; while the Greeks warn that "White hair is not a sign of wisdom, only age." The Irish suggest that "It is better to be a coward for a minute than dead for the rest of your life," and according to the Japanese, "The nail that sticks up gets hammered down," and "A man in love mistakes a pimple for a dimple."

Notwithstanding their heritage, some of these sayings seem to provide lessons that are universal; others are harder to understand unless we know more about their context. Consider the following Yiddish proverbs. Which of them make sense to you?

"When a poor man gets to eat a chicken, one of them is sick."

"When a father gives to his son, both laugh; when a son gives to his father, both cry."

"If God were living on earth, people would break his windows."

"One fool can ask more questions than ten sages can answer."

"What good is a cow that gives plenty of milk and then kicks over the pail?"

Social Institutions

Some solutions to problems are given special status—these solutions are called *institutions*. In everyday speech, people may refer to a specific organization as an institution ("This university is an institution of higher learning"). But to a sociologist, the term has a different meaning: *an institution is a set of ideas about the way a specific important social need ought to be addressed*. Institutional responses to problems tend to be justified by important social values and beliefs, and they tend to be slow to change. An institution, then, is part of nonmaterial culture.

Another way to put this is to say that once a particular pattern of responding to important social needs has become established, it becomes *institutionalized*. As parts of nonmaterial culture, institutions vary across societies, but (as you will see in chapter 9) all societies must address the same core of crucial problems.

Within a particular society, there is some latitude for difference in responding to basic social needs, but not too much. Take religion, for example. Even in our society, where people pride themselves on having freedom of religion, one's religious practices cannot stray too far from the accepted institutional pattern. If your religion requires you to participate in the sacrifice of the Eucharist or holy communion, that is okay. Sacrificing goats or chickens is getting a bit too far from the institutionalized line and may earn you an informal negative sanction. But sacrificing virgins is quite another thing—freedom of religion does not extend that far even in the United States.

Social Change: Cultural Diffusion and Leveling

Not every solution to a society's problems has been inherited from its ancestors. Depending on the extent of communication and contact between people of different cultures, people can adopt some of the solutions to life's problems from other cultures. Sociologists call the process by which cultural things are adopted *cultural diffusion*. For example, Americans have adopted sushi bars from the Japanese culture, and the Japanese have adopted baseball from American culture.

Elements of nonmaterial culture may diffuse, or spread, from one society to another as well. But the diffusion of nonmaterial culture is frequently more problematic. It is one thing to adopt American hamburgers, but quite another to adopt American ideas about women's role in society! Adopting a piece of material culture is easier because it is often easier to separate tangible things from their intangible meanings, which may not mesh or be congruent with a culture's values.

As cultural diffusion increases, the differences between cultures decrease. When you walk down a street in London, New York, Moscow, or Singapore and see someone eating a Big Mac or a Whopper while talking on a cellular phone or listening to Madonna on a portable compact disc player, you experience this sense of cultural *leveling*.

Subcultures and Countercultures

Especially in modern societies, it is misleading to speak of culture as if it were shared equally by everyone in a particular society. Some parts of a culture are shared only by specialized groups of people. When a group of people share enough specialized elements within a cultural system, they may constitute what is known as a *subculture*. *A subculture is any group of people whose shared specialized values, norms, beliefs, or use of material culture sets them apart from other people in society.*

Subcultures can exist for a variety of reasons. Some subcultures are occupational in nature. As a result of their work, for example,

---

From *Much Depends on Dinner* (1986)

MARGARET VISSER

The extent to which we take everyday objects for granted is the precise extent to which they govern and inform our lives [emphasis added]. The knee-high chair, the four-pronged fork, the corridor or hallway which enables us to walk into a room without having to pass through another room to do so: these determine (among other things) how and where we sit down, the manner in which we approach our food, and the thoroughness with which we live separately from others and respect the privacy and autonomy of their lives. None of these objects is necessary; many cultures eschew them altogether, and there was a time when our own ancestors lived very happily without them. We invented them, however, to fill needs: chairs, forks, and hallways were required by the sort of people we have become; *having them now prevents us from being different . . .* [emphasis added].

One of the great eye-openers of the twentieth century (like every discovery it sprung from our need) is the realization that the use of humble everyday objects is not only habitual—which is to say that we cannot do without them—but that these things are "ordinary" in the earliest and fullest sense of the word also: *they embody our mostly unspoken assumptions, and they both order our culture and determine its direction . . .* [emphasis added].

The English (and hence the American) tradition with roasts is still to bring in the whole bird or joint and carve it up in front of the guests—an extraordinarily old-fashioned procedure. Ever since the Middle Ages most European cuisines have been moving steadily away from such confrontations with the cutting of carcasses; the kitchen is in most cultures the place for such indelicacies, while the guests are protected by being seated safely in the dining-room. Even in Anglo-Saxon countries, however, modern capitulations to smaller joints, to convenience, and to the custom in hotels, often result in the less grand carving of a joint or a bird into pieces in the kitchen. The meat is then served . . . already on plates. Large joints are less popular than they used to be because families are smaller; added to which, North Americans in particular tend to classify "left-overs" with garbage, so that remainders of meat are wasteful. The result has been that joints and whole birds (huge turkeys, for example) have become especially festive in connotation: they are for relatively rare gatherings, when almost all of the meat will probably be consumed at a sitting.

---

police officers tend to see the world in similar ways. Many police officers come to feel uncomfortable hanging out with "civilians" and so tend to socialize exclusively with other officers. The same can be said of physicians.

Shared religious beliefs can also bring subcultures into being. Some religious groups, like the Amish, are examples of people whose practices and beliefs set them apart from the rest of society.

Regional differences are also at the root of some subcultures. For example, people who live in the southern United States tend to have in common special folkways, foods, and even accents that set them apart from other Americans.

Some subcultures are based on shared ethnic or racial heritage; others may be based on age, social class, and even sexual orientation.

Countercultures are different. When members of a subculture hold values or adhere to norms that are not only distinct from those of the larger culture *but in opposition to them,* sociologists call that group a *counterculture.*

7.3 Distinguish between subculture and counterculture. Give at least two examples of each.

7.4

STOP & REVIEW

    a. Margaret Visser states, "The extent to which we take everyday objects for granted is the precise extent to which they govern and inform our lives." What did she mean by that?

    b. Think of at least five ways in which culture has influenced your behavior today.

Chapter Review

1. Make a list of the sociological concepts that you learned in this chapter. Define each term. (*Hint:* You will learn the most from this exercise if, in addition to defining each concept, you create an example of it in your own words.)

2. Explain how culture can be both a product of action and a producer of action.

3. Was the author of the following sentence exhibiting enthnocentrism or cultural relativity? What do you interpret the quotation to mean?

   "Natives who beat drums to drive off evil spirits are objects of scorn to smart Americans who blow horns to break up traffic jams."

4. New norms must be created in response to changes in society. Describe the norms that have evolved governing the use of cell phones or e-mail. As far as you have observed, how widespread are these norms? What sanctions come to people who violate these norms?

STOP & REVIEW

Answers and Discussion

7.1   Check your examples. Is your example of a folkway a "gentle rule" about how things are usually done (blowing your nose in your handkerchief, not on your sleeve; eating with a fork, not a knife)? How about your example of a mos—is it a rule about something that is important? Is your example of a taboo something that is so disgusting you can't even imagine violating it (having sex with your brother)?

Remember, folkways, mores, and taboos are all types of norms. So, *norm* is the generic term for social rules of behavior.

7.2   There are many ways to answer this question. Here is how I filled in the boxes:

Types of Sanctions

	Positive	Negative
Formal	Good conduct medal Promotion on job	Getting fired Being fined
Informal	Cheers Being toasted	People not talking to you Being glared at Being hissed

Here are some things to remember about sanctions: They can be positive or negative, formal or informal. Formal positive sanctions are not necessarily better than informal positive sanctions; formal negative sanctions are not necessarily worse than informal negative sanctions. The point of sanctioning people—positively or negatively—is to encourage/force them to comply with social norms.

7.3   A subculture is a group of people whose values, language, dress, and so on set them apart from the larger society. A counterculture is a subculture whose values, language, dress, and so on are not only *different from* but are *in opposition to* those of the dominant culture. Most occupational subcultures (police, academics, and so on) are not countercultures. "Outlaw" groups (the Hell's Angels, the KKK) are subcultures that are also countercultures.

Because the defining characteristic of a counterculture is that it is in opposition to the dominant culture, you have to know something about the dominant culture to determine whether a subculture is also a counterculture. For example, in a communist or socialist country, a group of Young Republicans would be seen as a counterculture; but not so in U.S. society.

7.4

a. The power of everyday objects has to do precisely with the fact that *we feel as if* we can't live without them. I don't feel quite comfortable sitting on a chair that's lower than knee high. No matter how hungry I am, before I start on that baked potato, I have to find a fork. A spoon might work as well, but it wouldn't feel right. (Although I will use chopsticks when I am eating in a Chinese restaurant, I never feel as comfortable with them because I can't eat without thinking about what I'm doing.) Even though I keep my office door open and am not generally bothered by traffic in and out, I know I would be constantly annoyed if my colleague, whose office is next door, had to pass through my office to reach his—no matter how quietly he did so. Visser goes on to say that having these things now prevents us from being different.

b. If you had trouble with this one, look back to the quote from Ralph Linton. His point is that culture is everywhere, so it's hard to see (just as a fish likely would never have cause to notice it was swimming in water). Culture influences almost everything you do—so, what have you done today?

> I got up in the morning (instead of sleeping through the day). My culture demands that I participate during daylight hours!

> I ate breakfast. I wasn't particularly hungry, but "it's the most important meal of the day."

> I didn't take a nap. Naps are not prescribed for adults in my culture.

> I ate with a fork. I didn't have fried cat for lunch or dinner.

> I came to school and went to class. I spoke English all day.

Social Structure

When sociologists look at societies, or smaller groups such as colleges, or even families or Cub Scout troops, they see more than just assemblies of people; they see social structures. A social structure is a set of relatively stable *roles*, that is, patterned relationships among *statuses*. The definition is complicated, but in this chapter you will find the keys that will unlock that complexity.

Statuses

A social *status* is simply a position that a person occupies in a social structure. In modern Western societies, there is a wide variety of social statuses. These include *family* statuses (mother, father, child, grandparent), *occupational* statuses (president of the United States, lawyer, physician, firefighter, computer programmer), *social class* statuses (upper class, middle class, lower class). Other statuses are based on *age, race, sex, ethnicity,* and the like.

How do individuals come to occupy certain statuses? As you might guess from the examples given in the preceding paragraph, it varies. Some statuses are *achieved* by individuals. Achieved statuses in modern Western society might include being a spouse, sociology major, college graduate, chamber of commerce member, lawyer, or convicted mass murderer. These are all positions in the social structure that individuals achieve for themselves (though, as in the case of the convicted mass murderer, not always on purpose). Other statuses are *ascribed*. That is, individuals are placed, generally at birth, in a status—sex, race, ethnicity, age, and so on—that they cannot escape.

Understanding where people fit within a social structure is crucial to everyday life. For this reason, when we meet new people, our first inclination is to find out something about their social statuses. Knowledge of the social positions or statuses that people occupy helps us to know how to interact with them.

Imagine you're at a party where strangers are forced to mingle. What sorts of questions do people ask of one another under those circumstances? "What do you do for a living?" "Are you married?" "Do you have children?"

These are all questions about social status or position in the social structure: "What do you do for a living?" translates into "What is your occupational status?" Similarly, "Are you married?" translates into "What is your marital status?" And "Do you have children?" becomes "What is your parental status?"

The nature of your response to others is likely to depend on what you know (or assume) about their social statuses. Probably you will respond differently to someone who is married than to someone who is single. If someone tells you that she is the governor, you are likely to respond to her differently than if she says she is a carpenter.

Even if we do not have an opportunity to ask others about their social statuses, we can detect many clues simply by watching and listening. These clues are *status symbols*. The police officer's uniform is a symbol of his occupational status; his wedding ring is a symbol of his marital status. The microphone the professor wears while lecturing is a clue to her status. A book bag might be a symbol of the status of student, though it is not as clear a symbol as a wedding ring.

Once we know something about people's statuses, we generally feel more comfortable interacting with them. The reason for this is that each status is accompanied by certain expectations about how the *incumbent* (that is, the individual occupying the status) is supposed to behave and how others are to behave toward the incumbent. In other words, once we know an individual's status, we have some good ideas about how he or she may act and expect to be treated.

Usually we find out about people's statuses and respond appropriately without even being conscious of what we are doing. Things get interesting, however, when we arrive at the wrong conclusion about someone else's social status—because they withheld crucial status information or provided misleading data or simply because we misread the clues. The results can be embarrassing and make clear that it is really a myth that we treat people equally in this society.

> I can recall a number of occasions on which people have misguessed my status and found it can be embarrassing not only for me but for them! When I started driving, I was always losing the car keys. Finally my mother gave me a key ring that would attach to the belt

loop on my jeans. I've had that same key ring for more than 25 years now—and I still frequently wear it attached to the belt loop on my jeans. Of course, now that I am fully adult, I have a lot more keys (one of the status clues to adulthood?). And, when I attach these to my belt loop, they make a lot of noise. Because of this, and because of my casual attire, I have on several occasions been mistaken for one of the janitors or maintenance engineers on campus by people looking for someone to fix a light fixture or unplug a toilet! (A couple of times, I have helped to change a light bulb, but I've stopped short of helping to fix toilets.)

8.1

    a. List two of your ascribed statuses.

    b. List two of your achieved statuses.

Roles

Sociologists define a *role* as *the sum total of expectations about the behavior attached to a particular social status.*

Consider my sociology class. In that social structure, my *status* is professor. My *role* is to teach—I'm expected to stand up in the front of the classroom and say things that will provoke students into thinking profound thoughts about the nature of society.[1] I am also expected to give assignments that I will evaluate and grade. These are some of the expectations that are attached to my professorial status; these are some parts of my role.

You occupy the status of student, and the behavior expectations attached to your status are different. That is, your role is different. Your role is to come to class, be properly appreciative of your teacher's sociological insights, think profound thoughts about the nature of society, and prepare and turn in assignments.

Here is an important fact about statuses and roles: They exist independently of their incumbents or occupants. Regardless of who the professor is, he or she must meet certain minimal role expectations. If you were to look for the common denominator among all professors—putting their idiosyncrasies aside—you would discover the role of the professor.

Sociologists are interested in such things because knowing an individual's statuses and understanding his or her roles reveal a great deal about the life of that individual and how he or she is expected to behave. Sometimes living out one's statuses and play-

---

[1]A *social structure* is made up of social statuses and roles. A *status* is a position in a social structure; a *role* is the sum total of expectations attached to a status.

ing the accompanying roles is fairly straightforward. But sociologists have identified three major problems that come up—what I call "tricky situations"—role strain, status inconsistency, and role conflict.

TRICKY SITUATION 1: ROLE STRAIN

Some statuses are accompanied by very demanding roles. Take the status of student. Expectations about how students should act—that is, the student role—can be very demanding. You may have five different professors who seem to think that their class is the only one in which you are enrolled. And they expect you not only to attend class regularly but to come to class prepared, to write papers, and to study for exams.

As if all that were not enough, any incumbent in the status of student knows that the role involves more than completing course work. It also requires "extracurricular" activities—participating in residence hall or Greek events, going to football and basketball games, and attending to a variety of other time-consuming activities. Then there is that part-time job that helps keep the student in school.

According to sociologists, when the demands of a particular role are such that the incumbent is hard-pressed to meet them all, *role strain* is likely to occur.

Many occupational statuses expose incumbents to role strain. Consider the police officer who is expected to fulfill his or her quota of traffic tickets, respond to emergencies, solve crimes, and protect the rights of suspects. At times, it must seem to the police officer that these demands are impossible!

My mother, who is not a sociologist, nonetheless had a good sense of what role strain involved. I can remember her mentioning that being a parent involved (as she put it) "wearing many hats." She not only shopped for the groceries, cooked meals, cleaned house, and washed and ironed the clothes but also chauffeured us to music and dance lessons, was a den mother when my brothers were Cub Scouts, was my sister's Camp Fire Girls leader, and presided over the PTA for a couple of years.

TRICKY SITUATION 2: STATUS INCONSISTENCY

It's bad enough having to cope with one particular role that is very demanding. When you realize that most of us occupy more than one status and therefore have to play more than one role, you start to imagine how tricky that can be.

The problem of status inconsistency crops up when an individual comes to occupy multiple statuses that do not mesh with one another. For example, consider the case of a 50-year-old man, John Jones, who returns to college to obtain his degree. When he enrolled in school, Jones took on the status of student. The student's role is to study and to be deferential to the teachers. But Jones still retained his previous status of middle-aged man, as well as husband, father, and businessperson.

Suppose Jones has a professor who is half his age. Normally this middle-aged man expects 25-year-olds to be deferential to him. But Jones is now in a situation in which this young man (the professor) refers to him as John, and he (Jones) must address this kid as *Mr.* Smith.

Status inconsistency generally involves a situation in which a person with a particular *ascribed* status *achieves* an inconsistent status. For example, status inconsistency frequently exists when a woman (ascribed status) goes to work as a truck driver (a status traditionally achieved by men). Likewise, a man (ascribed status) who becomes a nurse (a status traditionally achieved by women) is viewed as having inconsistent statuses. So, just as with the phrase *nontraditional student* (which means students older than usual college age), when you hear the phrase *nontraditional work roles,* you can assume there is a perception of status inconsistency. The basis of this status inconsistency is the belief that the statuses that one achieves are not congruent with the statuses that others have ascribed to the individual.

There is nothing inherently contradictory about being a student and being middle-aged; nor is there anything contradictory about being a woman and a truck driver or being a man and a nurse. The inconsistency is not in the combination of statuses itself but in how people perceive particular combinations of statuses.

One very telling example of status inconsistency involved Justice Thurgood Marshall, the first African American to sit on the Supreme Court of the United States. He used to tell of one time when he was in the elevator that justices used to get to their offices. A couple of lost tourists got on the elevator and instructed Marshall to take them to a particular floor. (He did, and only later did the tourists discover that Marshall was not an elevator operator but a justice of the Supreme Court.)

TRICKY SITUATION 3: ROLE CONFLICT

Not only are some combinations of statuses perceived as inconsistent, but the actual demands of their roles can clash. Sociologists call this *role conflict.*

Consider the juvenile court judge who is also a parent. The status of judge in our society requires the incumbent to play a role in which he or she treats all defendants alike. The role of parent is different. Parents are supposed to be loyal to and love their children, and when their child gets into trouble, the parents are expected to be that child's advocate!

A serious role conflict would exist if Belinda Smith, daughter of Judge Smith, was arrested and brought into Judge Smith's court. No one would believe that Judge Smith could act as an impartial judge in such a case because of the conflict between the roles of parent and judge.

Role conflicts are not always so dramatic. Suppose you are baby-sitting some night for a 7-year-old kid. You have thus taken on the status of baby-sitter. The role expectations that accompany the status of baby-sitter are well known: watch and entertain the child and especially keep that kid out of trouble. But what if the person you are seeing calls and wants to come over to spend the evening with you. Now, the status of lover (or boyfriend or girlfriend) has its own role expectations, and these are in obvious conflict with the role demands of baby-sitting. You cannot play the roles of baby-sitter and lover at the same time. Attempting to mesh these two roles can only get you into serious trouble.

8.2 Define each of the following and give at least one example.

    a. role strain

    b. status inconsistency

    c. role conflict

Master Status

Sociologists know that most of us occupy a number of different statuses, and therefore we must play a number of different roles. But not all statuses are weighted the same in the minds of individuals (Hughes 1945).

I am a sociology professor, as is my colleague Jim. I have heard students refer to Jim as a sociology professor but refer to me as a *female* sociology professor. That is a clue to the fact that in those students' minds, my status as a female "filters" their perception of me as a sociology professor. This suggests as well that because I am a woman professor, these students may be tempted to treat me differently than they treat Jim and they expect me to act differently than they expect Jim to act. To the degree that students see me as a female professor, rather than simply as a professor, they are treating my gender as my *master status*. In their minds, it seems, my gender affects expectations about how I ought to and will play my role and how they ought to and will respond.

In modern society, gender is not the only master status. An individual's race or ethnicity can also be a filter through which other statuses are perceived. When you hear someone say, "He's an African American doctor," or "She's an Asian American lawyer," you can assume that racial and ethnic statuses influence people's perceptions of occupational roles.

In our society, we like to think that our achieved statuses are more important than our ascribed statuses. For this reason, when our master status is linked to a quality that is ascribed to us rather than to something that we have achieved, it can be upsetting. If I want to be taken seriously as a professor, it is annoying to be called a "professor-ette"—even if the person calling me that means no disrespect. (When I was doing research in the criminal courts of Cook County, Illinois, one of the [male] judges used to refer to any female lawyer as "little lady" but to her male counterpart as "counsel" or "Mr." As you can imagine, this mode of address really annoyed those professional women.)

Groups

A careful inspection of the list of statuses you occupy should lead you to an important sociological discovery: These statuses define who you are. Moreover, who you are (or so I predict) is frequently a result of your membership in groups: a family group, a marriage, a friendship group, some club or organization, some work group, and so on.

We do not spend our lives among random assortments of individuals. Rather, most of us live our daily lives in groups—that is, with *one or more other individuals with whom we share some sense of identity or common goals and with whom we interact within a specific social structure.* Group membership is so important to people that sociologists tend to focus almost exclusively on individuals in groups (large and small). Our assumption is that we can understand individuals' behavior only if we study individuals within the context of their own social groups.

There are, of course, many different sorts of social groups, and these vary in size and degree of intimacy among members, as well as in how open or closed they are to new members. But social groups are always something more than mere social aggregations. *A social aggregation is some collectivity of people who happen to be in the same place at the same time.* The aggregations of fans who gather at a football game or rock concert are not social groups.

PRIMARY AND SECONDARY GROUPS

Sociologists typically distinguish between *primary* and *secondary* groups. The concept of primary group comes to us from the work of sociologist Charles H. Cooley (1864–1929). Cooley was particularly interested in how humans become *socialized*—that is, *how they are taught to be functioning members of social groups*. Cooley believed that the most important kinds of socialization took place in primary groups like the family and friendship groups. In such primary groups, said Cooley, people learn the rules of social life and cooperation.

Secondary groups are different. Your family is a primary group, but your sociology class is a secondary group. You and your best friends are a primary group, but the university is a secondary group. The distinction between primary and secondary groups is, in part, frequently a matter of the size of each group—but only because it is impossible to experience the kind of intimacy a primary group affords with large numbers of people. However, the most important difference between primary and secondary groups has to do with the kinds of relationships that exist within them. Secondary relationships, or relationships in secondary groups, tend to be means-to-an-end relationships. Other members of the secondary group view you first as a member, or a worker, or a student, and only incidentally as a person with individual needs. In a secondary group, you may be little more than a spot on the organizational chart. In other words, in a secondary group, *what is important is your status, not your personal characteristics*. Table 8.1 summarizes the key differences between primary and secondary groups.

Recalling the distinction that Tönnies made (see chapter 1), we can say that secondary groups tend to be *Gesellschaft* while primary groups tend to be *Gemeinschaft*. Here is how Cooley described the primary group. As you read his description, what sorts of groups come to mind?

> By primary groups I mean those characterized by intimate face-to-face association and cooperation. They are primary in several senses, but chiefly in that they are fundamental in forming the social nature and ideals of the individual. The result of intimate association, psychologically, is a certain fusion of individualities in a common whole, so that one's very self, for many purposes at least, is the common life and purpose of the group. Perhaps the simplest way of describing this wholeness is by saying that it is a "we"; it involves the sort of sympathy and mutual identification for which "we" is the natural expression. One lives in the feeling of the whole and finds the chief aims of his will in that feeling. (1909, 23)

Table 8.1 Primary Versus Secondary Groups

	Primary Groups	Secondary Groups
Examples	Family, friendship group, work group, gang	Corporation, city, university, nation, sociology class
Size	Tend to be small	Can be *very* large
Nature of Members' Attachment	Socio-emotional (membership an end in and of itself); personal	Instrumental (membership often only a means to an end); impersonal
Duration	Long term	May be long term but can also be very short term
Demands on Members	Greedy; want to take in entire individual	Limited demands; only require performance of a specific role (such as worker)
Nature of Social Control	Informal	Formal
Boundaries	Relatively closed; tend to be hard to enter and exit	Relatively open; tend to be easy to enter and exit

Cooley emphasized that primary group relationships are not always "sweetness and light." In fact, he said, a great deal of competition will take place between members of a primary group:

> It is not to be supposed that the unity of the primary group is one of mere harmony and love. It is . . . usually a competitive unity, admitting of self-assertion and various appropriate passions; but these passions are socialized by sympathy, and come, or tend to come, under the discipline of a common spirit. The individual will be ambitious, but the chief object of his ambition will be some desired place in the thoughts of the others, and he will feel allegiance to common standards of service and fair play. So the boy will dispute with his fellows for a place on the team, but above such disputes will place the common glory of his class and school. (1909, 24–25)

STOP & REVIEW

8.3 Think of a primary group to which you belong. Which of the characteristics of primary groups (listed in table 8.1) does your primary group have?

 a. What is the name of your group (for example, "my family" or "friendship group")?

 b. How big is your group (number of members)?

 c. What is the nature of members' attachment? That is, what's your motive for staying a member of this group?

 d. How long has this group been in existence?

 e. What are the demands on individual members? That is, what sorts of things do others in your group expect of you?

f. What is the nature of social control? That is, if a group member gets out of line, what sorts of negative sanctions might he or she expect? Give examples.

g. What are the boundaries of the group? That is, how easy is it for a new person to join or an established member to leave this group?

FORMAL ORGANIZATIONS AND BUREAUCRACIES

The quintessential secondary group is the formal organization. Formal organizations come into being when groups of people *band together to achieve a specific goal* (for example, to make money for stockholders or to provide a specific service to the community) and *formalize their relationships with one another.* Generally, such organizations operate under some sort of charter or constitution that specifies the status positions with the organization (president, vice president, worker bee) and describes role expectations (job descriptions).

One of the most prevalent types of formal organizations is the bureaucracy. Max Weber claimed that modern life would come to be increasingly played out in bureaucracies. The bureaucracy, according to Weber, is one of the more important manifestations of the trend toward the rationalization of life.

Weber studied a number of different organizations and derived what he called the *ideal type* of bureaucracy (1920/1958). By ideal type Weber didn't mean the *best* kind of bureaucracy but rather the *pure* form of bureaucracy. The ideal-type bureaucracy is what is left when you strip away all the parts of an organization that are not necessary to it being a bureaucracy. Real-life bureaucracies may have a lot of characteristics that are not necessary for the organization to be a bureaucracy. In the next section I have highlighted some of what Weber saw as the most important characteristics of the ideal-type bureaucracy.

IDEAL-TYPE BUREAUCRACIES

I. There is the principle of fixed and official jurisdictional areas, which are generally ordered by rules, that is, by law or administrative regulations.

People who work within a bureaucracy have specific "jurisdictional areas," or places in the division of labor. That is, areas of authority are delegated to individuals. These are the workers' "official duties." Workers must stay within their jurisdictional areas and must carry out their duties according to the rules. Thus, in the Baker Shoe Company, the vice president of sales would never try to give a command to a factory line supervisor. Moreover, individuals are expected to become experts within their own areas.

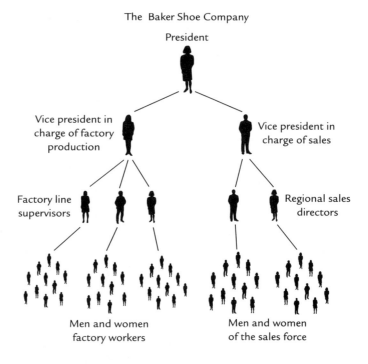

The Baker Shoe Company

II. The principles of office hierarchy and of levels of graded authority mean a firmly ordered system of super- and subordination in which the lower offices are supervised by the higher ones.

Bureaucracies have strict chains of command or authority structures. Generally these are shaped like pyramids—with fewer people at the top of the bureaucracy than at the bottom. Orders or commands travel from the top of the organization to the bottom. Every worker has a known supervisor to whom he or she is responsible. Going over one's supervisor's head (to complain, or whatever) is considered inappropriate.

III. The management of the modern office is based on written documents (files), which are preserved in their original or draft form.

Every significant move the organization makes (purchases, sales, hirings, promotions, firings, and so on) is recorded in writing. Orders or commands may be given verbally, but they are officially valid only if given in writing. If a subordinate disagrees with the legitimacy of a verbal order, he or she may demand that the order be put in writing and kept on file. (The files are the organization's "memory" and help ensure continuity.)

IV. Office management usually presupposes thorough and expert training.

Hiring and promotion are based on the individual's ability to do the job (or on merit), and not on such irrelevant factors as whom the individual knows. *Nepotism* (favoring one's relatives over others) is frowned on, as is accepting bribes from job candidates. Relationships within bureaucracies are impersonal, thus ensuring equal treatment for employees as well as customers and clients.

V. Official activity demands the full working capacity of the [bureaucratic] official.

In a nonbureaucratic organization, such as a one-person shoe shop, the shoemaker will spend most of his or her time making shoes and only do administrative stuff, like keeping the books, on the side. In an ideal-type bureaucracy, however, there is a specialized division of labor (as noted in characteristic I). Administrative work is a full-time commitment.

VI. The management of the office follows general rules, which are more or less stable and more or less exhaustive, and which can be learned. Knowledge of these rules represents a special technical learning, which the officials possess.

There is an established procedure or rule covering just about every situation. Knowledge of these rules and procedures is one of the tasks of bureaucratic administrators, because having such knowledge means knowing how to do the job.

Weber thus painted the ideal-type bureaucracy as a fully rationalized organization. By *fully rationalized* I mean having an organizational structure calculated to meet organizational goals most efficiently. In a rational organization there is a specialized division of labor, people follow rules, people are arranged hierarchically, and those at the top (presumably the most qualified) give orders to those at the bottom. In a rational organization someone keeps track of what the organization is doing (by keeping files) and people are hired, fired, and promoted according to their ability to do the job.

Again, Weber was talking about the ideal-type or pure-type bureaucracy. Weber knew that in real life, bureaucracies are never so pure—that nepotism happens and that people bend the rules. But his view of the ideal-type bureaucracy gives us a standard against which to measure the degree to which a particular organization is bureaucratized.

What we find when we examine a variety of formal organizations is that some are more bureaucratic than others. And even within a particular organization, some departments may be more bureaucratic than others.

It is easier to be highly bureaucratized (for example, to follow the rule book exactly) when the environment is regular and predictable. Thus, for example, we would expect that the part of the university that is organized to bill students to be fairly bureaucratized, because the work is routine and predictable.

On the other hand, academic departments, like the department of sociology, are likely to be less bureaucratized. First, you will likely have a large number of employees with Ph.D.'s, and these folks do not take kindly to others telling them what to teach or research. In the university, faculty justify their uppity behavior by citing such values as "academic freedom." And such values tolerate only a minimum of hierarchy and interference. Moreover, the work in academic departments varies from year to year as student demand for classes ebbs and flows and as professors come and go on sabbatical or research ventures.

The impersonal nature of the bureaucracy and the reliance on following rules restricts the ability of any particular supervisor or department head to act capriciously against employees. So-called red tape, which we commonly regard as so annoying, actually helps protect employees and clients from mistreatment.

Weber was ambivalent about the fact that modern life was being taken over by bureaucracies. He saw the positive functions of bureaucracies—they were organized to achieve tasks efficiently. But he also saw that bureaucracies had dysfunctional attributes—that they could become what he called "iron cages" of modern life, in which people become so trapped in following procedures and rules that they lose sight of the reason they are working so hard. In addition, if people get bogged down by procedures, they might lose their ability to adapt to changes in social circumstances. (Bureaucracies are, in effect, the slugs of the social world.)

The sociologist Robert Merton observed as well that it is easy for people who work in bureaucracies to lose sight of their ultimate purposes. "Paperwork" exists to help to communicate orders clearly, but when finishing the paperwork becomes more important than the task itself, this can cause problems. *When the process becomes more important than the outcome,* Merton noted, organizations and individuals experience *goal displacement.* For example, when filling out patients' charts is more important to health-care professionals than actually treating the patients, that's goal displacement. When doing well on an exam becomes more important than learning the material, that's goal displacement.

Chapter Review

1. Make a list of the sociological concepts that you learned in this chapter. Define each term. (*Hint:* You will learn the most from this exercise if, in addition to defining each concept, you create an example of it in your own words.)

2. Sociologists distinguish between ascribed and achieved social statuses. But do these different types of statuses have different

or similar origins? To what extent can we claim these for ourselves, and to what extent are they awarded or assigned by
others? Select two of your ascribed statuses and two of your
achieved statuses and discuss their origins.

3. At this stage of your life, what is your master status? What
will be your master status in ten years? In twenty years?
Describe what, if any, consequences your master status will
have on how you live your life.

Answers and Discussion

s T O p
&
R
E V I E w

8.1

a. Remember, ascribed statuses are those that are laid upon you;
frequently they have to do with the circumstances of your birth.
So, your ascribed statuses include your sex, race, and ethnicity.

b. Your achieved statuses are those that you earn through your own
efforts. College student is an achieved status, as is membership in
Phi Beta Kappa or the Girl Scouts.

8.2

a. Role strain exists when the demands of a specific role (that is, the
behaviors attached to a specific status) are very heavy and possibly even impossible to meet. Having role strain is like trying to
juggle four or five balls while people keep adding more. In the text
I used the examples of my mother (cook, clean, drive, PTA, Cub
Scouts, Camp Fire Girls) and of the student role (study, work,
recreate, go to class, attend football games).

b. Status inconsistency occurs when you have two or more statuses
that people perceive to be at odds with one another. Several years
ago, there was a television show about a brilliant 16-year-old who
became a physician. He experienced status inconsistency because
people found it difficult to treat a 16-year-old with the respect
that a physician is accorded in our society.

c. Role conflict involves a conflict between the expectations of two
or more roles (or the behaviors expected of people who hold two
or more statuses). In the text I used the example of the juvenile
court judge who was also a parent. She would experience role
conflict if her child were brought into court.

8.3 Your answers to this set of questions will vary depending on the primary group you choose to analyze. To illustrate, I will analyze my family
as a primary group—as it was when I was in college.

b. This group included seven members: two parents and five children. (I do not include my grandparents in my primary group
because they live pretty far away and we have never experienced
much "intimate, face-to-face association.")

c. I am attached to this group simply because they are my family. I
don't think I could escape them, even if I wanted to. (See part g.)

d. I choose to date this group from the time my oldest brother was born—in 1948.

e. They expect a lot of me. I am supposed to be a "good daughter"— which means that I show up for required family events (parental birthdays, Christmas, Thanksgiving, Fourth of July). If I can't be there, I have to have a good excuse, and I must phone. Once I got into trouble for not calling home on Labor Day—my dad didn't believe me when I later told him I didn't know that Labor Day was one of the family "biggies." If something bad happens to one of the members of the family, I am expected to return home immediately to share in the somber moments. Thus, when my father had a heart attack, I dropped out of school for a quarter and came home. Being in a primary group isn't necessarily a full-time occupation, but it is like being "on call" 24 hours a day. If you are needed, you must show up.

f. When I was younger, the negative sanctions were pretty tangible: "Because you did this, you can't watch television tonight" or "I'm taking the cost of that thing out of your allowance!" By the time I got to college, the negative sanctions were less tangible but still painful: "What do you mean you are going skiing over Christmas? *Do you want your father to have another heart attack* because he's disappointed in you?" (I hope that my mother never reads this book; otherwise, I might experience some negative sanctions for using her as a source of examples!)

g. There are very definite and rigid boundaries. No one can leave this group unless he or she dies, and no one can enter this group without being born into it or marrying into it.

Society and
Social Institutions

Here's a story I tell students in my introductory sociology class:

You've got about an hour before your sociology class begins and that's just enough time to pick up your scholarship check. So, you mosey on down to the administration building and wait in line in front of the comptroller's office. The line moves slowly, but finally it's your turn. The fellow working behind the counter, John Smith, tells you that your check hasn't arrived. You mutter to yourself about the inefficiency of bureaucracies as you leave the building. On your way out, you encounter Sam Johnson, the president of the university. Although you don't really know him, he waves at you and you wave back. He seems friendly enough, although you've heard many stories to the contrary. You start back through the campus to the classroom building. You pause for a moment to watch the college marching band rehearsing for Saturday's half-time show. Out of the corner of your eye you notice one of the campus parking cops is giving a ticket to a car parked illegally.

As you pass the Student Union, you check your watch and find there's enough time to get something to eat before class. You enter the union and the Go-Team Café. A friend of yours, Bill Peters, makes pizza in the café, and you say hello. After taking the biggest piece of pizza you can find, you stand in line (again) to pay for it. The cashier is a woman you know from your biology class, and you chat mindlessly with her as she gives you change from your five-dollar bill. You eat your pizza as you walk to your sociology class, gobbling the final bite as you enter the classroom. At the front of the room is Lisa McIntyre, your instructor. She's chatting with Mary Done, her teaching assistant, and several of her students about last week's quiz. One of the students, you think her name is Sylvia, seems pretty ticked off—she's speaking loudly and gesturing. You assume she's mad about the grade she got on the quiz. Then you spot Michelle and Aaron, your best friends in the class. The three of you always sit together in the back row. You settle in for class. McIntyre starts talking about statuses and roles, and although you should be taking notes, your mind wanders as you think about calling your parents and asking them for money to tide you over until your check arrives.

Twenty-five years later: Your daughter, Elizabeth, has about an hour before her sociology class begins. That's just enough time to pick up her scholarship check, so she takes herself on down to the administration building to wait in line in front of the comptroller's office. The line moves slowly, but finally it's her turn. The fellow working behind the counter, John Williams, tells her that her check hasn't arrived. She mutters to herself about the inefficiency of bureaucracy. On the way out of the building, she encounters Lisa McIntyre, the president of the university. Although she doesn't know McIntyre, your daughter waves back when McIntyre waves to her. McIntyre seems friendly enough, but Elizabeth has heard some stories! Elizabeth starts back through campus to the classroom building, and pauses for a moment to watch the college marching band rehearsing for Saturday's half-time show. She notices that one of the campus parking cops is giving a ticket to an illegally parked car.

As Elizabeth passes the Student Union, she checks her watch and figures she's got enough time to grab something to eat before class. She walks over to the student café, chats with Maryanne, the pizza maker, and picks out the biggest piece. Her pal, Andy, is working the cash register and gives her change from her hundred-dollar bill. Elizabeth eats her pizza as she walks over to the classroom building. When she enters the room, she notices the instructor, Mary Done, chatting with her teaching assistant and some of the students. One of the students, Elizabeth thinks his name is André, is speaking loudly and gesturing. Elizabeth assumes André is probably upset with the grade he got on last week's quiz. Elizabeth spots Craig and Kyoung-Joo, her best friends in the class. They always sit together in the back of the room. As Professor Done starts talking about statuses and roles, your daughter's mind wanders as she thinks about calling you and asking for money to tide her over until her check arrives.

That night, as Elizabeth describes her day to you over her IV (interactive video), you reflect that things haven't changed much. There's a new president, new financial aid officers, new campus cops, new cooks in the café, and new professors. But things are pretty much the same.

Amazing, isn't it? The entire population of the university has changed: new administrators and police; new faculty, staff, teaching assistants, students, new everything, *except things are pretty much the same.*

Things are pretty much the same because organizations like your college are more than just groups of people, they are social structures.

Sociologists understand that much of the enduring and repetitive nature of social life has to do with the fact that the statuses (positions in a group) and roles (the scripts that spell out the rights and duties of people in particular statuses) are enduring and repetitive. In this chapter we will examine why statuses and roles tend to be enduring and repetitive. More specifically, we will examine the nature of *social institutions*—phenomena that account for much of the fact that social structures tend to be enduring and repetitive.

Before we get to the idea of social institutions, however, we need first to consider the concept of *society*, because institutions start with society.

Society came into the English language from *socius*—the Latin word for fellowship or companion. The term *society* has a variety of uses in everyday language—sometimes people refer to the upper classes as high society; frequently, groups of people with similar interests join together as members of societies. (Spending even a minute on the Internet will demonstrate the incredible variety of these groups—National Multiple Sclerosis Society, Society for American Baseball Research, Society for Creative Anachronism, and even the International Ghost Hunters Society.)

When sociologists use the term *society*, however, generally it is to refer to *the totality of people and social relations in a given geographic space*. These days, societies tend to be coextensive with (i.e., having the same boundaries as) nation-states. Thus, for example, we speak of United States society or Canadian society. The defining characteristic of society—that is, the thing that distinguishes a society from any smaller group—is *self-sufficiency*. No group, no matter how large, qualifies as a society unless it provides the resources to answer all of its members' basic needs.

Sociologist Talcott Parsons explained the self-sufficiency criterion this way:

> Self-sufficiency by no means requires that *all* the role-involvements of members be carried on within the society. However, a society does have to provide a repertoire of [opportunities] sufficient for individuals to meet their fundamental personal exigencies [needs or requirements] at all stages of the life cycle without going outside the society, and for the society itself to meet its own exigencies. (1966, 17)

Again, what Parsons meant was that to be called a society, a group's resources must be comprehensive enough to meet all the basic needs of its members (food, clothing, housing, and so forth). But Parsons suggests something else: Self-sufficiency also means that the society must have enough resources to meet its own survival needs (social control, defense, membership replacement, etc.). This requirement, Parsons notes, means that a celibate group of monks cannot be considered a society, "because it cannot recruit new members by birth without violating its fundamental norms."

Societal Needs

No matter how different their peoples and cultures, all societies (big and small) must be self-sufficient. What this means exactly bears some thinking about. What do societies need to survive? Here's a short list of societal needs:

Have a continuing supply of new members.

Socialize new members.

Deal with members' sickness and health issues.

Select members for certain jobs and tasks.

Create knowledge.

Control its members.

Defend against its enemies.

Produce and exchange goods and services.

Promote social unity and the search for higher meanings.

How does a society meet these needs? The short answer is through social institutions. In chapter 7, I defined an institution as a recognized solution to a societal problem. Here is a more detailed definition: *An institution is an accepted and persistent constellation of statuses, roles, values, and norms that respond to important societal needs.*

Consider the societal problem of membership replacement. How is that problem solved? In large part, this societal problem is solved through the institution of the family. As I illustrate in table 9.1, the family is an accepted and persistent constellation of statuses, roles, values, and norms that together respond to society's need to replace its members.

Table 9.1 The Family as an Institution

Statuses	Mother, father, son, daughter.
Role expectations	Wives and husbands must be sexually faithful to one another.
	Parents protect, instruct, and nourish children.
	Children obey their parents, go to school, and do their chores.
Values	"All for one, and one for all."
	"Blood is thicker than water."
Norms	Help one another. Don't rat on family members.
	Parents treat children equally. Children treat parents with respect.

Here is an important point: The institution of the family described in table 9.1 is not the *best* type of family nor even the *normal* or average type of family in our society. But the table does represent what Max Weber would call the ideal-type family (the term *ideal type* was introduced in chapter 8). Although it may well be true that only a statistical minority of families exactly resemble the ideal-type family, the idea that families *ought* to follow the institutionalized pattern is widely accepted. Because of this, members of real-life families that depart from the ideal type may be subject to informal negative sanctions from others. For example, people who attempt to raise children without marrying will encounter both informal and formal negative sanctions (from raised eyebrows to problems with insurance companies); husbands and wives may feel a sense of shame, and children from families with single or divorced parents may be pitied as being from broken homes.

9.1 Describe the difference between a social structure and a social institution.

As shown in table 9.2, we can deduce a list of social institutions from the list of basic societal problems. Figure 9.1 shows how different statuses, roles, values, norms, and related social structures make up some of the basic institutions of society.

Table 9.2 Basic Societal Needs and Social Institutions

Societal Needs	Social Institutions
Have a continuing supply of new members	Family
Socialize new members	Family, education, religion
Deal with members' sickness and health issues	Medicine
Select members for certain jobs and tasks	Education, labor market
Create knowledge	Science, religion
Control its members	Law enforcement, judicial system, religion
Defend against its enemies	Government, military
Produce and exchange goods and services	Economic system
Promote social unity and search for higher meanings	Education, religion, politics

Social Institution	Institutionalized Statuses	Institutionalized Roles	Institutionalized Values	Institutionalized Norms	Examples of Social Structures
Family	Grandparent, mother, father, daughter, son, other kin	Support family, do chores	"Blood is thicker than water"	Don't speak of "private" family stuff to outsiders, "leave your brother alone!"	My family, your family
Religion	Rabbi, cantor, priest, shaman, disciple, worshiper	Teach about the sacred, worship the sacred	Respect the sacred and those who represent the sacred	Attend services, follow the holy teachings, "thou shalt not . . ."	Synagogues, temples, churches, prayer groups
Economy	Stock-holder, employer, employee, customer, creditor, debtor	Produce goods, supervise employees, get the job done	Profit is good; the customer is always right; *caveat emptor* (let the buyer beware)	Equal pay for equal work, forty-hour work week	General Motors, Bank of America, Consumer Credit Counseling
Law	Police officer, notary, attorney, judge, citizen	Enforce the law, resolve disputes, punish lawbreakers	Innocent until proved guilty; equality before the law	Tell the truth under oath, obey the law	Law firms, courts, police departments
Politics	Citizen, voter, elected and appointed official, lobbyist	Obey the law, vote, run society, look out for constituency's needs	One person, one vote; the will of the majority prevails	Do not stuff the ballot box, do not accept bribes	Democratic party, Republican party, political action committees
Science	Scientist, researcher, administrator, journal editor	Seek and publish knowledge	Do objective and unbiased research, disseminate findings	Do not steal others' ideas, do not "fudge" your data	Universities and colleges; American Sociological Association, scientific journals

Figure 9.1 *Examples of Institutional Constellations of Statuses, Roles, Values, Norms, and Related Social Structures*

STOP
&
REVIEW

9.2 Using figure 9.1 as a guide, complete the following chart to describe some of the statuses, roles, values, and norms that are involved in the social institutions of the military, education, and health care. Then indicate some social structures (e.g., groups or organizations) that bring each of these institutions to life.

Social Institution	Institutionalized Statuses	Institutionalized Roles	Institutionalized Values	Institutionalized Norms	Examples of Social Structures
Military					
Education					
Health care					

The Nature of Social Institutions

In addition to the fact that they respond to societal needs, institutions have other attributes in common:

1. Institutions are generally unplanned; they develop gradually.

2. Institutions are inherently conservative; they change, but slowly.

3. A particular society's institutions are interdependent; because of this, change in one institution tends to being about change in others.

4. The statuses, roles, values, and norms associated with an institution in one society frequently bear little resemblance to those in another society.

Let's take a closer look at each of these attributes.

INSTITUTIONS ARE GENERALLY UNPLANNED; THEY DEVELOP GRADUALLY

How do institutions come into being? The short answer is this: Faced with a particular problem, people try a variety of things to solve their needs. Some of these work better than others. The "best" way becomes a pattern for subsequent generations to follow.

I use the term *best* not to suggest the most efficient or even the most effective way. Institutions are constellations of statuses, roles, values, and norms. So, how a society solves its problems must fit with its existing social values and norms. For example, social control is a problem that all societies must solve. Perhaps the most effective and efficient method of social control would be to just execute everyone who violated a norm. But we don't do this because it goes against our values.

How Institutions Begin: A Hypothetical Example

A woman and a man are stranded on opposite ends of the same desert island. Finally, they happen to meet. Realizing that their chances of survival would be enhanced if they joined forces, they unite to form a group. As the days pass, they fall into a number of routines for everyday activities. Perhaps the man begins his day by chopping wood, and the woman makes the fire. Then the man spends the bulk of his mornings cooking and weaving grasses into useful domestic items, while the woman (who has a restless nature) explores the island and checks the tide pools for fish and other edibles. These routines quickly become habits and, in time, each morning begins as the one before without any great deliberation on the part of either the woman or the man. Occasional disruptions occur in their routines—one morning the man burns his fingers as he cooks the fish, so rather than weaving that day, he joins the woman on her inspection of the tide pools. But as soon as he heals, he returns to his usual routine.

Over time, then, the behavior of these two people has become *habitualized*. This habitualization would come as no surprise to a sociological observer. In their analysis of human interaction, Peter Berger and Thomas Luckmann explained the transformation of behavior into routine this way:

All human activity is subject to habitualization. Any action that is repeated frequently becomes cast into a pattern, which can then be reproduced with an economy of effort and which, *ipso facto*,[1] is . . . [seen] by its performer *as* that pattern. Habitualization further implies that the action in question may be performed again in the future in the same manner and with the same economical effort. This is true of non-social as well as social activity. Even the solitary individual on the proverbial desert island habitualizes his activity. When he wakes up in the morning and resumes his attempts to construct a

---

[1] *Ipso facto* is a Latin phrase meaning "by that very fact."

canoe out of match sticks, he may mumble to himself, "There I go again," as he starts on step one of an operating procedure consisting of, say, ten steps. In other words, even solitary man has at last the company of his operating procedures. (1966, 53)

Berger and Luckmann explained that following routines provides benefits to people: Routines free up mental space for thinking about more important things. (For example, each time I sit down to eat a bowl of Jell-O, the fact that I need not think anew about how to eat the stuff allows me time to ponder the lecture I'm going to give after lunch.)

Not all routines are institutions. Routine behavior is the way we do it, but institutionalized behavior is *the way it must be done*.

Why this is so is complicated but important: Our original islanders developed a routine that dictated that the man chops the wood and the woman builds the fire, that the man weaves and the woman fishes. They taught these routines to their children, and their children will teach them to their children. Initially, these routines need no explanation—the routines have been established, and following a routine makes life easier. The first generation of children and grandchildren knew how these routines came about (that the first woman was the restless sort and needed to walk around the island every day, while the man liked the intricacy of weaving). But among later generations, there may well be a child who asks "why must we do things this way?" His or her parents, who long ago accepted and became comfortable with the established routines (finding them effective, safe, and easy) may sense that the child needs to hear more than just "because that's the way we do things." Because the parents are invested in keeping disruption to a minimum and want the child to accept their routines, they are likely to answer both in terms of *logic* of doing things a particular way as well as the *rightness* of it.

Anthropologist Mary Douglas explained that institutions survive only if their rightness can be explained as both reasonable/logical and natural (1986, 53) Children's questions about why women fish and men weave, then, are not likely to be responded to with explanations about their great-great-great-grandparents' preferences. Indeed, the original reason for the routine may have been forgotten by then. Instead, children will be told that (1) it is reasonable to have a division of labor between men and women, and (2) the way labor is divided has to do with the fact that women, as child-bearers, have a God-given talent for dealing with nature (including fire) while men do not.

9.3 Describe the difference between behavior that is habitualized and behavior that is institutionalized.

INSTITUTIONS ARE INHERENTLY CONSERVATIVE; THEY CHANGE, BUT SLOWLY

The fact that institutions are legitimized by both logic and appeals to the nature of things makes them difficult to change, because any attempt at change seems to be an attack on nature as well as logic.

Consider the institution of the family in our own society. In recent times this institution has faced many challenges—gays and lesbians, for example, have called on the legal system to grant them many of the rights that until now have been accorded only to heterosexual partners. The obstacles faced by same-sex partners who wish to marry are great because their adversaries will call on both reason and nature to justify their opposition.

People who oppose same-sex marriage claim that it is not reasonable (logical) to grant legal rights to same-sex partnerships because such unions are prohibited by law. Marriages exist to facilitate the reproduction of members (children), and it takes a man and a woman to produce children. In case that logic is not persuasive (as it might not be to someone who points out that many gay men and lesbian women are parents and that many heterosexual couples choose not to have children), opponents respond by appealing to the belief that such homosexual unions are immoral by their very nature either because they are against God's law or because they are contrary to nature.

Not surprisingly, then, when the issue of same-sex marriage first came before the courts in Minnesota (in 1971), that state's supreme court ruled that the law prohibiting same-sex marriage is based in both legal statutes and, or so the court implied, God's will:

> [The Minnesota statute] which governs "marriage" employs that term as one of the common usage, meaning the state of union between persons of the opposite sex. It is unrealistic to think that the original draftsmen of our marriage statutes, which date from territorial days, would have used the term in any different sense. The term has contemporary significance as well, for the present statute is replete with words of heterosexual import as "husband and wife" and "bride and groom." We hold, therefore, that [the Minnesota statute] does not authorize marriage between persons of the same sex and that such marriages are accordingly prohibited. . . .
>
> The institution of marriage as a union of man and woman, uniquely involving the procreation and rearing of children within a family, is as old as the book of Genesis. . . . This historic institution manifestly is more deeply founded than the asserted contemporary concept of marriage and societal interests for which petitioners [the two men who sued to get the state to allow them to marry] contend. . . .

Petitioners note that the state does not impose upon heterosexual married couples a condition that they have a proved capacity or declared willingness to procreate, posing a rhetorical demand that this court must read such conditions into the statute if same-sex marriages are to be prohibited. . . . We are reminded that "abstract symmetry" is not demanded by [the Constitution]. (*Baker vs. Nelson* 291 Minn. 310, 191 N.W. 2d 185 [1971)].[2]

A PARTICULAR SOCIETY'S INSTITUTIONS ARE INTERDEPENDENT; BECAUSE OF THIS, CHANGE IN ONE INSTITUTION TENDS TO BRING ABOUT CHANGE IN OTHERS

Although institutions are inherently conservative, change does occur. Technological and economic changes, or even wars, for example, can require people to disrupt their routines and ultimately can cause institutional change. Once it was conventional wisdom that women—at least middle-class white women—should stay in the home and care for the children and household. In 1900 only about 5 percent of married women worked outside of the home. As a result of World War II, things started to change. Millions of men enlisted (or were drafted) into the military service, and this left U.S. factories literally unmanned just when they were gearing up to provide the goods that the country needed to wage war. Women stepped in to take men's places. When men returned to civilian life after the war, women were forced to leave the well-paying factory jobs. But the wartime experience proved

---

[2] The supreme court of the state of Vermont recently was called upon to make a decision in a similar case. Those opposed to same-sex marriages claimed that married couples should contain a male and female owing to the following "facts": "(1) Marriage unites the rich physical and psychological differences between the sexes; (2) sex differences strengthen and stabilize a marriage; (3) each sex contributes differently to a family unit and to society; and (4) uniting the different male and female qualities and contributions in the same institution instructs the young of the value of such a union." The court rejected those arguments, calling them illogical. As one of the justices who heard the case suggested, when it came to the importance of having diversity (i.e., a man and a woman) in marriage, the "rationale could require all marriages to be between people, not just of the opposite sex, but of different races, religions, national origins, and so forth, to promote diversity." In its very controversial decision, the Vermont court ruled that the state of Vermont had to make some arrangements that would make the benefits of marriage available to same-sex couples (*Stan Baker, et al. vs. State of Vermont, et al.*, No. 98-032, November Term, 1998). In response, the state legislature did not change the law that defined who could marry whom to include men marrying men and women marrying women. In what can be seen as an attempt to keep the institution of marriage intact, the legislature enacted An Act Relating to Civil Unions. This act did not allow same-sex marriages but allowed same-sex couples who contracted "civil unions" to have "all the same benefits, protections, and responsibilities under Vermont law as are granted to spouses in marriage" (H.847.17 March 2000).

that women could work outside of the home and that society would not collapse as a result. So, in the 1950s women began to respond to the needs of an expanding economy for more workers by taking jobs.

Today the evidence suggests that most married couples find it nearly impossible to survive financially unless both wife and husband work outside of the home. Indeed, by 1997 nearly 80 percent of all married couples were dual earners. This has led to changes in the kinds of child care arrangements that parents must make, a (slight) increase in the amount of work that married men do around the home, increased pressure (including legal pressure) on employers to open occupations to women that were traditionally filled by men, and stress on the educational system to provide after-school programs for students. In addition, women's increased participation in the labor force has led to many legal changes—equal opportunity laws and laws prohibiting sexual harassment in the workplace.

9.4 Suppose that our economy became almost totally reliant on computers, nearly all goods and services were manufactured by robots, and most people did their jobs from home. Over time, what impact on other social institutions might these changes in the institution of the economy have on other social institutions— for example, on the institutions of education, family, or even religion?

THE STATUSES, ROLES, VALUES, AND NORMS ASSOCIATED WITH AN INSTITUTION IN ONE SOCIETY FREQUENTLY BEAR LITTLE RESEMBLANCE TO THOSE IN ANOTHER SOCIETY

All societies have similar needs, but the ways in which they institutionalize their responses to these needs can vary a great deal. For example, the institutional response to the need to distribute political authority (i.e., government) may be organized as a *monarchy* ("rule by king or queen"), *aristocracy* ("rule by the 'best' few"), *tyranny* ("rule by an absolute or oppressive leader"), *theocracy* ("rule by God or God's representatives"), or *representative democracy* ("rule by representatives of the people").

Likewise, a society's response to the search for higher meaning or understanding of the sacred takes a variety of institutionalized forms: the idea that a life force exists in all living beings and that people ought to live in harmony with the rest of the natural world—*animism* (as practiced by some American Indian tribes); or the belief in a single supernatural sacred being—*monotheism* (as in

---

Polygamy and Monogamy

Anthropologist George Murdock (1897–1985) examined 554 societies and found that most societies allowed polygamous marriages. Here are his results:

415 polygyny

135 monogamy

4 polyandry

Even where polygamous marriages are permitted, *in practice monogamy prevails* because having multiple spouses tends to be more costly than having a single spouse. Morever, in most societies it seems that the ratio of women to men is such that there aren't enough members of either sex available for many people to have multiple partners. (1957, 59, 664–697)

Judaism, Christianity, and Islam); or the belief in many gods—*polytheism* (as in the Hindu religion).

In most of Western society, a family begins with *monogamous marriage*—that is, a marriage in which there is one wife and one husband.[3] In other societies some form of *polygamous* marriage serves as the foundation of family life: either *polygyny* (several wives with one husband) or much less frequently, *polyandry* (one wife, several husbands). And it is not just the forms of marriage that may differ; the values and norms that are the foundations of those forms can vary as well: In our society people believe that the normal progression is to fall in love and then marry. In other societies things proceed in the opposite direction. For example, in India nearly all marriages are arranged by the parents of the bride and groom. Love is expected to be a result of marriage (Sprecher and Chandrak 1992).

Social Change: The Trend Toward Increasing Specialization

Sociologists have found that as a society grows in size and complexity, its institutions tend to become more specialized. One

---

[3]It is frequently observed that in the United States, the institution of serial monogamy is practiced—that is, a monogamous marriage, followed by divorce, followed by another monogamous marriage, and so on.

illustration of this tendency is the fact that, in Western society, the role of the family used to be much broader than it is today. Prior to industrialization, the family not only had responsibility for nurturing children but for seeing to both their secular (nonreligious) and nonsecular (religious) training. Moreover, the family was the basic economic unit in society; people in families worked together in their farms, shops, or trades.

Similarly, the Church's role has become much more specialized in the West. A few hundred years ago, the leaders of the Catholic Church in Europe, for example, had control of such things as taxation and legal disputes. The Church even had its own armies and courts of law.

It's important to understand the idea of institutions—the statuses, roles, values, and norms that are organized responses to important societal needs. Understanding institutions is important because much of what people do—how they fall in love, make transactions in the marketplace, respond to law-breakers, and even how they worship—is in large part in response to institutions.

Institutions are established and accepted routines; their existence means that members of each generation need not continually find new solutions to society's needs; but by that very fact institutions also limit people's choices.

Chapter Review

1. Make a list of the sociological concepts that you learned in this chapter. Define each term. (*Hint*: You will learn the most from this exercise if, in addition to defining each concept, you create an example of it in your own words.)

2. At the beginning of this chapter, I assert that the values on which particular institutions are based must fit with the values of the larger society. Test this assertion: Look back to chapter 7 to the box entitled "What Do Americans Value?" Then pick two social institutions described in this chapter. How good is the fit between the values of that institution and the values of the larger society?

3. Sociologists have found that as societies grow in size and complexity, institutions become more specialized. That same growth in size and complexity may give rise to new institutions. Some sociologists have argued that one of the new institutions in society is the media. Do you agree that the media qualifies as an institution? Explain why or why not.

Answers and Discussion

9.1 A social structure always exists as some form of group—a particular family, business, platoon, or even society. An institution is a set of ideas or beliefs about how social structures ought to be organized. Thus, *my* family is a social structure, but *the* family as an institution is made up of ideas about how the statuses, roles, values, and norms of specific families ought to be organized.

9.2

Social Institution	Institutionalized Statuses	Institutionalized Roles	Institutionalized Values	Institutionalized Norms	Examples of Social Structures
Military	Commander in chief, general, sergeant, private	Give and obey orders, kill the enemy	Duty, honor, country	Obey orders!	Army, navy, marines, air force
Education	School board member, principal, teacher, professor, student	Administrate, teach, learn	All children should be treated equally, learning is a lifelong process, academic integrity	Prepare for class, do homework, have school spirit	Preschool, elementary school, high school, university
Health care	Physician, nurse, medical researcher, patient, American Medical Association	"First, do no harm," cure patients, discover new medicines	Give best medical care possible regardless of patient's status	Be careful, follow physician's advice, pay medical bills	Clinics, hospitals, drug stores

9.3 Habitualized behavior includes any routine that you follow because that's the way you like to do things—that is, it's your personal preference. For example, it's my routine to put on both socks before I put on either shoe; other people routinely put on one sock and then one shoe, then the other sock and shoe. Institutionalized behaviors are also routines, but institutionalized routines are ones that we believe we *ought* to follow. For example, I routinely prepare my lectures before class because I believe I ought to carry out my role of professor competently.

9.4 How you answer this depends on how good an imagination you have. One thing I am sure of, however, is that such a radical change in a single institution would bring about changes in others. For example, people might begin to accept "virtual interaction"—not just in the economic arena but in a variety of situations. Virtual education and perhaps even virtual religion might become commonplace. But if all this virtual interaction did become commonplace, and if people worked, learned, and even worshiped from home—it would undoubtedly have an effect on how parents and their children interact as a family. People might come to value their privacy more than ever and build more "walls" around themselves at home. Thus, ironically, doing everything at home might lead to members of the same family spending even less quality time together. On the other hand, spending so much time at home might drive people out of their homes during their free time and result in a refocusing on community life.

Socialization

A never-ending problem for every society is that people die. If a society is to survive, it must constantly replenish its membership rolls. Fortunately humans seem to have a built-in proclivity for reproducing themselves. But the simple biological production of new members does not entirely resolve a society's problem. The society must have new members who are capable of functioning effectively within existing social structures. In other words, a society needs people who can fill positions within the social structure (statuses) and carry out the behaviors expected (roles) of status incumbents.

Sociologists refer to the process by which society molds its members into properly social beings as *socialization*. More specifically, *socialization is the process by which people acquire cultural competency and through which society perpetuates the fundamental nature of existing social structures.* Although the socialization process is most intense for young people, it is a lifelong process.

Nature and Nurture: Biological and Social Processes

To say that infants are not yet social beings is not to say that they are not human. Of course, babies are human. And, of course, heredity plays a definite role in who a baby grows up to be. The color of the skin, eyes, and hair; the adult height and weight; perhaps even the sexual orientation as an adult—all depend primarily on the baby's genetic and biological nature.

But the personal attributes that sociologists deem most important in an adult—that is, *the social self, or the values, beliefs, ideas, and decision-making strategies, and the general way in which people live their lives*—are best explained by social rather than biological factors.

The importance of social factors in the development of humans is illustrated by stories of children raised outside a real social environment. "Anna" was a child born out of wedlock, the second such child to be born to her mother. Anna spent the first six years of her life locked in an attic-like second-floor room because her mother did not wish to incur her father's wrath by bringing Anna downstairs. Though she was fed, she was not otherwise nurtured—never really cuddled or talked to. When Anna was rescued at the age of 6, she could not do any of the things we expect of 6-year-old children: She "could not talk, walk, or do anything that showed intelligence" (Davis 1940, 119). Anna died about four years later. During her four years in the social world, she had progressed only to the level of a $2\frac{1}{2}$-year-old child.

"Isabelle" fared better. Like Anna, Isabelle was born to an unmarried mother and was kept in seclusion, away from most human interaction. When she was rescued at the age of $6\frac{1}{2}$, she responded to people as a wild animal might. But within a couple of years, Isabelle had managed to catch up with members of her age group. Why did Isabelle make more progress than Anna? One answer might be that Isabelle had better teachers. But there was another difference: Isabelle had never been cut off from human contact to the same degree that Anna had been. Isabelle was nurtured by her mother, and this early socialization seems to have made a difference—even though Isabelle's mother was a deaf-mute who communicated with Isabelle with gestures.[1]

It might be suggested that the real cause of Isabelle's and Anna's deficiencies was not a lack of social contact but rather physical factors such as malnutrition. Certainly Isabelle suffered the effects of a poor diet when she was found to have a severe case of rickets.[2]

But other research suggests that taking good care of an infant's *physical needs* is not enough to produce a healthy child. René Spitz (1945) compared the progress of infants in two institutions. The first was a nursery that had been established for babies born to women in a prison; the second was a "foundling" home (orphan-

---

[1]A more recent case of a child raised in extreme isolation (that of "Genie") is discussed in a book by Susan Curtiss (1997).

[2]Rickets is a children's disease caused by a lack of vitamin D and, especially, inadequate exposure to sunlight. Rickets is common in the tropics, due to the swaddling of infants and the confinement of women and children to the home. It causes dysplasia (an abnormal development) of the growing child's bones and can result in spinal deformity and distortion of the skull. In extreme cases, the child may grow up to be knock-kneed or bowlegged. The term *rickets*, or *rhachitis* (a synonym), comes from a Greek word meaning "disease of the spine." In adults, the same condition is called *osteomalacia* (Greek, *osteo* [bones] plus *malacia* [softness]) (Berkow 1987, 925).

age). The children in both settings were clean, well fed, and attended to by health-care professionals. The only real difference between the two environments was the amount of social interaction experienced by the children. In the prison nursery the infants were cared for mostly by their own mothers. In the foundling home six nurses cared for about forty-five infants. The outcome was that the children in the foundling home did not do nearly as well. Here's part of Spitz's report:

> In the ward of the children ranging from 18 months to $2\frac{1}{2}$ years, only two of the 26 children could speak a couple of words. The same two are able to walk. A third child is beginning to walk. Hardly any of them can eat alone. Cleanliness habits have not been acquired and all are incontinent [not toilet trained].

Spitz and his colleagues found a group of younger children (8 to 12 months) in the prison nursery to be an amazing contrast:

> The problem here is not whether the children walk or talk by the end of the first year; the problem with these 10-month-olds is how to tame the healthy toddlers' curiosity and enterprise. They climb up the bars of the cots after the manner of South Sea Islanders climbing palms. . . . They vocalize freely and some of them actually speak a word or two. All of them understand the significance of simple social gestures. When released from their cots, all walk with support and a number walk without it. (60)

Sociologists thus believe that without social interaction, humans find it difficult to survive. Without social interaction, humans cannot develop a *social self,* that *relatively organized complex of attitudes, beliefs, values, and behaviors associated with an individual.*

How Socialization Works

How does society socialize its members? How do people acquire cultural competency? As far as sociologists are concerned, socialization does not simply happen to people; socialization is a dynamic process of give-and-take between people and others in their environment. To say that socialization is a dynamic process means that people do not receive their social selves passively. Rather, individuals help to create their selves in the socialization process.

THE LOOKING-GLASS SELF: CHARLES HORTON COOLEY

Sociologist Charles Horton Cooley (1864–1929) gave us a great deal of insight into the socialization process. Cooley emphasized

According to one of his biographers, "Cooley's life was extremely uneventful. He shunned controversy and contention; any sort of conflict upset him and cost him sleep" (Coser 1971).

that the social self arises through interaction with others. According to Cooley, based on our perception of how others see us, we
develop our reflected or *looking-glass selves*. (A looking glass is a
mirror.) He explained the dynamic of self-creation this way:

> As we see our face, figure, and dress in the glass [the mirror] and
> are interested in them because they are ours, and pleased or other-
> wise with them according as they do or do not answer to what we
> should like them to be, so in imagination we perceive in another's
> mind some thought of our appearance, manner, aims, deeds, charac-
> ter, friends, and so on, and are variously affected by it. (1902, 152)

Cooley's idea of the social self had three principal elements. First,
we imagine how we look to the other person; second, we imagine
that other person's reaction to our appearance; third, we have
some self-feeling such as pride or shame.

Suppose it's the first day of class. I walk up to the front of the
room and begin to talk. I look at my students; I imagine how I
must look to them; I imagine the result of their appraisal of me—
and I feel good or bad about myself, depending on what I think
they think of me.

Suppose I trip as I walk into the room. Here's what's going on
in my mind: "They saw me trip; they must think I am a total
clod"; I am embarrassed. But suppose, as is more typical, I enter
the room gracefully and spend the class period making some brilliant observations about the nature of society and the importance
of sociology. I look at my students and think, "They think I am
brilliant and fascinating"; I am proud.

Cooley argued that the social self is constructed as a result of
this reflective process. According to Cooley, we learn to use this
looking glass, and thus learn who our selves are, in the intimacy
of primary groups—especially the family. Recall (from chapter 8)
what Cooley said about these groups. Primary groups are

> characterized by intimate face-to-face association and cooperation.
> They are primary in several senses but chiefly in that they are funda-
> mental in forming the social nature and ideals of individuals. The
> result of intimate association, psychologically, is a certain fusion of
> individualities in a common whole, so that one's very self, for many
> purposes at least, is the common life and purpose of the group. Per-
> haps the simplest way of describing this wholeness is by saying that
> it is a "we." (1909, 117)

Cooley believed that primary groups—family, friends, play
groups, work groups—were especially potent agents of socialization. It is in the primary group, he pointed out, that we learn to
read what other people are thinking and to discover what happens when we adjust our behavior according to what they are

thinking. Cooley recalls observing his own daughter as she developed her ability to use the looking-glass self:

In the case of M. I noticed as early as the fourth month a "hurt" way of crying which seemed to indicate a sense of personal slight. It was quite different from the cry of pain or that of anger, but seemed about the same as the cry of fright. The slightest tone of reproof would produce it. On the other hand, if people took notice and laughed and encouraged, she was hilarious. At about fifteen months old she had become "a perfect little actress," seeming to live largely in imagination of her effect upon other people. She constantly and obviously laid traps for attention, and looked abashed or wept at any signs of disapproval or indifference. At times it would seem as if she could not get over these repulses, but would cry long in a grieved way, refusing to be comforted. If she hit upon any little trick that made people laugh she would be sure to repeat it, laughing loudly and affectedly in imitation [of others' laughter]. She had quite a repertory of these small performances, which she would display to a sympathetic audience, or even try upon strangers. I have seen her at sixteen months, when [older brother] R. refused to give her the scissors, sit down and make believe cry, putting up her under lip and snuffling, meanwhile looking up now and then to see what effect she was producing. (1902)

Cooley said that society is made up of people's "imaginations" about one another: "Society is an interweaving and interworking of mental selves." People must not only imagine what goes on in the minds of others but take this into account in their own behavior. This is not to say that Cooley believed that people must conform to what others think. But, said Cooley, people must take into account and acknowledge what other people think of them.

Here's one of my favorite quotations from Cooley. (My guess is that you will find the quote easier to understand if you read it aloud to yourself.)

"I imagine your mind, and especially what your mind thinks about my mind, and what your mind thinks about what my mind thinks about your mind. I dress my mind before yours and expect that you will dress yours before mine. Whoever cannot or will not perform these feats is not properly in the game." (1902)

Children have strong motives to learn to use the looking-glass technique well—because it assists them in the competition for affection from other members of the primary group. As children age and interact with more and more persons, the self begins to grow as a result of these interactions. To Cooley, the child or person who lives in isolation from others is not fully human. Only with social experience, he argued, do people become truly human: "In these [primary groups] human nature comes into existence. Man does not have it at birth; he cannot acquire it except through fellowship, and it decays in isolation" (Cooley).

THE "I" AND THE "ME": GEORGE HERBERT MEAD

George Herbert Mead's (1863–1931) conception of the socialization process was similar to Cooley's but worked out in more detail.

After graduating from Oberlin College, George Herbert Mead tried his hand as a grade school teacher—he lasted about 4 months before being fired. He was more successful with older students; Mead taught at the University of Chicago for more than 35 years.

Mead said that the self actually involves two phases: the "Me" and the "I." The Me is that part of the self that is based on how one sees others as seeing oneself. The Me is what you see when you put yourself into the shoes of another and look back at yourself. (This is a tad complicated, so bear with me!) The I is the part of you that is uniquely you—your personal reactions to the situation.

The social self is a product of the ongoing interaction between the Me and the I. Consider the following interaction:

1. I am in class. Some students in the back row are making a lot of noise. (This strikes at the Me, which should be obeyed because I am the professor!)

2. I want to yell at them! (That's the I's reaction to being "dissed.")

3. But, I think, how will that make Me look? (The Me thinks about how a particular behavior will be perceived by onlookers.)

4. I am not going to yell at the noisy students because it will seem as if I am out of control.

According to Mead, this sort of dialog between the Me and the I is ongoing. The Me sees myself as an object, as others see me; the I is my response to my perception of how I think others see me in this situation.

Thus, my self is built up through the interaction of my I and my Me—the interaction between my own impulses (the I) and my understanding of other people's reactions to those impulses (the Me).

Here's another example:

1. A test is coming up in sociology class. Student X wants to do well because that's what is expected. (The wanting to do well is the Me's response.)

2. The student decides he would likely do well if he cheats. (That's the I, the impulsive response to the demands of the Me to get an A.)

3. The student says to himself, "But if I cheat, how would that make me look?" (The Me reacts with disgust.)

4. The student says to himself, "I will study and get an A. Then I will feel good about myself."

Children are not born with the I and the Me. According to Mead, these must be developed. Early on, children develop these parts of their selves and the ability to use them through play and games. Read through the accompanying excerpt from Mead and see if you can tease out how this process works.

For Mead play was an essential part of human development. By *play* he meant *simple imitative behaviors.* The child plays at being a police officer or astronaut by pretending to take on the role of police officer or astronaut. Often the child will take on a variety of roles in the same play period—both police officer and criminal, both doctor and patient. As they play, children (1) *begin to appreciate the perspectives of other people* and (2) *build up a sense of themselves as something that other people look at and make judgments about.*

> I have this vivid memory of playing "church" with my siblings. On the mantle in the living room was this enameled goblet. We would take Necco wafers, a flat candy, and put them in the goblet. Then I would stand in front of the altar/fireplace and distribute these wafers to my brothers and sisters. In other words, I would assume the role of priest and they would assume the role of churchgoers. (Of course, unless they knelt in front of me, I would not give them a piece of candy!)

Play is an important phase in children's development—it is their first exposure to taking on the roles of others and seeing themselves as others might see them. In other words, play is a first step to constructing a Me. In playing the priest and administering communion to my siblings, I got a chance to imagine how a priest would see me when I went for communion.

As children grow older they move from simple play to games. For Mead the thing that distinguished games from play is that games have rules that specify the roles people play and the behaviors associated with those roles. So, to successfully participate in a game, one must not only know what is expected but also have the discipline to take that into account. Thus, a child who plays the game of baseball must play a specific role that has rules to follow. A catcher catches, a pitcher pitches, and so on. The roles are impersonal in the sense that whoever is, say, the pitcher must pitch.

Participating in games enhances children's ability to do *role-taking*—that is, *to take on the role of another and see how things look from his or her point of view.* As the child begins more and more to be able to take on the point of view of others, we say that he or she has acquired a *generalized other.* As Mead described it, "The attitude of the generalized other is the attitude of the whole community. Thus, for example, in the case of such a social group as a ball team, the team is the generalized other insofar as it enters "as an organized process on social activity, into the experience of any one of the members" (1934).

Sociologists today also see the social self as a constantly evolving thing. Socialization is not something that simply happens to children; it is a lifelong process. The self is not taken in passively.

From *Play and Games in the Genesis of Self (1934)*

GEORGE HERBERT MEAD

Another set of background factors in the genesis of the self is represented in the activities of play and the game. . . . [For example, consider] the invisible, imaginary companions which a good many children produce in their own experience. They organize in this way the responses which they call out in other persons and call out also in themselves. Of course, this playing with an imaginary companion is only a peculiarly interesting phase of ordinary play. Play in this sense, especially the stage which precedes the organized games, is play at something. A child plays at being a mother, at being a teacher, at being a policeman; that is, it is taking different roles. . . . When a child does assume a role he has in himself the stimuli which call out [a] particular response or group of responses. . . . In the play period that child utilizes his own responses to these stimuli which he makes use of in building a self. The response which he has a tendency to make to these stimuli organizes them. He plays that he is, for instance, offering himself something, and he buys it; he gives a letter to himself and takes it away; he addresses himself as a parent or a teacher; he arrests himself as a policeman. He has a set of stimuli which call out in himself the sort of responses they call out in others. He takes this group of responses and organizes them into a certain whole. Such is the simplest form of being another to one's self. . . . The child says something in one character and responds in another character, and then his responding in another character is a stimulus to himself in the first character,

Rather, as Mead suggested with his description of the self as an interaction between the I and the Me, the self is a dynamic process.

More specifically, the self evolves continually as it interacts with a variety of *agents of socialization,* including the family, schools, peers, and the workplace.

FAMILY

The family is such a crucial agent of socialization in large part because it gets first crack at the job. In our society, until they go to school, most children are wholly dependent on their families. In this family setting children acquire some competency in nonmaterial culture—ways to communicate, a sense of right and wrong, basic beliefs about the nature of the world—as well as competency in the use of material culture—tying shoelaces and buttoning shirts; using forks, tissues, and telephones.

In introducing this topic, I noted that socialization is not only the process by which individuals acquire cultural competency but the process by which society perpetuates its existing social struc-

and so the conversation goes on. A certain organized structure arises in him and in his other which replies to it, and these carry on the conversation. . . .

When we contrast play with the situation in an organized game, we note the essential difference that the child who plays in a game must be ready to take the attitude of everyone else involved in that game and that these different roles must have a definite relationship to each other. Take a very simple game such as hide-and-seek. Everyone with the exception of the one who is hunting is a person who is hiding. A child does not require more than the person who is hunted and the one who is hunting. When a child is playing in the first sense [that is, doing imitative behaviors] he just goes on playing, but there is no basic organization gained. In that early stage he passes from one role to another just as the whim takes him. But in a game when a number of individuals are involved, the child taking one role must be ready to take the role of everyone else. When he gets in a baseball game, he must have the responses of each position involved in his own position. He must know what everyone else is going to do in order to carry out his own play. He has to take all of these roles. They do not have to be present in consciousness at the same time, but at some moments he has to have three or four individuals present in his own attitude, such as the one who is going to throw the ball, the one who is going to catch it, and so on. These responses must be, in some degree, present in his own make-up. In the game, then, there is a set of responses of such others so organized that the attitude of one calls out the appropriate attitudes of the other.

---

ture. Again, the family as an agent of socialization plays an important role in reproducing existing social arrangements. At a most basic level, the family is the main source of individuals' *ascribed statuses*. (The concept of ascribed statuses was introduced in chapter 8. If you cannot remember what this concept means, now would be a good time to review the first page of that chapter.)

As I show in table 10.1, depending on their social statuses (that is, their places in the social structure of society), parents tend to expect different things of their children as they work to prepare them for adulthood. The higher the parents' social status, the more they expect behaviors of their children that would prepare them for taking on higher social statuses. Thus, for example, intellectual curiosity is more valued than being a good student by parents from higher-status backgrounds. On the other hand, parents with lower socioeconomic status are more likely to value obedience. In the real world, such findings suggest this: Intellectual curiosity is the sort of quality that is required to do well in higher-status jobs; obedience is an attribute that is required if one is to do well in lower-status jobs.

Table 10.1 U.S. Adults Who Mention Particular Qualities as One of the Three Most Desirable for a Child to Have, by Adult's Income, Education, and Occupational Prestige

Adults' Status Attributes	Quality Mentioned				
	1 Good Sense	2 Obeys Parents	3 Considerate	4 Intellectually Curious	5 Good Student
Income					
Less than $4,000	19%	49%	29%	19%	32%
$4,000–$13,999	32	45	35	24	22
$14,000–$34,999	49	35	40	22	14
$35,000 and over	49	25	37	26	15
Education					
Less than high school	28	54	29	15	28
High school graduate	43	36	38	23	18
Some college	45	28	40	23	9
College degree	46	26	45	27	11
More than college	58	21	45	42	17
Occupational Prestige					
Low	27	49	27	14	22
Lower-middle	41	37	39	23	18
Upper-middle	43	35	36	25	16
Upper	46	23	48	35	11

NOTE: Data drawn from a national probability sample of 1500 adults in the United States.

SOURCE: Adapted from the *General Social Survey* (Chicago: National Opinion Research Center, 1986).

These findings are illustrative of what social scientists generally discover when they study socialization. As they raise their children, parents whose social status is relatively low typically value obedience to authority, neatness (for example, "coloring within the lines"), cleanliness, and good behavior. Middle-class parents, on the other hand, are more likely to stress such qualities as creativity, self-discipline, ambition, independence, curiosity, and self-direction. Thus, *parents tend to pass on to their children the outlooks that are suited to their own experiences in the world.* For example, the more parents are supervised in *their* lives, the more they tend to encourage and require obedience and conformity in their children. This tendency is one way in which the socialization process helps ensure the perpetuation of the existing social structure.

SCHOOL

The school is another important agent of socialization, but the socialization experience it offers is generally quite different from what the child receives in the family. At home, parents may have worked hard to treat each child as a unique individual. But in school the first lesson one learns is that everyone can expect to be treated in the same relatively impersonal manner.

The manifest function of the institution of education is to provide students with the knowledge and skills necessary for success in the adult world. The kinds of knowledge and skills taught in school, however, go beyond the academic course work. In every schoolroom where students recite the pledge of allegiance, for example, they are being taught the value of patriotism. Part of the latent function of education (sometimes called the *hidden curriculum*) is to prepare students to accept what teachers and administrators believe will be the students' places in the social structure. In some schools, for example, students are "tracked" into special programs (such as into vocational versus college preparatory classes). Although it is frequently said that students are tracked based on their individual aptitudes, there is a fairly strong association between a student's social class background and whether that student is, for example, encouraged to apply to college. (We will discuss this phenomenon of tracking in greater depth in chapter 13.)

PEER GROUPS

Unlike the institutions of family and school, which are formally charged with the task of socialization, the manifest function of peer groups is simply to have fun. Nonetheless, the latent function of peer groups is to act as a socializing agent. For the adolescent, the influence of the peer group can loom very large. Often peer groups grow into fairly elaborate subcultures, as kids develop their own peculiar values, norms, language, and use of symbols. As children interact with others in their peer groups, they learn a great deal about how they are expected to behave. The peer group is different from either family or school because it socializes children to become independent from adult authority. Still, much of what children experience in peer groups reinforces standard cultural conventions of statuses and roles. In other words, peer groups, too, can act to reinforce the existing social structure.

For example, peer groups play a large role in socializing children into "appropriate" gender-role behavior. One researcher found that girls are labeled "slags and sluts for many forms of independent behavior, such as going places on their own and talking aggressively to boys who insult them" (Eder 1995, 11).[3] And boys do not escape the socializing influence of their peers— in fact, one researcher argued that peer groups are the most important sources of "policing masculinity" in our society:

> The boys themselves often conveyed the importance of toughness through ritual insults. Many of the names the boys used to insult each other imply some form of weakness such as "pud," "squirt," and "wimp." Other names, such as "pussy," "girl," "fag," and "queer," associate lack of toughness directly with femininity or homosexuality. These names are used when boys fail to meet certain standards of combativeness. (Eder 1995, 63)[4]

It is within peer groups that children often encounter their first experiences with status distinctions: Very early on, children begin to distinguish between the kids who are valued and those who are not. In her study of adolescent culture, Donna Eder found many examples of this phenomenon in her interviews with middle-school students:

Eighth-Grade Interview (School Cafeteria)

Julie: And those kids who are poor and can't afford expensive clothes sit over there. [Points to the other side of the cafeteria]
Bonnie: Most of them . . .
Julie: [Laughs]
Donna: How does that get started? How does it get started that certain people sit over there and certain people sit at this table?
Bonnie: Like if there's a gross dirty kid that came and sat by this girl that was real clean and everything she'd go, "Oh, gross. You smell," or something like that. So they'd get up and go over there and most of those guys over there think that everybody over here is a snob and they don't want to sit by them.
Julie: Most of them are. (1995, 41)

THE WORKPLACE

Socialization does not end with childhood but is ongoing throughout an individual's life. For adults, a major agent of socialization is the workplace. Sociologists have found that workplace socialization involves several steps, some of which take place before the worker even finds a job! The first step is to make a career choice,

---

[3]Researchers have found that whereas there are more than 200 English words (including slang) for sexually promiscuous women and girls, there are fewer than two dozen words for sexually promiscuous men and boys.

[4]Such efforts at social control are not confined to the junior high playground; I have frequently heard college men taunt each other with such remarks as "What are you, chicken?" and "Are you a fag, or something?"

Rites of Passage

Many steps in the process of socialization are marked by *rites of passage*. These are ceremonies or rituals that mark important transitions from status to status within the life cycle. Anthropologist A. Radcliffe-Brown described part of the rite of passage of boys-to-men among the people of the Andaman Islands:

> The boy kneels down and bends forward until his elbows rest on the ground in front. One of the older men . . . makes a series of cuts on the boy's back. Each cut is horizontal, and they are arranged in three vertical rows, each row consisting of from 20 to 30 cuts. When the cutting is finished the boy sits up, with the fire at his back, until the bleeding stops. During the operation and a few hours following it the boy must remain silent. (1922/1948)

In a particular society, different rites of passage may be more important than others. In ancient Greece women counted their age from the date on which they were married, not from the day they were born, thus signifying that the wedding was the start of a woman's *real* life.

---

that is, to decide what you want to be when you grow up. The second step, called *anticipatory socialization,* involves learning about and even playing at a work role before entering it. Young children may play at storekeeping or teaching. Adolescents may join the Future Farmers of America to gain experience in agricultural jobs. High school and college students may do volunteer work, undertake internships, or research a particular sort of job. These activities constitute a rehearsal for the future in that they allow an individual to begin to identify with a work role and learn something about its expectations and rewards.

Finally, the individual finds employment and begins to learn the reality of the job—all of its disadvantages and advantages. This final stage can involve some difficult moments because workers generally find that no job is all that it's cracked up to be. New nurses may enter the hospital ward wanting to spend their time comforting the sick and injured but find they must spend most of their time doing administrative work and overseeing the work of nurses' aides. New college professors may expect that they will educate young adults to take their places in the world and then find that no one seems to be listening to their lectures. Factory workers may discover that the work is tedious beyond anything they could have imagined. And so it goes. Individuals

Socialization in the workplace "has diverse psychological consequences, including effects on intellectual flexibility, self concept, world view, and affective states." (Miller 1988)

have to find ways of coping with the reality of their jobs; generally, they learn these from more experienced co-workers. So, part of the on-the-job socialization involves not merely learning to do the work but learning to *cope* with doing the work.

Sociologists have found that people tend to become heavily invested in their work. Work is not simply another role to play in the social structure; work may become one's master status. Many adults, for example, when asked to explain who they are, preface all their other remarks by noting their occupation: "I am a nurse"; "I am a sociologist"; "I am a carpenter."

Resocialization and Total Institutions

Most socialization processes take place in the context of everyday life—in our families and peer groups, in school, in the workplace. But in some cases, socialization takes place in what sociologists call *total institutions*. This phrase was coined by Erving Goffman, who studied such places as mental hospitals and prisons. He found that in these kinds of organizations, an intense socialization experience takes place: "[A total institution is] a place of residence and work where a large number of like-situated individuals, cut off from the wider society for an appreciable period of time, together lead an enclosed, formally administered round of life" (Goffman 1961, xiii).

In a total institution, people are cut off from the rest of society and stripped of their individuality. They are no longer persons but objects; not men or women but "inmates," "patients," or "recruits." The goal of the total institution is to take away the individual's self and give him or her a new one more in keeping with the needs of the total institution. In other words, the goal is *resocialization*.

By way of example, Goffman offered this account of the resocialization of cadets in a military academy:

> For two months . . . the swab is not allowed to leave the base or to engage in social intercourse with noncadets. This complete isolation helps to produce a unified group of swabs, rather than a heterogeneous collection of people of high and low status. Uniforms are issued on the first day, and discussions of wealth and family are taboo. Although the pay of the cadet is very low, he is not permitted to receive money from home. The role of the cadet must supersede other roles the individual has been accustomed to play. There are few clues left which will reveal social status to the outside world. (1961, 46)

Peter Rose and his colleagues (1979) discovered a similar process in their study of Marine Corps recruits. Their account of the

---

Ponder

How might the central role of work in an individual's life increase the problems of socialization in retirement?

---

process reminds us that resocialization is generally begun by subjecting the individual to what sociologists call "degradation ceremonies." The goal of these is to degrade the individual, that is, take away the individual's self in preparation for giving him or her a new one.

Part of the Marine Corps resocialization began with *depersonalization*. The young men were no longer called by their names, their possessions were taken away, and they were subject to many new rules. Merging with the group was stressed: Recruits were no longer treated as individuals but had to speak, look, and act like every other recruit—or else. Uniforms and haircuts were important components of the transformation. To accomplish depersonalization, the men had to do some unlearning. It no longer mattered whether the recruit had been a high school football star, a talented carpenter, a big man on campus, or his parents' pride and joy. Former roles and identities simply did not count. The sooner they were forgotten, the better the recruit would get along.

10.1 Match the total institution on the right with the appropriate description on the left:

    a. for the incapable and harmless   i. monasteries

    b. for the incapable and   ii. prisons
       unintentionally harmful

                       iii. boarding schools,
    c. for the capable and   boot camps
       intentionally harmful
                      iv. mental institutions

    d. for the more efficient pursuit   v. nursing homes
       of tasks

    e. retreats from the world

STOP & REVIEW

Chapter Review

1. Make a list of the sociological concepts that you learned in this chapter. Define each term. (*Hint:* You will learn the most from this exercise if, in addition to defining each concept, you create an example of it in your own words.)

2. What is the most recent rite of passage in which you have participated (as the one making the passage)? Explain in what respects it was a rite of passage. What is the next rite of passage in which you anticipate you will participate?

3. Pick one of the statements below and discuss the extent to which a sociologist would agree with the sentiment expressed:

   a. "All children are essentially criminal" (Denis Diderot, 1713–1784).

   b. "I have never understood the fear of some parents about babies getting mixed up in the hospital. What difference does it make as long as you get a good one?" (Heywood Broun, 1888–1939).

Answers and Discussion

10.1

    a. nursing homes
    b. mental institutions
    c. prisons
    d. boarding schools, boot camps
    e. monasteries

Deviance
and Social Control

Deviance is one of the more intriguing topics studied by sociologists. The sociological study of deviance covers the gamut
of fascinating (if sometimes despicable) behaviors: alcoholism,
mental illness, gambling, murder, homosexuality, adultery, crime,
drug use, stripping, pimping, prostitution, bulimia, suicide, pedo-
philia, necromancy, pornography, panhandling—just to name a
few.[1] At first glance, gamblers, murderers, prostitutes, and the rest
may seem like the strangers among us. But just as deviance is the
flip side of conformity, understanding deviance contributes to our
understanding of conformity. And besides, although curiosity
about "perversion" may seem morbid, it's hard not to be fasci-
nated by deviant behavior.

The Relativity of Deviance
(What We Already Know)

Because of the close connection between norms and deviance, it is
fair to say that we already have a great deal of sociological knowledge about deviance.

For one thing, we know that *norms vary across societies*. So, we
also know that *what is considered to be deviant varies across societies*.
Different societies have different expectations about how people
ought to behave. A particular act may be regarded as normative
in society A but deviant in society B. In the United States, for example, it is expected that parents occasionally have to spank their
children. As long as the parent does not cause permanent harm to
the child, spanking is normative (because it is done "for the good

---

[1]When I was a college student, people referred to deviance courses as "the sociology
of nuts, sluts, and perverts."

Table 11.1 Percentage of People Who Think Specific Acts
Should Be Punished by Law, by Country

	India	Iran	Italy	United States	Former Yugoslavia
Homosexuality in Private Between Consenting Adults	74%	90%	87%	18%	72%
Public, Nonviolent Political Protest	33	77	35	6	46
Failure to Help Another Person in Danger	45	56	80	28	77

NOTE: Numbers have been rounded.

SOURCE: Adapted from Graeme Newman, *Comparative Deviance: Perception and Law in Six Cultures* (New York: Elsevier, 1967).

of the child"). On the other hand, it is against the law to spank children in Sweden!

Table 11.1 shows how people in different societies react differently to the same behavior. Compared to people in the United States, for example, more people in Iran strongly disapprove of homosexuality in private between consenting adults. In Italy and the former Yugoslavia, people are much more likely to regard failure to help another person in danger as such a seriously deviant act that it should be sanctioned legally. As this table suggests, the existence and strength of norms varies across cultures. Indeed, it is impossible to find any specific act that is regarded as deviant in every culture.[2]

Important: To define an act deviant is to say nothing about whether that act is inherently good or bad, or moral or immoral. Remem good, bad, moral, and immoral are not sociologic concepts. (If you need to, review chapter 4 on that point.) To say that an act deviant is only to say that violates the norms of a particular group of people a particular point in time.

For another thing, we know that *norms change over time—even within a particular culture.* So, we also know that *what is considered to be deviant at time 1 may be considered normative at time 2.* For example, in the 1950s college women were expected to wear skirts or dresses to class; today, on the other hand, no one thinks twice when a woman shows up for class wearing jeans. One hundred years ago, it was a crime for a worker to join a labor union. And 200 years ago, one person could own another person; today, slavery is considered deviant (in our society).

---

[2]Wait! You might be thinking, what about murder? Isn't murder regarded as deviant in all cultures? The trick here is that murder is not an act, but a category of acts that a society has elected to say are deviant. To put it another way, some form of killing is tolerated in nearly every society. But what sorts of killing are called murder and what sorts are not varies according to society. Similarly, what constitutes killing in self-defense varies across societies.

Finally, we know that *norms vary within a particular society*—that *different subgroups have different norms*. So, we also know that *what is considered deviant will vary from subgroup to subgroup within a particular society*. For example, according to the norms of many groups, dancing and playing cards are respectable, normative behaviors. But in some religious subcultures, dancing and card playing are regarded as deviant. Generally, drinking alcohol is normative, as long as the drinker does not drive or become drunk. But in some adolescent subcultures, on the other hand, "drinking until you pass out" *is* normative. (You may recall from chapter 7 that one of the things that defines a subculture is that its norms vary from those of the larger society.) We also have different expectations for different kinds of people. Thus, it is considered deviant for women to chew tobacco but not for men.

11.1 Which of the following statements about deviance are true, and which are false? Explain your answers briefly.

    a. Society can be divided into people who conform and people who do not conform to social norms.

    b. People generally agree on which behaviors are deviant and which are not deviant.

    c. Most people have violated one or more important mores at some time in their lives.

    d. Most deviant behaviors are regarded as deviant in all societies and at all times.

    e. Only acts that are harmful to people are judged deviant.

STOP & REVIEW

Nonsociological Theories of Deviance

Deviance has long intrigued social observers. For centuries many theorized that deviance was simply a product of sin and was caused by such factors as demonic possession. By the mid-nineteenth century, however, skeptical social observers began to look for different causes. The first attempts at scientifically explaining deviance focused on biological factors. For example, Cesare Lombroso, a physician who worked in Italian prisons, argued in 1876 that deviants were, in effect, biological failures. Claimed Lombroso, "Criminals are evolutionary throwbacks," or *atavists*.[3]

But Lombroso's study overlooked a couple of important factors. First, owing to heightened scrutiny on the part of police, Italian prisoners were most likely to be Sicilian—a group of people

---

[3]The term *atavism* refers to a biological state with a variety of physical manifestations, including low foreheads, prominent cheekbones, protruding ears, and lots of body hair.

who tended to have lower foreheads, more prominent cheekbones and protruding ears, and more body hair than the average Italian. Had Lombroso journeyed to Sicily, he would have found the same physical characteristics to be present among the general *nonimprisoned* population. British psychiatrist Charles Goring and others later probed the matter more carefully. Comparing thousands of convicts and nonconvicts, they found no evidence of any physical differences that would distinguish members of one group from the other.

Other researchers have attempted to identify physical characteristics typical of criminals. In the late 1940s William Sheldon contended that a person's body shape plays a role in criminality. He distinguished three general body types: (1) *ectomorphs* (tall, thin, fragile), (2) *endomorphs* (short and fat), and (3) *mesomorphs* (muscular and athletic). After analyzing the body structures and criminal histories of hundreds of young men, Sheldon reported that criminality was linked to mesomorphy. Later researchers found merit in Sheldon's findings but argued that he had misunderstood the cause-effect relationship between body type and crime. Mesomorphy itself was not the cause of criminality. Rather, the way mesomorphs tended to be socialized (to be tougher and to have less sensitivity toward others) created a kind of self-fulfilling prophecy that encouraged criminality.

Another category of nonsociological theories treats deviance as a result of personality factors—especially those arising from "unsuccessful socialization." Such researchers hypothesize, for example, that people with a strong conscience (or *superego*, to use Freud's term) tend to be good, while people with a weak conscience tend to be bad. Psychological theorists may also posit that some forms of deviance, such as violence, are a manifestation of an "aggressive personality," while other forms, such as homosexuality, may be seen as an expression of "psychological dependency." These theories do not explain, however, why such a small percentage of people with aggressive personalities commit homicide or why such a small proportion of people with dependent personalities become homosexual.

Sociological Theories of Deviance: Émile Durkheim and Suicide

Sociologists tend to be much more impressed by the fact that deviance is tied to social norms. Because social norms exist outside the individual, sociologists look for causes of deviance in the same place: *outside the individual.*

Deviance is relative—acts considered deviant today (smoking and other forms of air pollution) were not necessarily regarded as deviant in times past.

"Judge, my client is willing to plead guilty to bank robbery if you'll drop the charge of smoking in public."

THE COLLECTIVE CONSCIENCE
AND STRUCTURAL STRAIN

Émile Durkheim was one of the first to look for the causes of deviance in terms of social rather than individual factors. In his early research Durkheim focused on the act of suicide. Suicide was an interesting choice in that hardly anything seems more personal than the decision to kill oneself. Surely the causes of suicide must be within the individual! (In point of fact, Durkheim was not really interested in individual acts of suicide. He was concerned with suicide rates and what changes in suicide rates indicated about the health of a particular society.)

As we discussed briefly in chapter 1, Durkheim's primary concern was the nature of society and social order. What sorts of factors hold a society together? What sorts of factors can destroy a society? Durkheim envisioned society as a system made up of interrelated parts. Like a well-oiled machine, a well-functioning society depends on each of its parts working together. Each part of the social system—the institutions of family, religion, and education, for example—work together to make the entire system of society run well. Because of the close connection among all the social parts, when one part of this social machine is not working properly, the entire system ceases to work well.

According to Durkheim, in some societies the social machine was maintained in smooth working order because of the strength of what he called the *collective conscience*—"the totality of beliefs and sentiments common to the average members of the same society." The collective conscience, in other words, was made up of the values, beliefs, norms, and goals shared by people in a particular society. The collective conscience was a kind of social oil that makes things work smoothly.

As we also discussed in chapter 1, in the late nineteenth century, many people believed that society was in chaos and about to fall apart. For centuries society had seemed to be in a holding pattern, and social change, when it did occur, came slowly—almost unnoticed. But in the eighteenth and nineteenth centuries, social change became a fact of life. That sounds reasonable to us, because we live in a society in which change is a part of life. But a couple of hundred years ago, change was new and seemed to be undermining the very nature of what held society together. There were many prophets of doom.

To Durkheim, one of the symptoms of this "society falling apart" syndrome was the high rate of suicide. In many Western countries, the rate of suicide seemed to be increasing. Whereas many of his contemporaries were asking what was wrong with the people who were killing themselves, Durkheim started asking what it was about *society* that caused increases in the rate of suicide. Durkheim argued that changes in suicide rates could be explained not by focusing on individuals but only by focusing on different social factors.

Durkheim's study, entitled *Suicide* (published in 1897), was one of the first to use statistical analysis. One finding was that the rate of suicide was higher in industrializing societies than in nonindustrializing societies. This led Durkheim to suspect that suicide rates were manifestations of the amount of *structural strain* in a social system.

More specifically, as a result of his analysis, Durkheim argued that as societies grew larger, more complex, and more specialized, the things that traditionally had held people together would begin to fail. As the division of labor became specialized, people began to do different kinds of work; these differences meant that some people achieved a financial success that took them far from their original lifestyles. However, while people could technically improve their social class standing, they did not know any of the norms that accompanied their new stations in life. No longer was there a great deal of agreement on what values were most important and on which norms applied to whom.

EGOISM AND ANOMIE

Durkheim identified several sources of suicide, including *egoism* and *anomie*. Each is a manifestation of a different kind of structural strain. *Egoism occurs when people are not well integrated into society.* In a state of egoism, people lack ties to their social groups. For example, Durkheim found that unmarried people were less integrated into society than married people, who had ties to spouses, children, their children's friends' parents, and so on. Durkheim also argued that Protestants (whose religion encouraged independent thinking) were less integrated into their social groups than Catholics (who were encouraged to look to their priests for leadership). Integration is tied to suicide rates because people who lack ties to their social groups simply have less to live for (that is, less reason not to kill themselves).

> For example, while both married and unmarried individuals may occasionally entertain suicidal thoughts, the married have more social responsibilities, which deters them from committing suicide, than do the unmarried, who have no one to worry about . . . ; Catholics are socially integrated, they experience social support (comfort, understanding, and sympathy), which deters them from committing suicide in times of despair. (Liska 1987, 30)

Increases in suicide rates, according to Durkheim, also were linked to rapid social change, which resulted in a state of social confusion he called *anomie.* The word is taken from the Greek term for "lawlessness" or "normlessness." So, anomie (or anomy, as it is sometimes spelled) is a situation in which people do not experience the constraint of social norms—either because there are no norms or because they don't know the norms. More technically, anomie is *a state wherein society fails to exercise adequate regulation of the goals and desires of individual members.* To put it yet another way, anomie exists when things like the collective conscience are not powerful enough to affect the behavior of individuals. The lack of social constraint from social norms, like the lack of integration present in egoistic states, creates a situation in which behavior is not properly regulated and suicide is thus easier.

Durkheim hypothesized that anomie and egoism were both major influences on the rate of suicide in modern society. When people lived in a state of anomie (that is, when the collective conscience was not powerful enough to regulate their behavior) or egoism (as when people were not well enough integrated), they were more likely to kill themselves.[4] In short, Durkheim came up with *structural* explanations of suicide rather than individualistic ones. Durkheim never argued that the decision to kill oneself was

---

[4]Durkheim also identified other causes of changes in suicide rates. For example, he found that just as not enough moral regulation and integration would lead to an increased suicide rate, so would too much moral regulation. He called this sort of suicide altruistic suicide—as when someone dies to save others in his or her group. The lowest suicide rates require a balance between social freedom and social control.

anything other than a private one for the individual. Durkheim was concerned only with the *rate* of suicide within a particular social group. Or, in Mills's language, Durkheim treated what many had regarded a private trouble as a public issue and thereby broadened our understanding of the phenomenon of suicide.

More Structural Strain: Robert Merton and Anomie

The American sociologist Robert Merton rediscovered Durkheim's ideas about anomie in the late 1930s. Merton was not particularly interested in the problem of suicide, but he suspected that Durkheim's conception of anomie might help us to understand other forms of deviance.

ANOMIE AND MODERN SOCIAL STRUCTURE

Merton continued in Durkheim's footsteps by focusing on structural strain as a cause of deviance. But Merton applied the concept of anomie more broadly than Durkheim had. Durkheim had implicitly assumed that once society completed its transition from preindustrial to industrial, then anomie would go away. From his twentieth-century perspective, however, Merton realized that anomie was not about to go away; indeed, as far as Merton was concerned, *anomie is built into the structure of modern society.*

Merton refocused the meaning of anomie to make it speak more directly to twentieth-century society. Instead of seeing anomie as a situation in which there was a lack of norms (as Durkheim had), Merton said that *anomie occurs when the norms of a society do not match its social structure.* (This might sound complicated, but don't give up. Keep reading.)

Merton (1938) began his analysis by noticing that all social systems have two characteristics. First, they have commonly accepted *goals* for their members. These goals are simply socially valued things worth striving for. As we discovered in chapter 7, at the top of the list of things that people in the United States tend to value are achievement and success.

Second, each society establishes what it considers to be legitimate ways, or *means*, to reach these valued goals. In this society, for example, education and hard work are the legitimate and approved routes to achievement and success.

According to Merton, everything is fine in a society in which there is a good match between the culturally approved goals and the availability of legitimate means to reach those goals. In a well-structured society, everyone will understand what the goals are, and people will be able to reach those goals by following socially acceptable means.

In modern Western society, however, there tends to be a significant gap, or *disjunction*, between goals and legitimate means. Or, as Merton put it, anomie exists "when a system of cultural values extols, virtually above all else, certain common success-goals for the population at large while the social structure rigorously restricts or completely closes access to approved modes of reaching goals for a considerable part of the same population" (1938, 211). Under such circumstances, Merton argued, "deviant behavior ensues on a large scale."

Merton understood that the American Dream (the idea that hard work will lead to success) is frequently a myth.[5] As he looked around, he saw whole segments of society whose access to legitimate means to success was highly restricted. One must have a college education to achieve the best jobs, for example, and Merton realized that a college education was out of the reach of many—no matter how smart they were or how hard they worked. This was just the sort of situation in which, Merton said, there was a disjuncture between socially approved goals (success) and means (education). This disjuncture, for Merton, represented a form of structural strain—which he called anomie. But Merton did not stop there. He noted that when there is anomie, or a disjuncture between goals and means, people may respond (or adapt) in different ways. These modes of adaptation are summarized in table 11.2.

RESPONSES TO ANOMIE

Some people in society may not experience any disjuncture between goals and means. For example, for some people hard work may indeed lead to success.[6] In other cases, even when they keep running into obstacles (as when, for example, someone can't afford to pay the costs of a college education), people may ignore the disjuncture and keep on trying. In other words, they may continue to accept the goals of success and achievement and the

---

[5]Merton surely had a well-developed sociological imagination. Had it not been so well developed, he might never have come to this insight, because everything in his personal history seemed to be proof of the truth of the American Dream. Merton was born in 1910 on the "wrong side of the tracks" in north Philadelphia. He worked his way out of the slums by winning a scholarship to Temple University, where in 1931 he earned his B.A. Merton then won a fellowship to Harvard to pursue graduate studies, and in 1936 he was awarded the Ph.D. in sociology.

[6]As we will discuss more fully in chapters 13 and 14, such people tend to occupy specific places in the social structure. Upper- and middle-class people, for example, are less likely to experience the anomie of blocked opportunities (because they are less likely to experience blocked opportunities).

Table 11.2 Adaptations to Anomie

	Culture	Social Structure
	Culturally Emphasized Goals	Institutionally Available, Legitimate Means to Goal Attainment
I. Conformity	+ accept	+ accept
II. Innovation	+ accept	− reject
III. Ritualism	− reject	+ accept
IV. Retreatism	− reject	− reject
V. Rebellion	± reject old and substitute new ones	±

SOURCE: Adapted from Robert K. Merton, "Social Structure and Anomie," *American Sociological Review* (1938): 672–682.

means of hard work even when it isn't getting them anywhere. Merton calls this adaptation *conformity*.

Other people respond to anomie in a variety of ways. Merton called the first mode of adaptation that is obviously deviant *innovation*. Innovators accept and pursue the accepted goals of society but, when confronted with a lack of legitimate means, devise new ones. For example, if in the pursuit of the accepted goal of wealth, Mary finds she has no legitimate access to wealth, she might innovate by embezzling from her employer. The innovator, then, accepts the cultural goals but rejects the legitimate means for achieving these.

Some people reject culturally approved goals but continue to pursue the means. Merton calls this apparently odd form of behavior *ritualism*. Ritualists follow legitimate means without caring about the goals. Ritualists, then, simply go through the motions. Ritualism is the deviant response sometimes chosen by petty bureaucrats who, frustrated at not being able to achieve their goals, continue to stamp papers and file them even when there is no point to doing so. To the ritualist, following the rules becomes more important than achieving the goals. The professor who shows up in class but does not put any effort into teaching is another example of a ritualist who is only going through the motions. Notice that ritualism is an invisible form of deviance. Because the ritualist goes through the motions of conforming, he or she may be viewed as a conformist.

Retreatists are noticeably different in that they reject both the goals and the legitimate means to them. For example, like ritualists, retreatists do not care about the goal of success; but unlike ritualists, neither do they care about going through the motions. Some retreatists literally drop out of society by moving, say, to the mountains of Idaho and living in huts. (A generation ago, the hippies who "turned on, tuned out, and dropped out" were splendid examples of retreatists.)

The fifth mode of adapting to anomie that Merton identified was *rebellion*. Rebels are deviant in that they reject both cultural goals and means and then substitute new ones. It is the substitution of new goals and means that distinguishes the rebel from the retreatist. And it is the substitution of new goals and means that makes the rebel seem to be the greatest threat to society. The rebels' response to strain in the social structure is to tear it down and to build up a new one.

But Merton overlooked an important question: In a society in which there is a disjuncture between legitimate means and culturally approved goals, which mode of adaptation will people choose? How come some people choose to conform or to innovate? Why is it that still others choose to retreat or rebel?

LEGITIMATE VERSUS ILLEGITIMATE MEANS

Two students of Merton, Richard A. Cloward and Lloyd E. Ohlin (1964; see also Cloward and Ohlin 1959), extended Merton's analysis by suggesting that *just as legitimate means to success are unequally distributed in society, so are illegitimate means.* For example, to innovate successfully, one needs to learn certain skills. Suppose you want to be a bank robber. If your career is going to last longer than a few minutes, you need to learn how to select your targets (for example, banks located near freeway exits are much preferred to ones located on busy downtown streets). How do professional bank robbers signal to bank customers and employees that they are about to participate in a robbery and had best cooperate? How big a cut should the getaway driver be promised so that he or she won't fink to the cops?

Just as legitimate opportunity structures are unequally distributed in society, so, too, are illegitimate opportunity structures. If you are poor and illiterate, you probably will not have much of a future as a computer hacker or bank embezzler. If you are poor and want to steal, you are pretty much limited to taking on a single victim (or possibly two or three) at a time. But as an executive officer in a savings and loan, you have the unusual opportunity of swindling hundreds if not thousands of people.

11.2
    a. Merton wrote about deviance as an adaptation to "structural strain." What was the source or nature of this strain?
    b. What did Cloward and Ohlin add to Merton's theory of anomie?

Learning to Be Deviant:
Howard Becker's Study of Marijuana Use

Merton's conception of structural strain gives us some insight into *why* people might act in deviant ways, but it really does not tell us *how* people actually become deviant. Sociologists have noticed that one generally learns to be deviant through a kind of socialization—just as one learns to conform through socialization. In other words, deviance is frequently a learned social behavior.

One sociologist who made this point was Howard Becker. In addition to being a sociologist, Becker was a professional jazz musician in the 1950s, and one of the things he noticed was that jazz musicians tended to smoke marijuana—a practice that was not only deviant but illegal.

Why did people smoke marijuana? At the time it was widely thought that there was something wrong with the personality of marijuana smokers, that people who smoked marijuana suffered from some sort of psychological maladjustment. It was believed, for instance, that people who smoked marijuana did so out of a felt need for escape or because they were insecure, lacking in self-control, immature, or simply mentally ill. Conventional wisdom, then, regarded marijuana smokers as people with distinct psychological and/or emotional problems.

As a sociologist, however, Becker suspected that to truly understand the nature of this behavior, we would have to place it in its social context. And so it was that Becker began a sociological study of marijuana use. He conducted interviews with dozens of pot-smoking musicians. From his interviews, Becker found that marijuana use did indeed have important social qualities. For example, Becker found that becoming a marijuana smoker involved three separate social processes: (1) learning to smoke (gaining proper technique), (2) learning to perceive the effects, and (3) learning to enjoy the effects.

LEARNING TO SMOKE

According to Becker (1963), the novice smoker does not ordinarily get high the first time he (Becker's subjects were primarily male) smokes marijuana. Generally, it is necessary to smoke the drug several times to achieve a high. One explanation of this is that the novice does not know how to smoke "properly"—that is, in a way that ensures a large enough dosage of the drug. Most of Becker's interview subjects agreed that the drug cannot be smoked like tobacco if the user is to get high:

> "Take in a lot of air, you know, and . . . I don't know how to describe it, you don't smoke it like a cigarette, you draw in a lot of air and get

it deep down in your system and then keep it there. Keep it there as long as you can."

Unless one uses the proper technique, the effects of the drug will be minimal:

"The trouble with people [who are unable to get high] is that they're just not smoking it right, that's all there is to it. Either they're not holding it down long enough, or they're getting too much air and not enough smoke, or the other way around, or something like that. A lot of people just don't smoke it right, so naturally nothing's gonna happen."

Becker's interview subjects also reported that learning to smoke marijuana was a social thing:

"I was smoking it like I did an ordinary cigarette. He said, 'no, don't do it like that.' He said, 'suck it, you know, draw in and hold it in your lungs till you . . . for a period of time.' I said, 'is there any limit of time to hold it?' He said, 'no, just till you feel that you want to let it out, let it out.' So, I did that for three or four times."

Many reported that as first-time users they had been ashamed to admit their ignorance and so had pretended to already know how to inhale:

"I came on like I had turned on [smoked marijuana] many times before, you know. I didn't want to seem like a punk to this cat. See, like I didn't know the first thing about it. I just watched him like a hawk—I didn't take my eyes off of him for a second, because I wanted to do everything just as he did it. I watched how he held it, how he smoked it, and everything. Then, when he gave it to me, I just came on cool, as though I knew exactly what the score was. I held it like he did and took a toke just the way he did."

No one Becker interviewed had become a marijuana user without first learning the technique for smoking that allowed one to inhale a sufficient dosage—one that allowed the effects of the drug to be evident.

LEARNING TO PERCEIVE THE EFFECTS

Even after the novice learns the proper smoking technique, he or she may not evaluate the results as "being high." A remark made by one smoker pointed to the next step on the road to becoming a marijuana user:

"As a matter of fact, I've seen a guy who was high out of his mind and didn't know it." [Becker asks, "How can that be, man?"] "Well, it's pretty strange, I'll grant you that, but I've seen it. This guy got on [high] with me, claiming that he'd never got high, one of those guys, and he got completely stoned. And he kept insisting that he wasn't high. So, I had to prove to him that he was."

Becker's research suggested that getting high involves two things: (1) achieving the physiological effects of the drug and (2) recognizing and identifying these effects. Without the second element, one is not really high because one does not know one is high! Becker found that people who believed the whole thing was an illusion did not continue to use marijuana because there was no point to doing so. Thus, without social support, most people would not get beyond their first attempt. Generally, however, novice users said they had faith that eventually they would feel some real effects. Recognizing the effects of the drug frequently came as a result of interaction with more experienced users:

> "I didn't get high the first time. . . . I don't think I held it in long enough. . . . Probably let it out, you know, you're a little afraid. The second time I wasn't sure, and he [the more experienced smoker] told me, like I asked him for some of the symptoms or something, how would I know, you know. . . . He told me to sit on a stool. I sat on— I think I sat on a stool—and he said, 'Let your feet hang.' And then when I got down my feet were real cold, you know? And I started feeling it, you know. That was the first time. And then about a week after that, sometime pretty close to it, I really got on. That was the first time I got on a big laughing kick, you know? Then I really knew I was on."

One frequently reported effect of marijuana is intense hunger. One novice smoker remembers the first time he felt this:

> "They were just laughing the hell out of me because like I was eating so much. I just scoffed [ate] so much food, and they were just laughing at me, you know? Sometimes I'd be looking at them, you know, wondering why they're laughing, you know, like I'd ask, 'What's happening?' and all of the sudden, I feel weird, you know. 'Man, you're on, you know. You're on pot [high on marijuana].' I said, 'No, am I?' Like I don't know what's happening."

In essence, then, the novice smoker learns from more experienced users to experience the effects of marijuana use as a high. The ability to perceive the drug's effects must be achieved if use of the drug is to continue.

LEARNING TO ENJOY THE EFFECTS

Suppose the user has learned the proper smoking technique and has learned to identify the effects as a high. A final step is necessary before the user will continue to use the drug: He or she must learn to *enjoy the effects*. The sensations of a marijuana high are not necessarily pleasurable ones. The typical novice smoker feels dizzy, thirsty, hungry, paranoid, confused about time and space, and more. Are these responses enjoyable? As you might guess, the effects of the drug might be downright unpleasant. At best, the effects of the drug are ambiguous.[7]

The "taste" for sensations is in large part a socially acquired one. Remember your first sip of coffee? Yuck! What about oysters, green olives, and dry martinis? Double yuck! Yet many people begin to enjoy these. The same is true for the sensations produced by marijuana use. But it's not necessarily easy:

> "It started taking effect, and I didn't know what was happening, you know, what it was, and I was very sick. I walked around the room trying to get off, you know; it just scared me at first, you know. I wasn't used to that kind of feeling."

Another user reported:

> "I felt I was insane, you know. Everything people done to me just wigged me. I just couldn't hold a conversation, and my mind would be wandering, and I was always thinking, oh, I don't know, weird things, like hearing must be different . . . I get the feeling that I can't talk to anyone. I'll goof completely."

Over time, however, many people come to regard these sensations as desirable. As an experienced user explained:

> "Well, they get pretty high sometimes. The average person isn't ready for that, and it is a little frightening to them sometimes. I mean, they've been high on lush [alcohol], and they get higher that way than they've ever been before, and they don't know what's happening to them. Because they think they're going to keep going up, up, up till they lose their minds or begin doing weird things or something. You have to like reassure them, explain to them that they're not really flipping or anything, that they're gonna be all right. You have to just talk them out of being afraid. Keep talking to them, reassuring, telling them it's all right."

As you can see, what starts as an unpleasant experience becomes a desirable and sought-after one. In the end, with some help from a subculture, the user begins to regard being high as "fun." In simple terms, the individual not only has learned a deviant act but has learned to enjoy it.

The idea that deviance, like conformity, is learned behavior has added a great deal to our understanding of human behavior.

---

[7]In some important respects, Becker's portrayal of becoming a marijuana user may no longer reflect the reality of this process. The active ingredient in marijuana is THC (tetrahydrocannabinol). Fifty years ago, the level of THC in marijuana was quite low, and the effects of the drug were relatively subtle. But today, the level of THC in marijuana is very high (no pun intended), and the effects of the drug are much more noticeable. This probably means that it is much easier for novices to perceive the effects of the drug but more difficult for them to perceive its effects as enjoyable.

The Societal Reaction Perspective: Labeling Theory

The traditional view of deviance focuses on why and how in-dividuals commit deviant acts. These theories tend to take for granted that some acts are deviant and others are not. One impli-cation of this is that regardless of who commits the deviant act, they will be responded to in the same way as anyone else who commits that particular sort of deviance.

But sociologists know that this is not true. As William Cham-bliss (1973) found in his comparison of different youth gangs, in some cases it is not *what* you do but *who* you are. More specifically, Chambliss found that lower-class youths were more likely to be sanctioned than middle-class youths—even though the lower-class kids committed fewer deviant acts! The societal reactionist perspective in general, and labeling theory more particularly, focuses not on the one who commits the deviant act but on the re-sponse of the audience.

Labeling theorists take note of the fact that being judged and labeled deviant has significant consequences for people's behav-ior. The label of deviant is powerful!

Let's take the hypothetical case of Bob, who has just graduated from high school. One night Bob and three of his friends (includ-ing Melissa, his girlfriend) decide to steal a car and take it for a joyride. Actually Bob has chugged so much beer that he can barely walk, let alone go for a ride. But after listening to his friends cluck and call him a chicken, he goes along. As soon as he gets into the car, however, he throws up and passes out.

Meanwhile, John, the guy who's driving, has had a few too many beers himself and wanders all over the road. This catches the attention of the police in a patrol car, which comes up behind the stolen car with lights flashing. This strikes John as rude, and so he decides to speed up and outrun the cops. Inevitably, John's poor coordination lands them all in a ditch. The other three (who are relatively sober) take off and manage to outrun the cops. But Bob is still unconscious in the back seat—and the police are happy enough to arrest him as a reward for their crime-fighting efforts.

Bob is taken to jail, fingerprinted, and photographed. A few days later, Bob is brought to court to be arraigned. Being the upstanding fellow that he is, Bob refuses to fink on his friends, and so the court throws the book at him. He's found guilty of grand-theft-auto (a felony) and sentenced to 90 days in jail, with another nine months suspended.

Bob serves his summer in jail, but his real sentence is much longer. First, he loses his college scholarship. However, that hardly matters because Bob's only interest in college was so that he could

"With all that I've learned about sociology recently, establishing who's naughty and who's nice is not as simple as it used to be."

go on to law school and become an attorney. Bob knows that convicted felons can't become lawyers, so what's the point?

Bob's girlfriend, Melissa, still loves him, but her parents forbid her to date him. After all, Bob is a convicted criminal, and they don't want their daughter hanging out with an ex-con. His other friends are sympathetic, but they go off to college and lose touch. Bob tries to find a job, but every time he fills out an application, he has to deal with the question "Have you ever been convicted of a felony?"

Bob is the same guy he was before he went along on the joyride—but this Bob has an entirely different life than the old Bob. So what if he drinks too much now and gambles away what little money he has. It's not like he has any hope of leading a normal life.

Bob is a truly pathetic case, and I've exaggerated his circumstances to make a point: The label of deviant can trigger a self-fulfilling prophecy. If you treat people as deviant and cut off their opportunities to be anything other than deviant, you increase the chances that they actually will become deviant.

Sociologists would refer to Bob's initial foray into crime (his joyriding) as an instance of *primary deviance*. Primary deviance may be committed for all sorts of reasons, including, as in Bob's case, a desire to fit in with the group. Social labeling theorists seek to explain the acts of deviance that take place after the individual has been labeled as a deviant. These subsequent acts of deviance are called *secondary deviance*. Edwin Lemert explained the difference this way:

> Primary deviance is assumed to arise in a wide variety of social, cultural and psychological contexts and at best has only marginal

implications for the psychic structure of the individual; it does not lead to symbolic reorganization at the level of self-regarding attitudes and social roles. . . . Primary deviation, as contrasted with secondary, is polygenetic, arising out of a variety of social, cultural, psychological and physiological factors. . . .

Secondary deviation is deviant behavior [that results] as a means of social defense . . . or adaptation to the . . . problems created by the societal reaction to primary deviance. . . . Secondary deviation refers to a special class of socially defined responses which people make to problems created by the societal reaction to their deviance. (Lemert 1967, 17, 40)

Erving Goffman's work on social identity helps us to make sense of the power of labels. Goffman argued that the stigma[8] of negative social labels can work to spoil a person's identity. According to Goffman, a stigma is "any attribute that discredits a person or disqualifies him or her from 'full social acceptance'"(1963, 3).

Goffman identified three types of stigma. First, there are *abominations of the body*—clearly visible physical marks (deformities, scars, disfiguring injuries). Second, there are *blemishes of individual character*—labels of mental disorder, dishonesty, alcoholism, or bankruptcy. Finally, there are *tribal stigmas*—or being discredited for membership in a particular racial, religious, or ethnic group or subcultural group. In other words, a stigma can be either ascribed or achieved.

Goffman argued that a stigma can affect one's social interactions in two ways. When a stigma is visible or known, it can result in a *discredited identity*. Like Bob, who because he lived in a small town was publicly labeled as a criminal and treated as such, people with discredited identities have a tough time being nondeviant even if they want to be.

Frequently, however, individuals are able to hide attributes that, if visible, would stigmatize them. In other words, stigmatized individuals may try "to pass"—that is, to camouflage the attribute that would get them labeled as deviant. Successfully passing means that the individual is not discredited. But because the person is vulnerable to being found out, he or she is *discreditable*—that is, in danger of feeling the full force of the stigma.

Goffman observed that the results are the same regardless of whether the person achieves a stigma or has it ascribed to him or her: "In all of these various instances of stigma the same sociological features are found: an individual who might have been

---

[8]The term *stigma* comes from ancient Greece and Rome, where runaway slaves and criminals were branded with a hot iron or needle as a sign of their disgrace. These brands were called stigma, from the Greek verb *stizein*, meaning "to tattoo." When the word became part of the English language in the late sixteenth century, it was used as it had been by the ancients—to refer to visible signs of disgrace.

received easily in ordinary social intercourse possesses a trait that can intrude itself upon the attention and turn those of us whom he meets away from him, breaking the claim that his other attributes have on us" (1963, 18).

Others have found that a negative label, or a social stigma, can easily become a person's master status (the concept of master status was introduced in chapter 8). Edwin Schur noted, for example, that such negative social labels as drug addict, homosexual, prostitute, or juvenile delinquent "will dominate all other characteristics of the individual. Good athlete, good conversationalist, good dancer, and the like are subordinated to or negated by this trait, which is immediately felt to be more central to the 'actual' identity of the individual" (1971, 9).

11.3 Explain the difference between *primary* and *secondary* deviance. Why do some sociologists think it is important to distinguish between the two types?

STOP & REVIEW

The Functions of Deviance: Maintenance of the Status Quo and Social Change

According to conventional wisdom, society would be much better off if it could get rid of crime and deviance. Durkheim started changing at least sociologists' minds about this. His reasoning was this: If people continue to violate norms, their behavior must offer some benefit to society. What benefit does crime and deviance confer on society? Well, for one thing, criminals and deviants represent social enemies, and hating these social enemies can help unite society. Thus, Durkheim argued,

> crime brings together upright consciences and concentrates them. We have only to notice what happens, particularly in a small town, when some moral scandal has just been committed. They stop each other on the street, they visit each other, they seek to come together to talk about the event and to wax indignant in common. (1893/1933, 102)

Sociologist Kai T. Erikson extended Durkheim's idea that crime could be functional by noting that deviance *clarifies* society's norms and moral boundaries. Typically a group's norms are pretty vague, but societal reaction to rule breakers helps to clarify the limits of normative (appropriate) behavior:

> The reaction to some people as rule violators functions to clarify the meaning of the norm. Others learn "how far they can go." Consider the rule, "do not cheat on examinations." What does it mean for specific examination situations? In the case of a take-home examination,

> ### *Ponder*
>
> Generally speaking, the stigma that results from conviction for a white-collar crime is less than the stigma that results from conviction for a street crime. Why do you think this is so?

it clearly means that a student should not copy another student's answer. Does it also mean that students should not work together or talk over the assignment at all? How does the rule apply to term papers? Does it mean that students should not seek assistance from other students or other professors? Does it mean that one term paper should not be submitted in two classes? When some students "go too far" and exceed the academic community's boundaries or tolerance limits, the community reacts, and that reaction defines specific situational meanings of the rule. (Quoted in Liska 1987, 40)

Finally, deviance encourages social change. Durkheim noted that deviant people are sources of social change of the sort that can benefit society. As proved by the American revolutionaries of the eighteenth century, today's deviance may become tomorrow's morality, today's deviant may become tomorrow's hero.

11.4 In 1955 Rosa Parks, an African American woman, disobeyed an Alabama state law by sitting in the front of a city bus. At the time the law said that only whites could sit in the front. What function did her deviance play?

Chapter Review

1. Make a list of the sociological concepts that you learned in this chapter. Define each term. (*Hint:* You will learn the most from this exercise if, in addition to defining each concept, you create an example of it in your own words.)

2. Review Merton's typology of adaptation to anomie. Create an example of each type of adaptation (conformity, innovation, ritualism, and rebellion) and explain how each of your examples fits the definition of that type of adaptation. (Don't use examples given in the chapter; make up your own.)

3. Durkheim suggested that deviance can be a source of social change. Give an example of someone who, during your lifetime, was judged to be deviant or criminal but nonetheless brought about social change.

4. The relationship between conformity to norms and deviance is frequently a complicated one. Describe a situation in which conformity to the norms of some smaller group would result in nonconformity to the norms of the larger society. Then, discuss what implications this sort of conflict of norms might have for sociologists who want to understand why people deviate.

Answers and Discussion

STOP & REVIEW

11.1

  a. False—society *cannot* be divided into people who conform and people who do not conform to social norms. If we tried to make such a division, everyone would be on the same side of the line. Everyone deviates sometimes, and most people conform most of the time. (Even chainsaw murderers usually eat dinner with a fork and use toilet paper in the socially prescribed manner.)

  b. False—people generally do *not* agree on which behaviors are deviant and which are not deviant. In fact, there is a great deal of disagreement in society about what is deviant and what is not. It varies among subcultures and across time. However, within a particular society, there may be general agreement on the most important norms (for example, there is usually pretty solid agreement on what constitutes taboo behavior).

  c. True—most people have violated one or more important mores at some time in their lives. You may be the exception, but most of us will violate an important norm at least occasionally.

  d. False—Most deviant behaviors are *not* regarded as deviant in all societies and at all times. As I tried to emphasize, it is very difficult to identify a particular behavior that is deviant everywhere.

  e. False—it is *not* merely acts that are harmful to people that are judged to be deviant. There are many acts that really do not harm anyone but that are still regarded as deviant. It would be accurate, I think, to say that all deviant behaviors are offensive (if only in the sense that deviant acts offend social norms). Talking with your mouth full of food, for example, or picking your nose doesn't harm anyone, but these behaviors certainly do offend people.

11.2

  a. For Merton, the structural strain that led to anomie was the contradiction between socially approved goals and socially approved means. In our society, earning lots of money is a socially approved goal. But there are not enough socially approved/legitimate means for everyone to achieve this goal. This contradiction leads some people to deviate.

  b. Their contribution was to point out that just as not all people have the same access to socially approved/legitimate means, not all people have the same access to illegitimate means.

11.3   Primary deviance is deviance that people commit—on a whim or owing to particular circumstances. If they are caught and sanctioned for this act, they may be led to perform secondary deviance. Secondary deviance is deviance that people perform as a result of being labeled as a deviant.

11.4   She said that she did it because her feet were tired, but when Parks refused to give up her seat to a white person and was arrested for this "crime," she became a symbol that helped launch the civil rights movement.

Stratification and Inequality

Inequality is an inevitable fact of social life. In all societies, people are evaluated on the basis of some characteristic (or set of characteristics) and placed into higher- or lower-ranking groups. People in higher-ranking groups tend to receive disproportionately larger shares of valued social stuff (such as wealth, power, and respect). People in lower-ranking groups tend to receive correspondingly smaller shares of these social rewards.

Sociologists refer to this evaluation-ranking-reward system and its results as *social stratification*. The term *stratification* is one that we borrowed from the earth sciences because it conveys the fact that society is made up of social layers, or *strata*, that are arranged in a hierarchy. As figure 12.1 shows, like rocks in the earth, some people are at the bottom of society, some are in the middle, and some are at the top.

Be careful: The analogy between social strata and geological strata can be a little misleading. Yes, groups of people are arranged by strata in society just as rocks are in the earth. But geologists do not value a kind of rock simply because it is found in the top stratum. In every type of *social* stratification system, however, the people at the top are considered better than the people at the bottom. Sometimes, as I will describe shortly, *better* can mean purer, or smarter, or braver. But it always means more of something that is valued in that society (Barber 1968).

Although every society has some form of stratification, the forms vary from society to society. Notwithstanding their differences, all stratification systems have three related things in common. First, the systems tend to persist for a long time. Second, the systems are resistant to change. Third, each system is bolstered

Figure 12.1 *Perspectives on Stratification. Sociologists use the term stratification to refer to the different social strata that exist in society. People in higher strata receive greater rewards than do people in lower strata.*

by widely accepted *legitimating rationales.* These rationales help to account for the persistence of particular social stratification systems.

In the most general sense, legitimating rationales are widely accepted beliefs that something is fair and just. With respect to stratification, then, legitimating rationales are widely accepted beliefs that the inequalities that exist in a particular society (differences in power, wealth, prestige, and so on) are essentially "right and reasonable" (Della Fave 1980). In other words, the rationales that legitimate stratification systems reflect people's beliefs about why some people are ranked higher than others and why this is fair. To the degree that stratification systems differ across societies, we would expect them to have different legitimating rationales. Understanding these rationales will help us to make sense of people's acceptance of the kind of stratification that exists in their society.

Though there are perhaps as many forms of stratification as there are societies, sociologists generally group these into three major categories: caste, estate, and class.

Caste Systems

In a *caste system* one's rank is determined at birth. In other words, one's position in a caste system is based on ascribed characteristics. Caste membership generally determines a person's prestige, occupation, and residence, as well as the nature of his or her social relationships.

The most frequently cited example of a caste system is the one that originated in India some 4000 years ago. When Portuguese explorers visited India in the mid-sixteenth century, they were very impressed by the fact that each person was born into a particular subgroup and was more or less allowed to interact only with people from the same subgroup. The many prohibitions on interaction led the Portuguese explorers to call the subgroups *casta*—a Portuguese word meaning "pure" or "something that ought not be mixed." What the word reflects, then, is the sense the explorers had that the boundaries between the subgroups in India were so very strong that it was as if the people in different castes belonged to different races.[1] In 1908 Célestin Bouglé, a French social scientist, defined *caste* this way:

> The caste system divides the whole society into a large number of hereditary groups, distinguished from one another and connected together by three characteristics: *separation* in matters of marriage and contact, whether direct or indirect; *division* of labour, each group having, in theory or by tradition, a profession from which their members can depart only within certain limits; and finally *hierarchy*, which ranks the groups as relatively superior or inferior to one another. (Paraphrased in Dumont 1970, 21)

In a caste system, no one is allowed to wed, eat food cooked by, or drink from the cup of anyone from a lower caste. Many kinds of contact are judged to defile (contaminate) the higher-caste person. At one time, for example, members of the lowest castes were forbidden to move about in public during the daylight hours merely because of the possibility that their shadows might fall upon an upper-caste person.

The caste system of India finds its legitimating rationale in the Hindu religion. This rationale begins with the Hindu idea of *transmigration* (or what many Westerners would call *reincarnation*). It is generally believed that each person is born into a particular caste as a result of his or her actions and thoughts in a previous life. This has to do with the concept of *karma*— a Sanskrit word meaning "work" or "fate."[2] Those who subscribe to the Hindu faith view karma as the *inexorable application of the law of cause and effect*. That is, people who lead a good life, carefully follow the rules of the religion, and fulfill their *dharma*, or caste-based duties, will inevitably be born into a higher caste in the next life.

According to the Hindu religion, human beings *"do not start life with a clean slate. The soul of every newborn infant formerly inhabited some other body. Sometimes the soul came from another human being, sometimes from an animal. Wherever it had been before, it accumulated karma. Karma is a little like dust: it collects on the soul just through the process of living. Only a very wise and good individual, aided by ritual purification, can avoid accumulating a lot of it."* (McNeill 1987, 153)

---

[1] It was in this sense that Charles Darwin, in his *On the Origin of Species*, referred to different castes of insects.

[2] Sanskrit is the sacred language of the Hindu religion.

But those who fail to carry out their dharma will lose caste in the next life (Smith 1958).

According to the Hindu religion, there are four *varnas*, or "colors" or "grades of being." As told by the Hindu creation story found in the Rig Veda (an ancient religious text), the universe was born from the sacrifice of the male/female entity Purusha. Purusha was dismembered by the gods, and the detached parts became the stuff from which the entire universe was fashioned. More specifically, from the different parts of Purusha's body came the four *varnas*: (1) the *brahmans*, or priests, seers, and philosophers; (2) the *kshatriyas*, or warriors, royalty, and administrators; (3) the *vaishyas*, or producers, merchants, farmers, artisans, and other skilled workers; and (4) the *shudras*, or peasants and unskilled workers. A final group of people, the *scheduled castes*, or untouchables, complete India's stratification system, though for thousands of years they were deemed too impure to be part of the caste system itself.[3]

Within each *varna*, or grade of being, are castes (*jatis*) numbering in the thousands. As with their *varna*, people's membership in a *jati* begins at birth and lasts until death. Each *jati* is associated with a particular occupation (for example, shoemaker, teacher, animal herder, or leather worker). However, it is no longer the case that all the members of a *jati* necessarily work in that occupation—especially in urban areas.

"Thousand-faced Purusha, thousand-eyed, thousand footed—he, having pervaded the earth on all sides, still extends ten fingers beyond it. Purusha alone is all this—whatever has been and whatever is going to be. . . . He is the lord of immortality and also of what grows on account of food.

When they divided Purusha, in how many different portions did they arrange him? What became of his mouth, what of his two arms? What were his two thighs and his two feet called?

His mouth became the brahman; his two arms were made into the [kshatriyas]; his two thighs the vaishyas; from his two feet the shudra was born."

—Rig Veda

In 1949 the concept of untouchables was outlawed in India, and in 1950 the Constitution of Independent India outlawed the entire caste system. Did this mean the end of the caste system in India? No. What it meant was that the *formal* laws of India no longer enforced the system. Because of its tie to important religious beliefs, however, the caste system has retained much of its strength and is still enforced by very strong informal norms and sanctions. Recently, as some lower castes have sought to claim their legal rights, these informal sanctions have tended to be quite violent. In the city, it is possible to get past some of the constraints of the caste system because of the anonymity of urban life. In the coun-

---

[3] During his tenure as the great modern leader of India, Mohandas Gandhi (1869–1948), nicknamed Mahatma ("the Great Soul"), worked to bring the untouchables into mainstream society in India. Mahatma called the untouchables the Harijan (sons of Hari). Hari is the name commonly used to refer to Vishnu, an important Hindu deity. In other words, Gandhi was renaming the untouchables "creatures of God. " Today, many members of this caste prefer the less euphemistic term *scheduled caste*, wanting to make clear their less-than-enviable position in society.

tryside, however, everyone knows who belongs to each caste, and the caste system still has a great deal of power.

Estate Systems

As in a caste system, a person's place in the hierarchy of an *estate system* is determined at birth. Contacts between members of different estates are permitted, though generally this contact is fairly impersonal (as between a boss and an employee). So, for example, marriage between people of different estates is generally forbidden by law. The feudal system that prevailed in Western Europe during the Middle Ages is frequently cited as a good example of an estate system of stratification.

In England, as in much of the rest of Europe, there were three estates, or social strata. The highest stratum, the first estate, was made up of the aristocracy or nobility. The first estate, which persisted nearly into modern times in England, came into power after William the Conqueror (also known as William the Bastard) came from Normandy to proclaim himself king of England (in 1066 C.E.). William and his soldiers eventually confiscated most of the property owned by the original English (the Saxons). To show his appreciation, William granted these lands (or *feuds*) to the men who had helped him to conquer England. The earliest members of this first estate, then, were those with distinguished records of loyalty and military service to William (and later, to subsequent kings). Originally royal land grants were more like land loans, and in theory, when the individual grantee died, the lands reverted to the king, who could then grant them to someone else. Over time, it became customary for the king to regrant the lands to the heirs of the previous owner. In this way membership in the first estate came to be inherited, or ascribed.

The clergy made up the second estate. Like the members of the first estate, the church had a great deal of power, in large part because it owned a great deal of land. Membership in the second estate was not based on ascribed characteristics. But the highest-ranking churchmen (and churchwomen) came from the ranks of the first estate, and the lowest-ranking from more common stock.

Originally the third estate included only the peasants (sometimes called *villeins*, or serfs). These were the people who were tied legally to specific parcels of land. So, when the king granted a piece of land to a member of the first estate, the aristocrat—or lord of the manor—got the people, too! The lord–peasant relationship was supposed to be for their mutual benefit. The lord of the manor pledged to protect his peasants from outside threats and keep the peace. In return, the peasants pledged their labor and loyalty.

A Year in the Life of the Peasant

"From the 29th of September until the 29th of June he must work two days a week, to wit on Monday and Wednesday; and on Friday he must plough with all the beasts of his team; but he has a holiday for a fortnight at Christmas and for a week at Easter and at Whitsuntide. If one of the Fridays on which he ought to plough is a festival or if the weather is bad, he must do the ploughing on some other day. Between the 29th of September and the 11th of November he must also plough and harrow half an acre for wheat, and for sowing that half-acre he must give of his own seed the eighth part of a quarter: Whether that quantity be more or less than is necessary for sowing the half-acre he must give that quantity, no more, no less: and on account of this seed he is excused from one day's work. At Christmas time he must make two quarters of malt and for each quarter he is excused one day's work. At Christmas he shall give three hens and a cock or four pence and at Easter ten eggs. He must also do six carryings in the year within the county between the 29th of June and the end of harvest at whatever time the bailiff shall choose, or, if the lord pleases, he shall between the 29th of June and the 29th of September work five days a week, working the whole day at whatever work is set him, besides carrying corn, for he shall carry but four cartloads of corn for a day's work. If at harvest time the lord shall have two or three 'boon works,' he shall come to them with all the able-bodied members of his family save his wife, so that he must send at least three men to work" (Pollock and Maitland 1898/1968, 267).

Vocabulary

bailiff: overseer

boon works: days of work the lord could require of a peasant as a favor

carrying: transporting crops

fortnight: 14 days

harrow: cultivate

malt: barleywater or barley added to water (the first step in beer making)

plough: plow

quarter: 8 bushels (8 gallons or 4 pecks)

sow: plant seed

Whitsuntide: Whitsunday/Pentecost (a Christian holiday celebrated in spring)

Each lord of a manor likewise owed duties to the king or some other overlord. Typically, these duties could be discharged by paying off any taxes assessed by the king. But some duties were different:

> A Kentishman was required to "hold the King's head in the boat" when he should cross the Channel. Even more peculiar was the case of a certain [minor lord] obliged every Christmas to make before his lord, *unum saltum et siffletum et unum bumbulum* ("a leap, whistle and audible gaseous expulsion"). (Bishop 1968, 111)

In time the third estate came to include merchants and craftsmen as well as peasants. When they were few in number, the merchants and craftsmen were regarded as free men and existed on the periphery of the estate system. But, beginning in about the twelfth century, the nobles came to fear the growing power of these ambitious individuals. To keep them in their place (that is, below the first estate), the aristocrats enacted laws officially designating merchants and craftsmen as members of the third estate. In this way, the third estate came to be the estate of commoners.[4]

What beliefs legitimated the feudal system? Early on, the privileges that came from being a member of the first estate were justified because of the personal qualities of each aristocrat—his military prowess, bravery, loyalty, and so on. When rank in society (and land ownership) became hereditary, of course, even the proverbial 90-pound weakling could become lord of the manor. In time, people came to believe they belonged to the estate that suited them. As far as the people were concerned, social rank was assigned by God. As one historian explained, members of the aristocracy were perceived to be "noble," and "everyone else was judged 'ignoble' or 'churlish'"—that is, rude and ill-bred:

"In the fifteenth-century, Lady Luliana Berners wrote about 'the common conviction that Seth and Abel, sons of Adam and Eve, were gentlemen, but Cain a churl and ancestor of the churls of the world. Christ [she said] was a gentleman on his mother's side.'"

—Morris Bishop
(1968, 115)

> The gentleman or nobleman was a man set apart to govern. He was independent and leisured: he derived his income without having to work for it, that income made him free from want and from being beholden to or dependent upon others, and he had the time and leisure to devote himself to the arts of government. He was independent in judgment and trained to make decisions. Not all gentlemen served in the offices which required such qualities (justice of the peace, sheriff, militia captain, high constable, etc.). But all had this capacity to serve, to govern. (Morrill 1984, 297)

---

[4] Occasionally, people speak of the fourth estate. This refers to the members of the media/press. The "term has its source from a reference to the reporters' gallery of the British Parliament whose influence on public policy was said to equal that of the Parliament's three traditional estates, the clergy, nobility, and commons" (Black 1979, 591).

As industrialization came to Europe, the estate system broke down. Industry created new jobs and pulled people away from the land. Still, remnants of the estate system can be found even today. For example, membership in the upper house of the English Parliament, the House of Lords, is open to all holders of hereditary *peerages,* or noble rank—these are the *Lords Temporal*.[5] Moreover, the upper house includes the *Lords Spiritual*—the archbishops and the most senior bishops of the Church of England (other religions are not officially represented in Parliament). At the same time, membership in the lower house of Parliament, the House of Commons, is limited to commoners—no one of noble birth can stand for election to the House of Commons without repudiating (giving up) his or her title.

Class Systems

The social class system of stratification was made possible by industrialization and urbanization. Workers moved from farms and agricultural occupations to cities and factory positions. Geographic mobility and industry presented many more opportunities to change one's life circumstances. A class system seemed to be an inevitable result.

Recall that in the estate system it was commonly believed that God placed the best people in the highest ranks. In the *class system,* by contrast, it is commonly thought that the best people work their own way into the highest ranks. In theory, at least, a true class system is supposed to turn on achieved rather than ascribed characteristics. Those who are smart, talented, and hard-working (and a little lucky) can rise to the top of the class system. Of course, people who are not as smart, talented, or hard-working (or who have bad luck) can just as easily sink to the bottom. In brief, this is the sort of belief that justifies class-based stratification systems as fair and just. To paraphrase James Kluegel and Eliot Smith (1981, 29–32), the opportunity to get ahead is available to all. Because of this, the position you reach in the stratification system is the direct result of your own efforts, traits, and abilities, and *not* the result of economic or social factors. The fact that your efforts determine where you end up means that you are personally responsible for the rewards you receive. Because people determine their own class standing, the current system of inequality is fair and appropriate.

---

[5]This group does not include those lords who are not yet 21 years of age or who are disqualified owing to being foreign-born, bankrupt, insane, or in prison for a felony or treason. Since 1963 women of noble rank have been allowed to sit in the House of Lords.

Theoretical Conceptions of Class

What it is, exactly, that determines one's place in a class system has been a matter of great debate. One of the first to take a stand on this matter was Karl Marx. According to Marx, the most important thing about any society was its economic system, especially the means by which it produced the stuff that people needed to survive. In the earliest days of humanity, the *means of production* was hunting and gathering; in the Middle Ages, it was agriculture; in modern times, it is industry. Marx said that to understand an individual's resources, personality, values, and beliefs, we need to understand where he or she stands relative to the means of production.

From Marx's perspective, people in industrial society fell into one of two social classes. The upper class was made up of the capitalists—those who owned the means of production (for example, the factory owners). The lower class was made up of workers who supported themselves by selling their labor to the capitalists.

Marx called the capitalist/owner stratum the *bourgeoisie*—a French word meaning "shopkeeper." In the Middle Ages, the bourgeoisie were relegated to the third estate. But, as Marx observed, as the means of production changed from agriculture to industry, the landowning aristocrats lost power to the spirited entrepreneurial shopkeepers who had risen up to become the factory owners.

Marx called the worker stratum the *proletariat*—from the Latin *proletarius*, a term that was used to refer to the lowest class of citizens in ancient Rome.

Max Weber had a different take on the nature of modern stratification. First, he said, Marx's conception of economic class was too narrow. The crucial thing was not where one stood in relation to the means of production (that is, whether one was an owner or a worker), but where one stood in the market situation. Weber defined class this way:

> The term *class* refers to any group of people . . . [who have the same] typical chance for a supply of goods, external living conditions, and personal life experiences, insofar as this chance is determined by the . . . power . . . to dispose of goods or skills for the sake of income in a given economic order. . . . *Class situation* is, in this sense, ultimately *market situation*. (Weber 1920/1958, 180)[6]

---

[6]Weber distinguished between lifestyle and life chances: *Lifestyle:* distinctive ways in which people consume goods and services; the social customs associated with each class. Lifestyle differences tend to reflect people's financial and social resources. *Life chances:* phrase coined by Max Weber to indicate the probabilities concerning the fate an individual can expect in life. Life chances include the probability that the individual will obtain good health, education, autonomy, and a long life.

Ponder

Economist Simon Kuznets suggested that the graphic relationship between the means of production and the level of social stratification is a parabolic one (that is, one shaped like ∩). I've illustrated this relationship in figure 12.2.

Given your understanding of the different kinds of stratification systems, why do you think that industrial societies might have more equality than agrarian societies (that is, those based on agriculture)?

Figure 12.2 *Kuznets's Curve—Social Stratification and Technology*

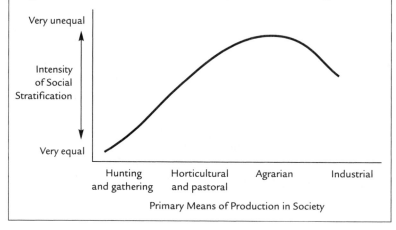

Marx's version of class would place professional baseball players (who in 1993 earned average salaries of $859,499 a year) in the same class as secretaries who earned less than $30,000 a year, because they all earn a living by selling their labor. But from Weber's point of view, baseball players would be in a much higher economic class than secretaries owing to the differences in their respective market situations.

Furthermore, according to Weber, Marx's emphasis on economic factors to the exclusion of all else was misguided. For Weber social stratification was *multidimensional,* and economic situation was only one dimension of social position. For example, a college professor who earns less than $40,000 a year still has a higher social standing than the automobile factory worker who makes $50,000.

Weber argued that to truly understand the nature of social stratification, sociologists had to take into account not only economics (market system) but the dynamics of power and status in society. As Weber defined it, *power* "is the probability that one actor within a social relationship will be in a position to carry out his own will despite resistance." Thus, according to Weber, power is the ability to impose one's will or to get one's way even when faced with opposition from others.

Weber distinguished between different types of power. Legitimate power (which he called *authority*) is power that is seen as justified. For example, when a police officer stops a bank robber and takes her loot, this is a legitimate use of power. When a mugger stops a pedestrian and takes his wallet, this is an illegitimate use of power. According to Weber, the extent to which people have power (especially authority or legitimate power) has a big impact on their overall position in the stratification system.

Frequently money and power are related, but not always. A local district attorney, for example, will earn less money than the executive officer of a large corporation, but the DA can exercise the power of her office to prevent the corporate officer from breaking the law.

Finally, Weber said, we must also take into account the degree to which people have social *status*. In this context status has to do with prestige—or the degree to which an individual has social honor.[7] Most research on social status or prestige has focused on occupations. As illustrated in table 12.1, sociologists have found that people in different occupations fairly consistently receive different amounts of social honor.[8]

Here's an important point: In view of what I have just stated, to refer to our stratification system as one based on class is rather misleading. So, you should firmly implant the following fact in your brain: When sociologists use the word *class*, they tend to mean more than economic factors. Most sociologists follow Weber's example in treating social class as a multidimensional thing. Thus, for example, when sociologists use the word *class*, they frequently mean *socioeconomic standing*, or SES. Measures of SES look at people's income, education, occupational prestige, and wealth and provide some overall assessment of people's place in the social stratification system.

---

[7]This may seem confusing to you because in chapter 8 I defined *status* as "a position that a person occupies on a social structure." Weber used the word *status* differently—to specify the degree to which a position in the social structure is respected or deferred to.

[8]Occupational prestige is usually determined by asking survey respondents to rank a number of occupations on a scale of 0 to 100. The average score given an occupation determines its prestige rating.

Table 12.1 Occupational Prestige Rankings
of Selected Occupations in the United States

Occupation	Prestige Score	Occupation	Prestige Score
Physician	86	Bookkeeper	47
Lawyer	75	Machinist	47
College professor	74	Mail carrier	47
Architect	73	Secretary	46
Chemist	73	Photographer	45
Aerospace engineer	72	Bank teller	43
Dentist	72	Tailor	42
Secret Service agent	70	Welder	42
Clergy	69	Farm owner	40
Psychologist	69	Telephone operator	40
Pharmacist	68	Carpenter	39
Registered nurse	66	Radio/TV repair	38
Secondary school teacher	66	Security guard	37
Accountant	65	Brickmason	36
Athlete	65	Childcare worker	36
Electrical engineer	64	File clerk	36
Elementary school teacher	64	Hairdresser	36
Veterinarian	62	Baker	35
Computer programmer	61	Bus driver	32
Sociologist	61	Auto mechanic	31
Reporter	60	Sales clerk	30
Police officer	60	Cashier	29
Actor	58	Assembly line worker	29
Dietician	56	Garbage collector	29
Radio/TV announcer	55	Taxi driver	28
Librarian	54	Waitress or waiter	28
Aircraft mechanic	53	Bellhop	27
Fire fighter	53	Bartender	25
Dental hygienist	52	Farm laborer	23
Social worker	52	Household maid	23
Electrician	51	Door-to-door salesperson	22
Funeral director	49	Janitor or cleaner	22
Realtor	49	Shoe shiner	9

SOURCE: Adapted from *General Social Survey, Cumulative Code Book, 1972–1990* (Chicago:
National Opinion Research Center, 1990).

STOP & REVIEW

12.1 Mary Beth received an associate degree in plumbing from the
local community college. Now she owns a small plumbing firm
(where she employs three other plumbers). She brings home about
$25,000 a year.

Elizabeth graduated from Harvard Law School. Now she works
as in-house counsel (attorney) for General Motors. She brings home
about $145,000 a year.

a. According to Marx, who occupies the higher class position—Mary Beth or Elizabeth? Why?
b. What would Weber say about who occupies the higher class position? Why?
c. Suppose the stock market crashes, times are really tough economically, and people stop making major purchases. Who is more economically vulnerable—Mary Beth or Elizabeth? Why?

Some Words About Slavery

Although slavery is a major source of inequality everywhere it exists, I have not included it as a system of stratification in and of itself. The reason for this is that slavery can exist (and has done so) within caste, estate, and class systems. Slaves are people whose function is to serve others and who have no political rights of their own—no right to own property, to sign legal contracts (and then go to the courts to get their contracts enforced), to legally marry, or to maintain legal custody of their children. Slaves may be given certain freedoms by their masters, but these are dependent on the goodwill of the master. In the most extreme form of slavery, slaves are treated as if they were the property of their masters, in much the same way as goats or cattle. This extreme type of slavery is called *chattel slavery*—*chattel* being a legal term for "movable property" (like farm animals) as opposed to "real property" (like land). This is the sort of slavery that existed in southern states prior to the Civil War.

Slavery is most frequently found in societies that are heavily agricultural (as opposed to industrial). Depending on the society, people can be enslaved in a number of ways. The earliest forms of slavery involved people who had been captured in war or kidnapped. In many societies people have been enslaved because they could not pay their debts (or the debts of a family member). Often, criminals have been sentenced to slavery. In some societies children are sold into slavery by their parents (frequently as an alternative to infanticide, or infant killing, which usually involves only girl babies). Finally there is *self-enslavement*, which occurs when people sell themselves into slavery as a way to overcome serious economic insecurity.

Historian Orlando Patterson (1982) found that regardless of how groups of people originally find their way into the position of being slaves, if slavery persists in a society for more than a couple of generations, it tends to become hereditary. In other words, there is a tendency for slavery to change from being an achieved to an ascribed status.

Some social scientists have suggested that a slave system is just like a caste system and that slaves are simply the outcastes. They have a point—but Patterson argues that there are important differences between slaves and outcastes:

> There was never any marriage, or even illicit sexual relations, between the outcaste group and ordinary persons, whereas such relations were common between "free" males and slave women. . . . Slaves universally were not only sexually exploited in their role as concubines, but also in their role as mother-surrogates and nursemaids. However great the human capacity for contradiction, it has never been possible for any group of masters to suckle at their slave's breasts as infants, sow their wild oats with her as adolescents, then turn around as adults and claim that she was polluted. (1982, 50)

Moreover, slaves can be freed, or manumitted[9]—but outcastes cannot lose their caste status. Finally, in a variety of societies, slaves were drawn from even the highest caste. "Indeed, in order to perform the various duties imposed on domestic servants, to be permitted to cross the threshold of an owner's dwelling, it was imperative for the slave to enjoy a degree of ritual purity conferred only by membership in certain castes." Thus, for example, in Nepal "even Brahmins were enslaved without losing caste" (Patterson 1982, 51).

Social Mobility and Open Versus Closed Systems

At the most abstract level, sociologists distinguish between *open* and *closed* stratification systems. The distinction depends on the amount of *social mobility* that the system allows.

Sociologists also distinguish between different types of social mobility. *Horizontal* mobility refers to movement, say, from one occupation to another in the same stratum. *Vertical* mobility refers to movement up or down in a stratification system (for example, from lower to middle class). A truly open system of stratification will have a great deal of both horizontal and vertical mobility. A truly closed system will have neither.

Sociologists further distinguish between *inter*generational and *intra*generational mobility. *Intergenerational* mobility refers to changes in position in the stratification system by different generations of family members. When a son attains a higher (or lower) class than his father, the son has experienced intergenera-

---

[9]Manumission was a formal process by which a slave was made free. The term comes from the Latin *manu* (hand, power) and *mitter* (to let go).

tional mobility. *Intragenerational* mobility—or *career* mobility—has to do with the mobility that occurs within a person's lifetime. For example, a woman who starts her life in poverty and grows up to be a justice of the Supreme Court has experienced intragenerational, or career, mobility. In an open system of stratification, we would expect to see a great deal of intragenerational or career mobility—people should have opportunities to work their way up (or down). And we would also expect a great deal of intergenerational mobility—if a system is truly open, where you start out (such as poor or rich) should not determine where you end up.

A word of caution is in order here. Recall from chapter 8 Weber's concept of the ideal type. The ideal type of a thing is that thing considered in its *pure form*. As we discussed in chapter 8, the ideal-type bureaucracy is a step removed from real bureaucracies, because real bureaucracies often are not pure. The concepts of open and closed stratification systems are also ideal types. No known system of stratification is either totally open or totally closed. Table 12.2 lists some of the major differences between ideal-type open and closed systems.

It is fairly easy to see where each of the major systems of stratification—caste, estate, and class—would fit in this classification. The caste system is the most closed system. In India the differences between people in different *varnas* and even *jatis* are perceived to be related to differences in the purity of the individual's soul. This means that there is no real chance of changing one's caste (or the caste of one's children) during one's lifetime.

The estate system is also mostly closed, but there is some room for advancement. As noted previously, one could change one's estate by joining the church. Even men without religious vocations could at least hope for advancement because "here and there

Table 12.2 Attributes of Ideal-Type Open and Closed Systems of Stratification

Open Systems	Closed Systems
Boundaries between strata are permeable (open).	Boundaries between strata are impermeable (closed).
Positions within the system are achieved.	Positions within the system are ascribed.
The opportunity to change ranks exists.	No opportunity to change ranks exists.
The law permits exogamy (marriage outside of a stratum), but informal norms promote endogamy (marriage within a stratum).	The law requires endogamy.

little men became big through astuteness, prowess, or royal favor. Valiant fighters were knighted on the field of battle." At the same time, some not-so-valiant "knights sank into the peasantry or lived as robbers" (Bishop 1968, 115). In general, however, distinctions between the estates were seen as fixed by God.

The class system is the closest thing to a truly open stratification system. As I suggested, one's class is supposed to be determined by what one does, not by who one's parents are—that is, by achieved rather than ascribed characteristics. In a class-based system, then, we would expect to see a great deal of all kinds of mobility—vertical and horizontal, intragenerational and intergenerational. The degree to which that is true in real life (as opposed to theory) is something we will examine in the next two chapters.

12.2 Give two examples of each of the following:
 a. vertical mobility
 b. horizontal mobility
 c. intragenerational mobility
 d. intergenerational mobility

Chapter Review

1. Make a list of the sociological concepts that you learned in this chapter. Define each term. (*Hint:* You will learn the most from this exercise if, in addition to defining each concept, you create an example of it in your own words.)

2. Suppose that your much younger brother or sister (a 7-year-old) has just watched a television show about poverty in the United States that featured many clips of children dressed in shabby clothes and looking hungry. Your little brother or sister poses a question to you—"How come some people are so poor and others have so much money?" Explain how you would respond.

3. Something terrible happens, and you have to drop out of college. The only job you can find pays $7.50 an hour. Create a budget for how you would spend that money—for rent and other necessities. Would you be able to live a "comfortable" life? (Check the local paper to find out about rent, visit a grocery store to discover what different foods cost.)
   Then assume that on the same level of wages, you had to support two children. What would their lives be like?

4. Describe the differences in the kinds of rationales or principles that justify caste, estate, and class systems.

Answers and Discussion

12.1

 a. Marx would say that Mary Beth, the plumber, has a higher class position than Elizabeth, the attorney. The reason is that Mary Beth owns (part of) the means of production, while Elizabeth makes her living selling her labor.

 b. Weber would say that Elizabeth has the higher class position, because her salary puts her in a better position with respect to the marketplace. She can purchase more stuff and increase the quality of her life chances and lifestyle.

 c. This could be argued either way, but in my opinion, it's possible that Elizabeth is the more economically vulnerable. During depressed economic times, General Motors might have to down-size. And given that lawyers are not necessarily central to the business of General Motors, they might be the first to be laid off. Unless she has other sources of wealth, without a regular paycheck coming in, Elizabeth could experience some financially stressful times. Mary Beth, on the other hand, is less vulnerable to economic disaster because toilets, sinks, and the like are not luxuries in society. If they break, people have to get them fixed.

12.2

 a. Vertical mobility occurs when someone goes up or down the "occupational ladder." A promotion from typist to executive secretary is vertical mobility, as is a demotion from executive vice president to sales representative.

 b. Horizontal mobility is movement in which someone changes jobs but not necessarily for the better or worse. If I quit my present teaching job and moved to a new university, this would probably be a horizontal move. Sociologists and other observers of the modern labor market predict that the current generation of workers will change careers more than a half dozen times in their lifetimes. Many of these changes will be horizontal.

 c. The prefix *intra* means "within." So, intragenerational mobility is career mobility, or mobility within the lifetime of a person. Movement from graduate student to instructor, to assistant, to associate, and then to full professor is intragenerational mobility.

 d. The prefix *inter* means "between." So, intergenerational mobility is mobility between generations. Suppose your dad was a blue-collar worker and you became a physician. You would have experienced intergenerational mobility. (Of course, it could be that your mom was a physician and you became a bum. That would be intergenerational mobility, too.)

Inequality and Achievement

Social Class

When I introduce students to the concept of stratification, they often react as if it's a topic that is relevant only to other societies. More specifically, I have observed in my students a tendency to believe that in the United States, there are no such things as social classes, let alone, social class differences.

My students are not unusual in this respect. Many researchers have reported that people in the United States are reluctant to admit the existence of class. This was something that Paul Fussell discovered early on when he was writing his *Class: A Guide Through the American Status System*. The subject of class, he concluded, is "always touchy":

> You can outrage people today simply by mentioning social class, very much the way, sipping tea among the aspidistras [a kind of lily] a century ago, you could silence a party by adverting too openly to sex. When, recently, asked what I am writing, I have answered, "A book about social class in America," people tend first to straighten their ties and sneak a glance at their cuffs to see how far fraying has advanced there. Then, a few minutes later, they silently get up and walk away. . . . It is as if I had said, "I am working on a book urging the beating to death of baby whales using the dead bodies of baby seals." Since I have been writing this book I have experienced many times the awful truth of [economist] R. H. Tawney's perception, in his book *Equality* (1931): "The word 'class' is fraught with unpleasing associations, so that to linger upon it is apt to be interpreted as the symptom of a perverted mind and a jaundiced spirit." (1983, 15)

Why *is* class such a touchy issue in the United States? It's touchy because asking questions about social class violates an important social myth: that people in the United States are pretty much alike. As one respondent to a survey explained to sociologist Richard Scase, "Class is not as important as it used to be, most people are middle class nowadays." Indeed, study after study has found that most everyone (well, anyway, at least 80 percent) in the United States will describe him- or herself as a member of the middle class. So, when you ask people about class and class differences, they will typically respond that such differences do not exist—at least not where they come from.

> Being told that there are no social classes in the place where the interviewee lives is an old experience for sociologists. "'We don't have classes in our town' almost invariably is the first remark recorded by the investigator," reports Leonard Reissman, author of *Class in American Life* (1959). "Once that has been uttered and is out of the way, the class divisions in the town can be recorded with what seems to be an amazing degree of agreement among the good citizens of the community." (Fussell 1983, 17)

How much inequality is there in the United States? When we measure it in terms of income,[1] we find that there is a great deal of inequality. Examine figure 13.1. It shows that if we divide the U.S. population into five groups, the highest fifth (the top-earning 20 percent of the people) receives nearly half of the money that is paid out in income each year.

Figure 13.2 shows that the level of inequality of wealth[2] is even more striking. The top fifth (the richest 20 percent of society) owns more than 80 percent of the wealth. That means that the remaining four-fifths of the U.S. population share one-fifth of the wealth.

Still, the existence of inequality does not necessarily mean that class is all that important. And, in fact, for many Americans, class is not seen as very important because most people believe that regardless of social class, everyone has about the same chance to get ahead in society. As we observed in chapter 12, what really justifies the U.S. stratification system is the idea of "equality of opportunity." Ask people and they will tell you: What matters is how hard you work and how smart you are. Because of our socialization, such reasoning is compelling to Americans. Even children understand and believe it—at least, that is what Scott Cummings and Del Taebel discovered from their survey of schoolchildren. Here's how one of their young respondents explained the logic of the stratification system:

> "People are rich because they have the know-how and the opportunity, and to an extent most of them are wealthy because of some type of motivation that causes them not to settle at one step or one degree;

By 1990 the most affluent (wealthiest) 1 percent of Americans (834,000 households, with about $5.7 trillion in net worth) owned more than the least affluent 90 percent of Americans (84 million households, with about $4.8 trillion in net worth).

---

[1] *Income* is the amount of money that an individual or family group receives each year (from wages, salaries, investments, and so on).

[2] *Wealth* is the total value of the assets owned by an individual or family group.

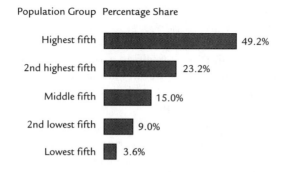

Figure 13.1 How
the Nation's Income
Is Distributed

SOURCE: U.S. Bureau of the
Census, 1999.

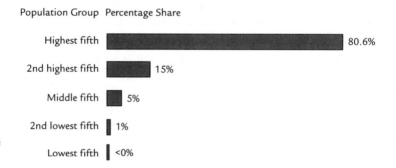

Figure 13.2 How
the Nation's Wealth
Is Distributed

SOURCE: U.S. Bureau of the
Census, 1991.

*"In the United States,
40 percent of the
nation's wealth is
concentrated in only
1 percent of American
households. Even
Britain, a nation with
a history of severe eco-
nomic stratification,
doesn't come close;
the richest 1 percent
of families there hold
18 percent of the coun-
try's wealth."*

—Sarah Boxer (1995, 1)

they wanted to reach higher heights. . . . People are poor because they are not educated enough to know that there is something for them out there; that they can make money. . . . They are ignorant and uneducated; a lot of them just don't care. . . . They are happy the way they are. . . . *If you really want to have some money, you can get it no matter how poor you have been*" [emphasis added]. (1978, 207)

If equality of opportunity does exist, an individual's class origins should not determine the level of his or her economic and social achievements. That is, if there is equality of opportunity, neither poverty nor wealth should be necessarily intergenerational; people who grew up in poor families should be no more likely to be poor as adults than people who grew up in nonpoor families.

One of the most ambitious attempts to test the validity of this rationale began in 1968 with the Panel Study of Income Dynamics, in which researchers followed 5000 families and their children over the course of twenty years. As sociologist Margaret Corcoran discovered, where one begins does have a big effect on where one ends up. Consider table 13.1—the data presented there suggest one thing: It matters if one's parents are poor, and *"it matters a lot"* (Corcoran 1995).

Table 13.1 Childhood Poverty and Adult Outcomes

	Black Children		White Children	
	Poor	Not Poor	Poor	Not Poor
Percent Who Are *Poor as Adults*	24.6%	9.6%	9.3%	1.2%

NOTE: Adults were 27 to 35 years of age in 1988. A respondent was defined as poor if the cost of his or her family's needs (shelter, clothing, food) exceeded the family's income. Food stamps and other government aid were counted as income.

SOURCE: Adapted from Margaret Corcoran, "Rags to Rags: Poverty and Mobility in the United States," *Annual Review of Sociology*.

Social scientists have extensively documented that parents' social class has a tremendous effect on their children's life chances. Simply put, people have a greater chance of succeeding in life if their parents are not poor. In what respects are people's life chances affected by their class origins? We can focus on four areas in particular:

"Nobody cares more about free enterprise and competition and about the best man winning than the man who inherited his father's store or farm."

—C. Wright Mills (1959)

1. *Health:* Parental class position has long-term health consequences for children. In general, mortality (death) rates and morbidity (sickness) rates are negatively related to social class. For example, studies have demonstrated that poverty is related to delays in children's physical development. "Physically underdeveloped and ill children might become less healthy and hence less employable as adults, a process perhaps arising from the inadequacies of the physical environment that poverty affords or from inadequate treatment of children's ailments directly due to lack of economic resources or indirectly to parental inattention or resignation: better to ignore things that you cannot alter" (Corcoran 1995, 262–263). Poor children are also more likely to suffer from serious psychological distress (Braun 1995; Johnson et al. 1991; McLeod and Shanahan 1993; Nelson 1992).

2. *Education:* Parental income has an effect on whether children finish high school and attend and graduate from college. Poverty has an impact even on really young children. In 1986, for example, only about 25 percent of poor children were enrolled in a preschool program compared to 40 percent of children from more affluent families (Entwisle and Alexander 1993).

3. *Working life:* Men who grew up in poor families tend to work many fewer hours per year and to earn less per hour than men who grew up in middle-class homes. Growing up in poor families reduces men's annual earnings by more than 40 percent (Corcoran 1995).

The Matthew Effect

As figure 13.3 suggests, the advantages that come with wealth tend to endure even during troubled economic times. The figure shows that during the 1980s, the rich got richer while the not-so-rich got poorer. This dynamic is one example of what some people call the *Matthew effect* (from the passage in the Gospel of Matthew that says, "For whosoever hath, to him shall be given, and he shall have more abundance: but whosoever hath not, from him shall be taken away . . ." [13:12]).

Economist Lester Thurow explained it this way: "Once wealth is accumulated, opportunities to make more money multiply, since accumulated wealth leads to income-earning opportunities that are not open to those without wealth" (1996, 243).

Figure 13.3 *Change in Share of Nation's Wealth, 1980–1992*[a]

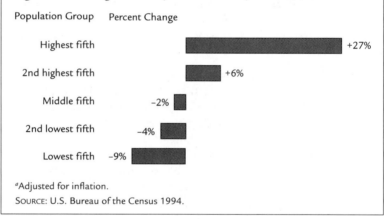

Population Group	Percent Change
Highest fifth	+27%
2nd highest fifth	+6%
Middle fifth	–2%
2nd lowest fifth	–4%
Lowest fifth	–9%

[a]Adjusted for inflation.
SOURCE: U.S. Bureau of the Census 1994.

4. *Crime and justice:* Poor people are more likely to be victims of all kinds of crime. People from the lower classes who break the law are more likely to be arrested, less likely to be released on bail, and more likely to be convicted and sent to prison than people from higher classes who break the law (Bureau of Justice Statistics 1992, 1993; Tittle and Meier 1990; Tittle, Villenez, and Smith 1978).

13.1 Can you think of any other examples of the *Matthew effect?*

Explaining Social Stratification

Most people end up in a class position that is the same as or close to the one occupied by their parents. Another way to state this is to say that members of each new generation tend to reproduce the class structure in which they were raised. When sociologists try to explain the dynamics that underlie this reproduction of the class structure, they typically draw on one of two sorts of perspectives: cultural and structural.

CULTURAL EXPLANATIONS

Cultural explanations of the reproduction of the class structure hinge on two assumptions. First, people in different social classes have different patterns of values, beliefs, and behavioral norms, which they pass on to their children through the socialization process. Allison Davis, writing in the late 1940s, was an early proponent of this sort of cultural perspective. According to Davis, "Social class patterning of the child's learning, as exerted through the family, extends from the control of the type of food he eats and the way he eats it, to the kinds of sexual, aggressive and educational training he receives" (1948, 12). The second assumption of the cultural perspective is that the values, beliefs, and behavioral norms of lower classes are not very compatible with success in society.

Probably the most famous advocate of the cultural perspective on the reproduction of the class system was Oscar Lewis. Based on his studies of the lower classes in a variety of societies, Lewis coined the term *culture of poverty.* According to Lewis and others who have followed in his footsteps, the culture of poverty turns poverty into a vicious cycle. Once it comes into existence, he said, the culture of poverty "tends to perpetuate itself from generation to generation because of its effects on the children" (1966, 50). Lewis argued that "by the time slum children are age six or seven they have usually absorbed the basic values and attitudes of their subculture. Thereafter they are psychologically unready to take full advantage of changing conditions or improving opportunities that may develop in their life time" (1966, 7).

Most proponents of the cultural explanation emphasize that it is not so much that the values, beliefs, and behavioral norms of poor people are bad; more to the point is the degree to which these values, beliefs, and behavioral norms are out of whack with those of mainstream society. Social psychologist Morton Deutch argued, for example, that

> we know that children from underprivileged environments tend
> to come to school with qualitatively different preparation for the
> demands both of the learning process and the behavior equipments
> of the classroom. There are various differences in the kinds of social-
> ization experiences these children have, as contrasted with the

middle class child. The culture of their environment is a different one from the culture that has molded the school, its educational techniques and theories. (1964, 172)

STRUCTURAL EXPLANATIONS

Structural explanations of the reproduction of the class system reject the notion that the best way to understand poverty is to look at cultural attributes of the poor. Proponents of the structural point of view argue that it is much more appropriate to focus on the limited access to opportunities that poor people have compared to the more affluent. They suggest that the differences in the values, beliefs, and behavioral norms that seem to exist are better explained as the *consequences* of poverty rather than as the causes. Sociologist Elliot Liebow, who explored the life of the urban poor in great depth, explained the significance of what might *seem* to be cultural differences between rich and poor this way:

> The streetcorner man *does not appear as a carrier of an independent cultural tradition* [emphasis added]. His behavior appears not so much as a way of realizing the distinctive goals of his own subculture, or of conforming to his [values and beliefs], but rather as his way of trying to achieve many of the goals and values of the larger society, of failing to do this, and of concealing this failure from others and from himself as best he can. (1967, 222)

Again, the structuralist point of view is that it is not their culture but the lack of opportunities open to the poor that holds them back. For example, the important thing is not that poor children tend to be less prepared for the realities of school than middle-class children, but that the schools themselves are inadequate.

13.2 Recently a student shared with me an example of his experiences with the stratification system in the United States:

> *"In high school I was an all-American basketball player even though I played in a ghetto school. . . . I got letters from coaches from top college programs saying, 'I've heard you are a great player, are you going to any camps?' The point was that they didn't want to come to my school to watch me play because it's in a rough place. They were willing to come see me if I could go to camp. But I wasn't able to afford to go to any of the camps."*

In your informed judgment, which point of view on the reproduction of class does this student's experience support—the *cultural* or the *structural*? Why? In your answer, summarize the two points of view—cultural and structural.

More recently, Jonathan Kozol compared schools in poor neighborhoods to those in more affluent ones. The differences he found are reflected in the title of his book—*Savage Inequalities: Children in America's Schools*. Here he quotes a teacher who works in an inner-city high school:

> "Very little education in this school would be considered academic in the suburbs. Maybe 10 to 15 percent of students are in truly academic programs. Of the 55 percent who graduate, 20 percent may go to four-year colleges . . . another 10 to 20 percent may get some kind of higher education. An equal number join the military." (1991)

It is hard to blame cultural factors when even the most highly motivated students have a tough time getting an education in such schools. One young woman told Kozol,

> "I don't go to physics class, because my lab has no equipment. . . . The typewriters in my typing class don't work. The women's toilets . . ." she makes a sour face. "I'll be honest," she says, "I just don't use the toilets. If I do, I come back into class and I feel dirty." (1991)

Kozol observed that things were bad all around at that school and are not likely to get better in the foreseeable future:

> The science labs . . . are 30 to 50 years outdated. John McMillan, a soft-spoken man, teaches physics at the school. He shows me his lab. The six lab stations in the room have empty holes where pipes were once attached. "It would be great if we had water," says McMillan. . . .
>
> Teachers are running out of chalk and paper, and their paychecks are arriving two weeks late. The city warns its teachers to expect a cut of half their pay until the fiscal crisis has been eased. (1991)

The situation in suburban schools tends to be quite different. Typical was one school where Kozol found, for one thing, that members of the faculty were not so worried about chalk and paper:

> According to the principal, the school has 96 computers for 546 children. The typical student, he says, studies a foreign language for four or five years, beginning in the junior high school, and for a second language (Latin is available) for two years. Of 140 seniors, 92 are now enrolled in AP [advanced college placement] classes. Maximum teacher salary will soon reach $70,000. (1991)

When Kozol asked students at this high school how they felt about their privileged positions, he found that students not only understood their advantages but accepted them as just:

> "I don't think that busing students from their ghetto to a different school would do much good," one student says. "You can take them out of the environment, but you can't take the environment out of *them*. If someone grows up in [the inner city], he's not going to be prone to learn." His name is Max and he has short black hair and speaks with confidence. "Busing didn't work when it was tried,"

he says. I ask him how he knows this and he says he saw a television movie about Boston.

"I agree that it's unfair the way it is," another student says. "We have AP courses and they don't. Our classes are much smaller." But, she says, "putting them in schools like ours is not the answer. Why not put some AP classes into *their* school? Fix the roof and paint the halls so it will not be so depressing." (1991)

Jennifer, whose family had recently moved up from a poorer neighborhood, agreed. She pointed out to Kozol that though her family had managed to bring itself up, some people simply weren't prepared to do what it takes to be mobile:

"It has to be the people in the area who want an education. If your parents just don't care, it won't do any good to spend a lot of money. Someone else can't want a good life for you. You have got to want it for yourself." Then, she adds, however, "I agree that everyone should have a chance at taking the same course." (1991)

According to proponents of the structural perspective, the cultural theories of poverty themselves may be contributing to the problem. By stressing the inadequacies of poor people, they seem to encourage a cover-up of the inadequacies of the structure in which those poor people live. William Ryan called the kind of reasoning implicit in the cultural perspective a form of "blaming the victim" (1971). For proponents of the structural point of view, then, blaming poor people's culture for their poverty is like blaming the rape victim because she wore provocative clothing; such blame is simply misplaced. Just as the rapist is the major cause of rape, the major cause of poverty is a lack of opportunities.

To what extent do these theories obscure more basic reasons for the educational retardation of lower status children? To what extent do they offer acceptable and desired alibis for educational default: the fact that these children, by and large, do not learn because they are not being taught effectively and they are not being taught because those who are charged with the responsibility of teaching them do not believe they can learn, do not expect that they can learn, and do not act in ways which help them to learn. (Clark 1967, 130–131)

Public education in the United States is supposed to prepare children to compete with one another in the real world; the famous educator Horace Mann (1796–1859) called the U.S. public school system "the great equalizer." Research by Kozol and others suggests that when it comes to schools, the playing fields are not all that equal.

Even within the same school, the playing field is likely to be uneven. This unevenness manifests itself in the practice of tracking. In *Keeping Track: How Schools Structure Inequality,* Jeannie Oakes defined tracking this way:

> Tracking is the process whereby students are divided into categories
> so that they can be assigned in groups to various kinds of classes.
> Sometimes students are classified as fast, average, or slow learners
> and placed into fast, average, or slow classes on the basis of their
> scores on achievement or ability tests. Often teachers' estimates of
> what students have already learned or their potential for learning
> determine how students are identified and placed. Sometimes stu-
> dents are classified according to what seems most appropriate to their
> future lives. Sometimes, but rarely in any genuine sense, students
> themselves choose to be in "vocation," "general," or "academic" pro-
> grams. (1985, 3)

Although some schools claim they do not track their students,
Oakes and others have found that most if not all schools have
some mechanism by which they divide their student populations
into groups of students who are "alike": "In fact, this is exactly the
justification some schools offer for tracking students. Educators
strongly believe that students learn better in groups with others
like themselves. They also believe that groups of similar students
are easier to teach" (Oakes 1985, 4).

What are the consequences of tracking? Maureen Hallinan studied research on tracking and summed up the evidence this way:

> The general conclusion that can be reached from this research is that
> tracking and ability grouping have a negative effect on the achieve-
> ment of lower track or ability group students, a negligible effect on
> students in the middle groups, and a weak to modest positive effect
> on high track and ability group students. . . . Moreover, the research
> reveals a considerable number of disadvantages of tracking and abil-
> ity grouping for students in the lower groups in terms of the develop-
> ment of negative attitudes and behaviors related to learning.
>
>   In addition to these immediate consequences of tracking and abil-
> ity grouping for student achievement, the practice has been shown to
> have important consequences for future course selection and place-
> ment and for educational aspirations. . . . The research shows that
> placement in a college preparatory track has positive effects on a num-
> ber of educational outcomes, including academic achievement, mea-
> sure by grades and standardized test scores, measures of motivation,
> and educational aspirations and attainment. And this positive rela-
> tionship persists even after family background and ability differences
> are controlled for. (Hallinan 1988, 260; see also Thernstrom 1992)

Teachers' expectations and students' learning vary by track.
Oakes asked teachers in different tracks, "What are the most critical things you want your students to learn?" Then she asked students, "What was the most important thing you learned in school
this year?" Representative quotes from teachers and students in
the different tracks are given in table 13.2.

On what basis do schools divide their students into tracks?
School officials report that their tracking systems reflect students'

Table 13.2 High School Teachers' Goals
and Students' Learning Experiences, by Track

What teachers say are their most important goals for their students	
High Track	**Low Track**
Ability to reason logically, in all subject areas.	That they know that their paychecks will be correct when they receive them. Punctuality, self-discipline, and honesty will make them successful in their jobs. They must begin and end each day with a smile. . . .
Logical thought processes. Analysis of given information.	
Ability to understand exactly what is asked in a question.	
That their own talents and thoughts are important.	Properly planning to ensure favorable performances.
Development of imagination. Critical thinking.	How to fill out insurance forms, income tax returns.
To gain some interpretive skills. Scientific reasoning and logic.	Content—minimal. Be realistic about goals. Develop ones they *can* achieve. Practical math skills for everyday living. A sense of responsibility.

What students report is the most important thing they have learned in class during the school year	
High Track	**Low Track**
To understand complex concepts and ideas and experiment with them. Also to work independently.	I have learned that I should do my questions for the book when [the teacher] asks . . .
The most important thing that I have learned in this class is the benefit of logical and organized thinking; learning is made much easier when the simple processes of organizing thoughts have been grasped.	To learn how to listen and follow the directions of the teacher.
	To be a better listener in class.
	The most important thing I have learned in this class is to always have your homework in and have materials ready whenever [the teacher] is ready.
I have proved to myself that I have the discipline to take a difficult class just for knowledge, even though it has nothing to do with my career plans.	Learn to get along with the students and the teacher.

SOURCE: Jeannie Oakes, "More Than Misapplied Technology: A Normative and Political Response to Hallinan on Tracking," *Sociology of Education*.

academic abilities and aptitudes. Yet kids from lower-class backgrounds are disproportionately placed in lower tracks, while kids from more affluent backgrounds are disproportionately placed in upper tracks. Often the tracks in which kids are placed have less to do with their abilities than with their parents' social class. A parent from a higher stratum, for example, can ensure that his or her child is placed on a fast track even if the kid hasn't been doing all that well in school. Of course, when that happens, it means there is one less place on the fast track for a less affluent child who is doing well. The result is a highly stratified school—and the stratification within the school tends to reproduce the economic stratification outside of it.

> I have this rather vivid memory of the first day of school in the ninth grade. Mr. Mullen, my teacher, warned us to watch our step—now that we were in the high school, our every move would be noted and would become part of our PERMANENT RECORD. Whatever we did from that day forward would have a big impact on our success in high school and beyond. It was scary to realize that one could have such a thing as a permanent record. But Mr. Mullen had implicitly conveyed a more comforting message as well—at least, I remember feeling relieved that my permanent record had not started earlier without anyone warning me.

I am glad that I didn't know it at the time, but most kids' trajectories are set as soon as or even before they enroll in the first grade. And by the time they get to high school, it has practically been set in stone.

> Entering the first-grade classroom is a big step for a child. It can be a glowing or a devastating experience. The teacher smiles at the children, looking at them to see what the year will bring. The well-groomed white boys and girls will probably do well. The black- and brown-skinned ones are lower-class and will have learning problems unless they look exceptionally clean. All the whites who do not look tidy and need handkerchiefs will have trouble. If the teacher sees a preponderance of lower-class children, regardless of color, she knows her work will be difficult and unsatisfying. The teacher wants her children to learn, all of them, but she knows that lower-class children do not do well in school, just as she knows that middle-class children do do well. All this she knows as she smiles at her class for the first time, welcoming them to the adventure of first grade, measuring them for success or failure against the yardstick of middle-classness. The children smile back at her, unaware as yet that the first measurements have been taken. The yardstick will be used again when they speak to her, as she hears words spoken clearly or snuffled or stammered or spoken with an accent. And later they will be measured for readiness for reading or intelligence. Many times that first year the children will be examined for what they are, for what they bring with them when they come to school. (Oakes 1985, 47)

But surely a child's actual performance is more important than the teacher's expectations? So what if the teacher assumes that little Johnny will have trouble learning? Can't little Johnny simply prove her wrong? Possibly. But students' performances most often prove teachers' expectations right. Does this mean that teachers have especially accurate intuition? Or could it be that teachers' expectations influence the way children perform in school?

13.3

    a. In your own words, summarize the major differences between teachers' expectations for high- and low-track students.

    b. In your own words, summarize the major differences between the expectations of high- and low-track students.

The Pygmalion Effect: The Power of Expectations

In the 1960s Robert Rosenthal and Lenore Jacobson conducted an experiment to test the existence of the Pygmalion effect in schools.[3] These researchers hypothesized that teachers' expectations influenced children's performance. The design of their experiment was simple but elegant: Rosenthal and Jacobson administered a special test to all the students in a school. The teachers were told that the results of this test could predict how students would do in school during the coming academic year. When teachers were given their class lists for the new school year, each of them found that about 20 percent of their students were labeled as being on the threshold of "spurting" or "blooming" academically. But the "special test" was actually a little-known version of an intelligence test—it could not predict future achievement. Rosenthal and Jacobson had simply *randomly* assigned one out of every five children to the spurter/bloomer group. They said nothing at all about the other children in the class. Really, all these researchers did was to create an impression in the teachers' minds that great things could be expected of some of their students in the coming year. Then they sat back and waited to see what would happen.

At the end of the year, Rosenthal and Jacobson retested the students using the same intelligence test they had used the year before. Most of the students showed some gains in points on the test (just as we would expect of children as they get older). But as

---

[3]According to Greek legend, Pygmalion was the king of Cyprus who sculpted a beautiful woman out of ivory. He fell in love with the statue (Galatea) and prayed to the goddess Aphrodite to bring it to life. Aphrodite granted his wish, and Pygmalion married her. In 1913 the George Bernard Shaw play *Pygmalion* was a big hit (and in 1956 was adapted as a musical called *My Fair Lady*). In his version Shaw's male protagonist, Professor Henry Higgins, created a fine English lady out of a street-wise Cockney girl, Eliza Doolittle. The Pygmalion effect, then, refers to situations in which some piece of raw material (ivory, Cockney girls, elementary school students) are molded by their creators into something finer.

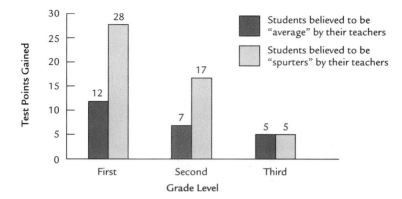

Figure 13.4 *Spurters' and Average Students' Gains on Intelligence Test Performance*

SOURCE: Adapted from Robert Rosenthal and Lenore Jacobson, *Pygmalion in the Classroom: Teacher Expectations and Pupils' Intellectual Development* (New York: Holt, Rinehart & Winston, 1968).

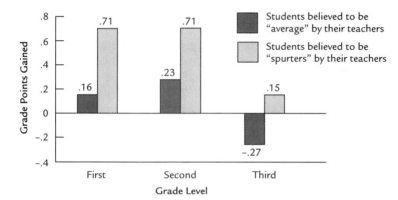

Figure 13.5 *Spurters' and Average Students' Gains or Losses in Reading Grades (Assigned by Teachers)*

SOURCE: Adapted from Robert Rosenthal and Lenore Jacobson, *Pygmalion in the Classroom: Teacher Expectations and Pupils' Intellectual Development* (New York: Holt, Rinehart & Winston, 1968).

figure 13.4 shows, *the kids who were expected to spurt made larger gains than nonspurters.* On their report cards, the kids who had been labeled as spurters showed even more improvement compared to the kids who hadn't been labeled. Figure 13.5 shows the grade point changes for reading. Similar increases for spurters compared to nonspurters were found in arithmetic grades.

13.4 What might account for the fact that the differences between spurters' and nonspurters' *grade increases* were larger than the differences between the spurters' and nonspurters' *scores* on the intelligence test?

The Fallacy of Hard Work

It is important to recognize that while everyone faces significant obstacles, some people's obstacles loom quite large. For many people, this is a very difficult concept to accept, because they are so socialized into the "work hard and you can succeed" theory of social life. I am reminded of this periodically when students tell me what they think about sociological approaches to stratification. Last semester a student explained her point of view this way:

> "I'm sorry, I just don't agree. People do have opportunities, it's just that some people aren't willing to work hard and take advantage of them. Look at me—my parents can't afford to pay my way through college, so I work two jobs part time to support myself. If I can do it, anyone can!"

Her point was a reasonable one. She *is* putting a lot of effort into staying in college. I agreed with her that not everyone would be so willing to put in the time and effort, and I congratulated her on her willingness to work so hard to achieve her goals. However, I also suggested to her that even though she has to work hard, she still has some advantages that other people do not.

Willingness to work hard is no guarantee that one will succeed in our competitive social system. In fact, willingness to work hard doesn't even guarantee that one can get into the race. Katherine Newman and Chauncy Lennon (1995) studied low-wage job opportunities in inner-city neighborhoods. Focusing on minimum-wage jobs at places like McDonald's or Burger King, they found that "the ratio of applicants to hires is approximately 14 to 1." Moreover,

> among those people who applied but were rejected for fast-food work in early 1993, 73% had not found work of any kind a year later, despite considerable effort. Even the youngest job-hunters in our study (16- to 18-year-olds) had applied for four or five positions before they came looking for these fast-food jobs. The oldest applicants (over 25) had applied for an average of seven or eight jobs. . . . (Newman and Lennon 1995, 66)

Perhaps the rejected applicants were not as qualified as those who actually got hired? Newman and Lennon suggest that even in competitions for the lowest-paying jobs, qualifications are not the only things that count:

> The rejection rate for local applicants is higher than the rate for similarly educated individuals who live farther away [that is, not in the inner city]. Other studies in the warehouse and dockyard industries report the same results. These findings suggest that residents of poor neighborhoods are at a distinct disadvantage in finding minimum-wage jobs near home. (1995, 67)

According to Newman and Lennon, "it is simply not the case that anyone who wants a low-wage job can get one. As is true for

---

Ponder

Alexis de Tocqueville (1805–1859) was a French historian, political scientist, and lawyer. After touring the United States in the early 1830s, Tocqueville published his thoughts about Americans in a book entitled *De la Démocratie en Amerique*, or *Democracy in America* (1835). Here's one thing he had to say about the American class system:

> I am aware that among a great democratic people there will always be some members of the community in great poverty and others in great opulence; but the poor, instead of forming the great majority of the nation, as is always the case in aristocratic communities, are comparatively few in number, and the laws do not bind them together by ties of hereditary [poverty] . . .
>
> As there is no longer a race of poor men, so there is no longer a race of rich men; the latter spring up daily from the multitude and relapse into it again. Hence, they [the rich] do not form a distinct class which may be easily marked out. . . . Between these two extremes . . . stands an innumerable multitude of men almost alike, who, without being exactly rich or poor, possess sufficient property to desire the maintenance of order, yet not enough to excite envy.

In your own words, summarize Tocqueville's view of the American class system. Then, given what you have read in this chapter about the nature of social inequality in the United States, specify the degree to which you agree or disagree with Tocqueville, and state why.

---

almost any glutted labor market, there is a queue [line] of applicants and employers can be fairly choosy." In the inner city, they conclude, people are "locked into a fierce struggle for scarce opportunities at the bottom."

Social Mobility, Social Structure, and Social Change

Those who study social stratification and mobility in the United States agree that most people do not experience vertical social mobility either between or within generations. For the most part, people who start out in blue-collar jobs tend to stay in them their entire working lives; people who start out in white-collar jobs tend to stay in them their entire working lives. In other words, most people do not experience either intergenerational or intragenerational mobility.

Nonetheless, social mobility is not exactly rare in this country. Overall, there has been a great deal of upward social mobility in the United States and in many European countries over the past century. But this mobility generally involves short steps rather than long leaps. Most occupational mobility, for example, tends to be between closely related occupations.

One crucial fact: Sociologists have found that most of the mobility that has occurred over the past century can be better explained by *social factors* than by individual effort. For example, early industrialization created a number of new jobs—jobs that allowed people to move away from the farm. As industrialization and technology continued to evolve, larger numbers of the new jobs were higher paying. Most of the social mobility that took place in the twentieth century can be accounted for merely by the increases in good jobs.

Class differences in birthrates have facilitated social mobility as well. People in the upper classes traditionally have tended to marry later and have fewer children than people in the lower classes. This has meant that when new jobs opened up toward the top of the occupational structure, the children of the upper classes couldn't fill them all. The difference in birthrates, then, has been another social fact that has drawn people up the occupational ladder.

Finally, immigration has played a role. As new residents settle in this country, they tend to be relegated to the lowest rungs on the occupational ladder. This pushes nonimmigrants out of the lowest jobs and into higher ones (or it does when better jobs exist).

Sociologists refer to mobility that results from such social facts as changes in the occupational structure, immigration, and birthrates as *structural mobility*. Structural mobility has little or nothing to do with changes in the quality of individuals; structural mobility has to do with changes in the social structure of society.

Most sociologists agree that structural factors will continue to be crucial determinants of mobility rates. But evidence suggests that the upward trend may not continue. Since the 1970s, for example, technological change has tended to make obsolete the lower- and entry-level positions in the occupational structure—as when robots replace factory workers and computers replace accountants—while not opening up higher-level ones. In the 1960s and 1970s, most of the newly created positions in the occupational structure paid fairly decent salaries; in the 1980s and 1990s, however, most of the newly created positions paid close to minimum wage. If this trend continues, we may well see a great deal of downward structural mobility in the twenty-first century.

Chapter Review

1. Make a list of the sociological concepts that you learned in this chapter. Define each term. (*Hint:* You will learn the most from this exercise if, in addition to defining each concept, you create an example of it in your own words.)

2. As a potential college graduate, you are poised to join an important American minority group—college graduates. How did you come to be so fortunate?
   a. Create a (brief) cultural explanation of your status as a potential college graduate.
   b. Create a (brief) structural explanation of your status as a potential college graduate.
   c. Briefly describe which explanation you find more believable and why.

Answers and Discussion

STOP & REVIEW

13.1 I first read about the Matthew effect in a book by Robert Merton entitled *Sociological Ambivalence and Other Essays* (1976). At one point in the book, Merton made reference to the Thomas theorem. (As you may recall from the Introduction, the Thomas theorem is "If people define situations as real, they are real in their consequences.") Then Merton attached the following footnote:

> What we may call the Thomas Theorem appears just once in the corpus [body] of W. I. Thomas's writing: on page 572 of the book he wrote with Dorothy Swaine Thomas entitled *The Child in America*. I ascribe the theorem to W. I. Thomas alone rather than to the Thomases jointly not because of his gender or great seniority but only because Dorothy Thomas has confirmed for me what many have supposed: that the sentence and the paragraph in which it is encased were written by him. There is thus nothing in this attribution which smacks of "the Matthew Effect," "[as] in which cases of collaboration between scholars of decidedly unequal reputation has us ascribe all credit to the prominent scholar and little or none to the other collaborator(s)." (1976, 175 n. 20)

13.2 The cultural explanation essentially holds that lower-class people do not advance because their cultural situation does not prepare them to advance. The structural explanation suggests otherwise: that there are social structural obstacles facing people in the lower classes that don't hinder people in the more affluent classes. This student seems to have had the talent and willingness to succeed at basketball; what stood in his way was a structural obstacle (the fact that he lived in a scary place and didn't have enough money to go to camp and thereby showcase his talents for college coaches).

STOP & REVIEW

13.3

a. The teachers' expectations of the low-track students are quite low; it is as if they expect the students only to learn to be obedient, to be respectful of authority, and to do their work—period. They expect much more from the high-track students—they want them to use higher-order thinking: to learn to work independently and creatively and to ask questions. [One can almost imagine that if a kid in the lower track started doing the things that the kids in the higher tracks were doing, he or she would get into trouble!]

b. Not coincidentally, the students' experiences are closely related to their teachers' expectations. Higher-track students report that they learned to work independently and think abstractly; lower-track students report that they learned to be obedient little students.

   Here's an interesting question to ask yourself: Looking back at table 10.1, do you see any correspondence between the data presented in that table and the information presented in table 13.2? (You should!)

13.4 What we might be seeing is another example of the power of the teachers' expectations. The test provides an objective measure of the students' gains in IQ. The presumption here is that the spurters advanced more because they were treated differently by the teachers. The reading scores, because they are assigned by the teachers, are subjective measures of not only students' advances but the teachers' perceptions of the degree to which students advanced.

Inequality and Ascription

Race, Ethnicity, and Gender

"Citizens, you are brothers, but God has made you differently. Some of you have the power to command, having been made of gold; others, of silver, to be assistants; and others, of brass and iron, to be farmers and craftsmen."

—Plato, *Republic*, c. 400 B.C.E.

References to social inequality are scattered throughout the writings of Western philosophers and political thinkers, from the ancients to the moderns. In the olden days, however, the issue of stratification didn't provoke so many questions. And why should it? It made about as much sense to question why, say, Richard Fitzhugh was noble and John Smith common as it did to wonder why a seed would grow in fertile soil and not in barren sand. That was simply the way things were.

Centuries later, of course, industrialization changed everything, making traditional understandings of the social hierarchy obsolete. As industrialization proceeded, the political powers of the old landowning aristocracy were undercut by the financial resources of the capitalistic entrepreneurs. At the same time, the legal and customary restrictions that had kept even the most talented and determined individuals from being socially mobile gradually eroded. The principle that "all men are created equal" made the class system more of an open competition. In modern industrial society, the highest positions in the stratification system were to be won by the most talented and determined individuals. Money was money, and whoever earned the most of it would come out ahead—notwithstanding any snobby pretensions to aristocracy.

In chapter 13, however, we found that the social structure is not as open as it might seem. If the stratification system is like a footrace, some people are given a boost by their parents and get to start a lap or two ahead of others. Of course, if someone can run *really* fast, he or she might still beat the racers who started in front.

217

Why a Dollar Is Not Always a Dollar

Take a dollar bill out of your pocket and look at it. You would think that your dollar bill is the same as anyone else's dollar bill—right? After all, your dollar cost you the same amount as it cost anyone else to own a dollar—4 quarters, 10 dimes, 20 nickels, or 100 pennies. Your dollar will buy the same amount of stuff as anyone else's dollar. Everybody knows that, and that's why money is believed to be the great equalizer.

Although it is the basis of the conventional understanding of capitalism, the idea that a dollar is a dollar is misleading. In reality, *some people's dollars cost more and buy less.*

Take education, for example. Many people think of education as an investment. Students (and their parents) are willing to go into debt to pay tuition because they expect that down the road the investment will pay off in better jobs that, among other things, pay higher salaries.

The fact of the matter is, however, that education pays higher dividends for some people than for others. Look at table 14.1. The data show that on average the payoff of a college degree is greater for whites than for Hispanics or blacks, and higher for men than for women.

Table 14.2 suggests a further point: Even when education pays off in the same sort of job, how much you earn depends on who you are. When we compare how much men and women earn in the same occupations, for example, we find that men's income beats women's income by a substantial amount.

The next point is this: Even if you have money in hand, it will buy more or less depending on who you are. For example, in the

Table 14.1 Median Income by Years of School Completed for Black, Hispanic, and White Full-Time Workers, 1990

	Years of Schooling Completed					
	8 Years or Less	9–11 Years	12 Years	Some College	College Degree	Graduate School
Males						
Black	$16,961	$16,778	$20,271	$25,863	$28,263	$36,851
Hispanic	13,913	17,868	20,932	26,380	30,532	42,315
White	16,906	21,048	26,526	31,336	33,074	47,787
Females						
Black	$11,364	$13,643	$16,531	$19,922	$26,881	$31,119
Hispanic	11,231	12,586	16,298	20,881	22,555	30,133
White	11,826	14,010	17,552	21,547	26,822	31,991

SOURCE: U.S. Bureau of the Census 1991.

Table 14.2 Median Income of Full-Time, Year-Round Workers, by Gender (1999) and Ratio of Women's Earnings to Men, 1999, 1998, 1997[a]

Occupational Category	1999 Median Income		Ratio: How Much Women Earned for Each Dollar Men Earned		
	Men	Women	1999	1998	1997
Executives, administrators, and managerial	$55,261	$36,141	65¢	68¢	65¢
Professional	$54,616	$37,533	69¢	70¢	70¢
Technical and related support	$41,700	$30,001	72¢	69¢	73¢
Sales	$38,267	$23,778	62¢	62¢	60¢
Administrative support, including clerical	$31,767	$24,581	77¢	77¢	76¢
Precision production, craft, and repair	$34,429	$24,946	73¢	76¢	69¢
Machine operators, assemblers, and inspectors	$29,156	$18,928	65¢	68¢	66¢
Transportation and material moving	$30,754	$20,720	67¢	71¢	74¢
Handlers, equipment cleaners, helpers, and laborers	$21,206	$18,432	87¢	76¢	73¢
Farming, forestry, and fishing	$18,949	$13,230	70¢	84¢	99¢
Total (all workers)	$36,476	$26,324	72¢	73¢	74¢

[a]Ratio is calculated by dividing the median amount of money women in each category earned by the median amount of money earned by men in that category.

SOURCE: U.S. Bureau of the Census 2000.

early 1990s, the Federal Reserve (the government agency charged with overseeing the banking industry) found that banks distinguished between loan applicants based on criteria other than money. As figure 14.1 shows, at all levels of income, whites found it easier to obtain mortgage loans than blacks and Hispanics.

Ian Ayres and his colleagues (1991) found more evidence for the differential value of a dollar. Armed with extensive knowledge of the value of cars and techniques of negotiating, a team of researchers visited a number of car dealerships in a large midwestern city. Table 14.3 (page 221) shows what happened. The left-hand column lists the average initial offers made by the dealer to different types of buyers. White men were offered the best deals—$818 over the dealer's cost. Of course, the dealer's initial offer is only the beginning of the process; it's a place from which to start negotiating. But the final outcomes of negotiation were different depending on who the buyer was, as you can see in the right-hand column of table 14.3 Again, whites, and especially white males, were offered the better deals. It seems almost paradoxical: People

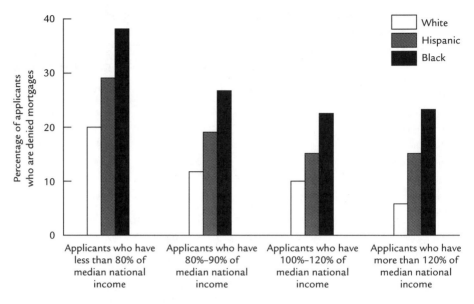

Figure 14.1   *Percentage of Applicants Who Are Denied Mortgages,*
by Income Level and Race/Ethnicity

SOURCE: Federal Reserve Board 1990; Michael Quint, "Mortgage Race Data Show Gap.
Fed Has Apprised Bankers of Disparity in Loan Approvals," *New York Times*, October 14,
1991.

who on average earned the least money were asked to pay the
most for their cars.

The same sort of relationship between how much money people have and how much they have to pay to purchase consumer
goods holds for less expensive items. Of course, rich and poor
alike will pay $1.99 for some doodad in Smithville's Bigco Shop-
per store. But the price of milk in the inner-city stores where many
of the less affluent shop is a great deal higher than in the suburbs
where many of the more affluent shop.

Moreover, suppose you want to purchase a refrigerator or television or even a mattress set. If you use a credit card, you can
expect to pay the cost of the item and anywhere from 15 to 20 percent interest on top of that. But what if you don't have a credit
card? If you don't have the cash, you might go to a rent-to-own
store and buy one—because rent-to-own stores will sell you the
item and let you pay for it over time. But renting-to-own costs a
lot: In 1997 the U.S. Public Interest Research Group found that
more than half of rent-to-own stores charged at least 100 percent
annual interest, and some charged as much as 275 percent. What
if you want to buy a refrigerator that costs $739.95? If you use
your credit card, that refrigerator will cost you an additional
20 percent or so, or about $120 in interest. But for the same refrig-
erator in a rent-to-own store, a consumer would pay annual inter-

Table 14.3 Average Car Dealer Profits, by Race and Gender

	Initial Offer	Final Offer
White males	$ 818	$ 362
White females	829	504
Black males	1534	738
Black females	2169	1237

SOURCE: Adapted from Ian Ayres, "Fair Driving: Gender and Race Discrimination in Retail Car Negotiations," *Harvard Law Review* 104:821.

est of 87 percent, or $620.05, in addition to the refrigerator's listed price. Because the rent-to-own stores technically do not extend credit but rather rent their products to consumers, they aren't required to follow laws—such as those contained in the Truth in Lending Act and the Consumer Leasing Act—that exist to protect consumers. As a result of their investigation, the researchers concluded that "purchasing appliances, furniture, computers, jewelry or other merchandise from rent-to-own stores costs two to five times as much as buying those items at department or discount stores" (reported in *New York Times*, June 13, 1997).

This sort of differential treatment of people based on their gender or race is not only unfair but, according to basic economic theory, irrational and (supposedly) self-defeating. Let's say there are two doodad factories—A and B. The owner of factory A pays fair wages to all her workers. The owner of factory B pays less than fair wages to some of his workers.

Common sense suggests that the best workers will apply for employment at factory A. These workers will produce more and better doodads. On the other hand, the only workers willing to work at factory B will be those who could not get hired at factory A. These will be the less qualified/less productive workers who produce fewer doodads of dubious quality. Because of the difference in quality, consumers will be more likely to buy the doodads from factory A than from factory B. The owner of factory A will thus make higher profits than the owner of factory B. In time the owner of factory B will not be able to compete successfully and will go out of business. That's the way the free market works—or is supposed to work.

Overcharging consumers is likewise irrational. If store C charges more for milk than store D, then people will choose to shop at store C. Eventually store D will either have to lower its prices or go out of business.

The theory is simple: To compete successfully in the marketplace, one must pay one's workers fair wages and charge one's customers fair prices. There is no need for governments to regulate the market; the market regulates itself.

The reality seems to be more complex than the theory. In fact, businesses do survive even when they pay some of their workers less than others for the same job (see table 14.2). Likewise, some retailers seem to be able to charge some customers more than others. This suggests that some social facts are complicating the more straightforward economic facts. What's going on?

Prejudice

The roots of the word *prejudice* can be traced to the Latin term *praejudicium*, which means "prejudgment." Strictly speaking, then, a prejudice involves a prejudgment—or a judgment of some thing, person, or situation on the basis of prior experience with similar things, persons, or situations. There is nothing inherently wrong with prejudgment. In fact, prejudgment underlies the whole principle of learning by experience.

Prejudice is a negative and persistent judgment based on scant or incorrect information about people in a group. Prejudice involves beliefs and attitudes. More technically, we might define it this way: Prejudice is a negative or hostile attitude toward a person who belongs to a group, simply because he or she belongs to that group and is therefore presumed to have the objectionable qualities ascribed to the group.

Prejudice has a different flavor from mere prejudgment, however. As social psychologist Gordon W. Allport pointed out in his book *The Nature of Prejudice*, the difference between prejudice and prejudgment has to do with the fact that prejudice is based on inaccurate information and/or illogical arguments. To put it another way, *a prejudice is an unjustified prejudgment*; that is, prejudice involves not only *pre*judgment but *mis*judgment.

Allport pointed out that one of the things that helps us to distinguish prejudgment from prejudice is the fact that people tend to hold onto their prejudices even in the face of contradictory information. By way of example, Allport cited an imaginary conversation between Mr. X (who is prejudiced against Jews) and Mr. Y (who is annoyingly persistent in his nonprejudice):

> *Mr. X:* The trouble with Jews is that they only take care of their own group.
>
> *Mr Y:* But the record of the [United Way] campaign shows that they give more generously, in proportion to their numbers, to the general charities of the community, than do non-Jews.
>
> *Mr. X:* That shows they are always trying to buy favor and intrude into Christian affairs. They think of nothing but money; that is why there are so many Jewish bankers.
>
> *Mr Y:* But a recent study shows that the percentage of Jews in the banking business is negligible, far smaller than the percentage of non-Jews.

Mr. X: That's just it; they don't go in for respectable business; they are only in the movie business or run night clubs. (1954, 13–14)

Thus, as Allport concludes, prejudices have a way of "slithering around" the facts in order to find ways of justifying ill feelings toward members of another group.

Prejudice is sustained by *stereotypes*—oversimplified generalized images about members of a particular group. Stereotyping essentially categorizes all members of a particular group as having a specific set of characteristics. Stereotypes deny the existence of individual differences among the members of a specific social category.

Discrimination

It is crucial to distinguish between prejudice and stereotypes on the one hand and discrimination on the other. Prejudice and stereotypes involve attitudes and beliefs; *discrimination involves behavior.* Moreover, there is no guarantee that prejudiced attitudes will manifest themselves in discriminatory behaviors:

> What people actually do in relation to groups they dislike is not always directly related to what they think or feel about them. Two employers, for example, may dislike Jews to an equal degree. One may keep his feelings to himself and may hire Jews on the same basis of any workers—perhaps because he wants to gain goodwill for his factory or store in the Jewish community. The other may translate his dislike into his employment policy, and refuse to hire Jews. Both men are prejudiced, but only one of them practices *discrimination.* (Allport 1954, 14)

Sociologist Robert K. Merton added another wrinkle to our understanding of the links between prejudice and discrimination. As figure 14.2 shows, Merton suggested that just as not all people

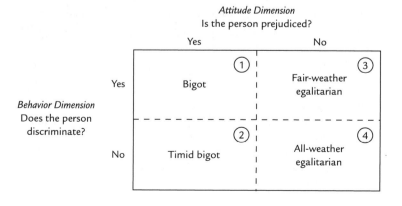

Figure 14.2
A Typology of Prejudice and Discrimination
SOURCE: Adapted from Robert K. Merton, *Sociological Ambivalence and Other Essays* (New York: Free Press, 1976).

who are prejudiced practice discrimination, not all people who practice discrimination are prejudiced.

Cells 1 and 4 represent the people whose behavior is consistent with their beliefs. Cell 1 represents that person who is prejudiced and does discriminate—no matter what. Cell 4 represents the unprejudiced person who does not discriminate—no matter what.

But cells 2 and 3 represent people whose behavior is not necessarily consistent with their beliefs. Cell 2 represents the person who is prejudiced but will not discriminate unless it is convenient to do so. So, for example, the store owner who is prejudiced against minorities but who needs their business may not discriminate against minorities. Merton calls this person a "timid bigot."

Cell 3 is the final case. This person is not prejudiced but does discriminate when it's convenient to do so. Suppose you work at Benny's Food Shack as a waiter or waitress. Your boss tells you to do all that you can to discourage minorities from eating in the restaurant (provide really slow service, mix up their orders, overcharge them, and so on). You don't want to do this because you aren't prejudiced. However, your boss makes it clear that you will either do things her way or be fired. You really need this job, so you go along. Under these circumstances, you are a "fair-weather egalitarian."

There are many types of discriminatory behaviors. Allport identified five general categories that range, as he put it, "from the least energetic to the most":

1. *Verbal rejection* ("antilocution"): using derogatory nouns ("epithets") to refer to people in particular groups; telling jokes that put down entire groups of people

2. *Avoidance:* avoiding interaction with people from particular groups

3. *Active discrimination:* acting to exclude members of particular groups from education, employment, housing, political, or recreational opportunities

4. *Physical attacks:* using violence or the threat of violence against members of particular groups or their property, such as burning churches or desecrating graves

5. *Extermination:* participating in lynchings, massacres, genocide, or pogroms

Although they vary in seriousness, all the behaviors associated with these five categories are discriminatory because they involve treating people unequally because of their membership in some group.

It is especially important to distinguish between two levels of discrimination: individual and institutional. *Individual discrimina-*

tion occurs when an individual discriminates against another individual (or group of individuals). The apartment house owner who refuses to rent to someone because of his or her race, religion, or whatever is practicing individual discrimination.

Institutional discrimination involves a denial of opportunities and equal rights to individuals and groups that results from the normal operation of society. This term was introduced in the 1960s by political activist Stokely Carmichael and his co-writer Charles Hamilton (1967). Their intent was to distinguish between the outcomes of the practices of individuals (say, members of the KKK) and the outcomes of the practices found in everyday society that lead, for example, to the deaths of young African American children. As Carmichael and Hamilton pointed out, institutional discrimination is "built into" the usual operations of society. Unlike individual discrimination, institutional discrimination can occur even when people have "no intention of subordinating others because of color [or other ascribed characteristic] or are totally unaware of doing so" (Downs 1970, 5).

Here are two examples of institutional discrimination:

> Height requirements in a police or fire department that are geared to the average height of white males—thereby systematically excluding most women and male members of some minority groups—even when height has no bearing on one's ability to do the job. (The average Asian, for example, may be judged too short to work as a fire fighter in many U.S. cities; yet who does the fire fighting in Asia?)

> Preferences given to children of alumni ("legacies") for admission to prestigious universities (including law and medical schools)—thereby discriminating against worthy individuals not fortunate enough to be born into wealthy families

14.1 Define *prejudice* and *discrimination,* and explain how they differ.

14.2 Explain the difference between *individual* and *institutional* discrimination.

Discrimination and "Isms"

A particular act of discrimination may be more or less injurious depending on the social context. Many sociologists group particularly potent kinds of discrimination into one of the "isms" categories: ageism, anti-Semitism, heterosexism, racism, sexism.

"Isms" are different from ordinary discrimination. For example, ageism is not simply age-based discrimination; nor is racism the same as race-based discrimination or sexism the same as sex-based discrimination. The suffix *ism* is generally applied to acts of discrimination that occur at the institutional level or, when they occur at the individual level, are consistent with institutional patterns of discrimination. When an African American tells an anti-white joke, it is as discriminatory as when a white person tells an anti–African American joke. But, because the patterns of institutional discrimination in our society tend to be against African Americans, only the anti–African American joke falls into the racism category. From the sociological perspective, the *ism* is used to signal the differences in potency of different types of discrimination. More generally, then, discriminatory acts are "isms" when their source is a member of the dominant group and their target is a member of a minority group in society.

Why make such a distinction? Why not categorize all race-based discrimination as racism and all sex-based discrimination as sexism? These are crucial questions. We make the distinction because, as sociologists, we know that when we take into account the larger social context, the impact of discriminatory acts is different for minorities than it is for members of the dominant group.

Michael Schwalbe came to a similar conclusion as a result of his study of the "Men's movement" in the United States:

> To [some of the men] any word of disparagement by members of one sex for another was an example of sexism. Women's joking about men's foibles or atrocious behavior was thus supposedly just as sexist, and just as unacceptable, as anything some men might do to demean or oppress women. . . . There was blindness here to power differences. Women as a group do not have the institutional power to demean, oppress, or exploit men as a group. In the context of male supremacy, women's verbal criticism of men is an act of *resistance,* not sexism. Similarly, blacks may think of whites as evil, and may even be "prejudiced against" whites. But it is perverse to call this racism, since blacks as a group do not have the institutional power to hurt white people. In fact, when blacks do disparage whites, they must do it in the safety of their own communities, lest they become victims of truly racist retaliation. (1996, 266 n. 13)

Understanding the difference between race discrimination and racism, or sex discrimination and sexism, involves taking into account the institutionalized relationships that exist between members of different groups. We can begin by examining the concepts of *minority* and *dominant groups.* What do those terms mean? Sociologist Louis Wirth explained them this way:

> We may define a minority as a group of people who, because of their physical or cultural characteristics, are singled out from the others in the society in which they live for differential and unequal treatment, and who therefore regard themselves as objects of collective discrimination. The existence of a minority in a society implies the

existence of a corresponding dominant group enjoying higher social status and greater privilege. *Minority status carries with it the exclusion from full participation in the life of the society.* Though not necessarily an alien group, the minority is treated and regards itself as a people apart. (1945, 347)

Any person may be the target of discrimination—or of unequal treatment because of his or her group membership. On the playground, little girls may exclude boys from their jump rope game just as little boys may place a "NO GIRLS ALLOWED" sign on their tree house. But overall, the experience of discrimination is different for members of the dominant group than it is for members of minority groups.

For a member of the dominant group, being the target of discrimination is not only upsetting but shocking! After all, the defining characteristic of dominant-group membership is that one enjoys greater privilege. David Gates (1993), a reporter for *Newsweek*, provides a series of revealing quotes in this context. Tom Cole, a retired marketing executive in Chicago, claims, "The white male is the most persecuted person in the United States." Tom Williamson, president of the National Coalition of Free Men, "complains that Clinton 'has brought in a feminist administration that has no conception of men's problems. They are self-serving and self-pitying. We're going to be in for it.'" A white male fire fighter says of minorities, "They stole my pay, they stole my promotion, and I couldn't say I didn't like it. White guys are being pushed around big time to make up for past wrongs. If you're black and belong to a black group, you're an activist. If you're white and you belong to a white group, you're an asshole. Nobody supports the KKK—*I* don't. But there's nothing for a white guy to join." Then there is Steve, age 29, who "sold his Jeep CJ7 to put himself through the police academy. . . . He was a finalist for a job in a rural northern California town, but got bumped down the list by three women he says didn't go through the same application process. 'When they take the chance that I had and allot it to three women just because they're female, that burns me up,' he says. 'I got shot out of the saddle.'"

When *Newsweek* polled white American men in 1993, it found that a majority believed they were losing influence in American society. More to the point, the survey found that the average white male felt that he was losing his *advantage* in terms of jobs and income.

Research suggests that when rights and privileges are extended to members of minority groups, members of the dominant group perceive their *loss of advantage as discrimination.* Moreover, the cost to dominant groups tends to be exaggerated by them. It is in this context that we can make sense of statements like "the white male is the most persecuted person in the United States"—a nonsensical statement in the light of empirical reality:[1]

> It's still a statistical piece of cake being a white man, at least in comparison with being anything else. White males make up just 39.2 percent of the population, yet they account for 82.5 percent of the Forbes 400 (folks worth at least $265 million), 77 percent of Congress, 92 percent of state governors, 70 percent of tenured college faculty, almost 90 percent of TV news directors. They dominate just about everything but NOW and NAACP; even in the NBA, most of the head coaches and general managers are white guys. (Gates 1993, 49)

Generally members of minority groups tend not to be as shocked when confronted with discrimination—frequently it's part of their daily lives. Here's how a black student at a mostly white university described the feeling he had as he walked home each night from a campus job to his apartment:

> "Even if you wanted to, it's difficult just to live a life where you don't come into conflict with others. Because every day you walk the streets, it's not even like once a week, once a month. It's every day you walk the streets. Every day you live as a black person you're reminded how you're perceived in society. You walk the streets at night; white people cross the streets. I've seen white couples and individuals dart in front of cars to not be on the same side of the street. Just the other day, I was walking down the street, and this white female with a child, I saw her pass a young male about 20 yards ahead. When she saw me, she quickly dragged the child and herself across the busy street. What is so funny is that this area has had an unknown white rapist in the area for about four years. [When I pass] white men tighten their grip on their women. I've seen people turn around and seem like they're going to take blows from me. The police constantly make circles around me as I walk home, you know, for blocks. I'll walk, and they'll turn a block. And they'll come around me just to make sure, to find out where I'm going. So, every day you realize [you're black]. Even though you're not doing anything wrong; you're just existing. You're just a person. But you're a black person perceived in an unblack world." (Feagin 1991, 111–112)

Being bombarded by discriminatory behaviors can take a big toll on people. Sometimes it may seem to members of the dominant group that minorities take "small slights" and blow them

---

[1]The phenomenon that *loss of advantage* is experienced as discrimination can be found in other cultures. In India, to integrate the Harijan into the mainstream of society, the government instituted a policy of "protective discrimination," or affirmative action, in which some university scholarships and a certain percentage of government jobs are reserved for Harijan. Lelah Dushkin (1979) found that upper-caste members tended to exaggerate both the costs that they were paying (for example, in terms of lost jobs) and the benefits that the Harijan were receiving.

out of proportion, because they are "just too sensitive." Here is one middle-class black woman's account of the time that she "overreacted":

> "We had a new car . . . and we stopped at 7-11 [store]. We were going to go out that night, and we were taking my son to a baby-sitter. . . . And we pulled up, and my husband was inside at the time. And this person, this Anglo couple, drove up, and they hit our car. It was a brand new car. So my husband came out. And the first thing they told us was that we got our car on *welfare*. Here we are able-bodied. He was a corporate executive. I had a decent job, it was a professional job. . . . But they looked at the car we were driving, and they made the assumption that we got it from welfare. I completely snapped; I physically abused that lady. I did. And I was trying to keep my husband from arguing with her husband until the police could come. . . . And when the police came they interrogated them: they didn't arrest us, because there was an off-duty cop who had seen the whole incident and said she provoked it." (Feagin 1991, 112)

Sociologist Joe Feagin found that most white Americans believe that these days middle-class blacks can live their lives substantially untouched by race discrimination. He wanted to find out whether this was true. In his research, he found evidence that race discrimination against even middle-class blacks is fairly widespread. It may lack the crudity of the era when blacks encountered "No Negroes Served Here" signs in restaurants, but it is noticeable. One of Feagin's respondents, a female black professor at a predominantly white university in the Southwest, explains how she copes when she encounters the police:

> "When the cops pull me over because my car is old and ugly, they assume I've just robbed a convenience store. Or that's the excuse they give: 'This car looks like a car used to rob a 7-11 [store].' And I've been pulled over six or seven times since I've been in this city—and I've been here two years now. Then I do what most black folks do. I try not to make any sudden moves so I'm not accidentally shot. Then I give them my identification. And I show them my university I.D. so they won't think that I'm someone that constitutes a threat, however they define it, so that I don't get arrested." (114)

She explained the overall effect of daily encounters with race discrimination this way:

> "[One problem with] being black in America is that you have to spend so much time thinking about stuff that most white people just don't even have to think about. I worry when I get pulled over by a cop. I worry because the person that I live with is a black male, and I have a teen-aged son. I worry what some white cop is going to think when he walks over to our car, because he's holding on to a gun. And I'm very aware of how many black folks accidentally get shot by cops. I worry when I walk into a store, that someone's going to think

I'm in there shoplifting. And I have to worry about that because I'm not free to ignore it. And so, that thing that's supposed to be guaranteed to all Americans, the freedom to just be yourself, is a fallacious idea. And I get resentful that I have to think about things that a lot of people, even very close white friends whose politics are similar to mine, simply don't have to worry about." (114)

Feagin explained that "particular instances of discrimination may seem minor to outside white observers when considered in isolation. But when blatant acts of avoidance, verbal harassment, and physical attack combine with subtle and covert slights, and these accumulate over months, years, and lifetimes, the impact on a black person is far more than the sum of individual instances" (115). Feagin refers to the cumulative impact of encounters with racist behavior as having a *pyramiding effect.* Another of his respondents explained it this way:

". . . if you can think of the mind as having one hundred ergs of energy, and the average man uses fifty percent of his energy dealing with the everyday problems of the world—just the general kinds of things—then he has fifty percent more to do creative kinds of things that he wants to do. Now that's a white person. . . . A black person also has one hundred ergs; he uses fifty percent the same way a white man does, dealing with what the white man has [to deal with], so he has fifty percent left. But he uses twenty-five percent fighting being black, [with] all the problems of being black and what it means. Which means he really only has twenty-five percent to do what the white man has fifty percent to do, and he's expected to do just as much as the white man with that twenty-five percent. . . . So, that's kind of what happens. You just don't have as much energy left to do as much as you know you really could do if . . . your mind were free." (115)

14.3 Why do sociologists distinguish racism from race-based discrimination and sexism from sex-based discrimination?

The Social Construction of Minority Groups

Louis Wirth stressed that minorities are people who have been "singled out" as different. Naive observers tend to believe that the things that distinguish members of minority and dominant groups are direct reflections of inherent biological or psychological differences.

Take, for example, the concept of race. The term *race* was first applied to humans in 1775 by the German naturalist and physiologist Johann Friedrich Blumenbach. Blumenbach, one of the founders of anthropology, came up with a taxonomy (classification) scheme that divided people into five racial categories: Caucasian, Mongolian, Malay, American, and Ethiopian or African. Although Blumenbach did not make much of racial differences (instead he stressed the essential unity of humankind), many of the scientists who followed him invested the concept of race with great meaning. In the nineteenth century, in fact, many scientists adhered to *polygenism*—or a belief that different races evolved from different origins, that different races constituted different subspecies of humanity.[2] Here's how this was explained by one such "scholar":

> [The] mass of scriptural and scientific evidence clearly indicates that the pure-blood White is the creature whom God designed should perform the mental labor necessary to subdue the earth; and that the Negro is the creature whom God designed to perform the manual labor. The Negro, in common with the rest of the animals, made his appearance upon the earth prior to the creation of man. With the Negro and the animals of draft, burden and food, it was possible for [white] man to develop all the resources of the earth and not personally till the ground. (Carroll 1900/1991, 101–102)

Race has proved to be a slippery concept. Consider the original five categories proposed by Blumenbach. His placement of groups of people within each category does not mesh with contemporary conceptions of race. Under the category of Caucasian, for example, he placed not only Europeans but Hindus. Under the category of Mongolian, on the other hand, he lumped Chinese, Turks, and Eskimos.[3]

Later anthropologists argued for different taxonomies of race. The English anthropologist Ashley Montague showed that these taxonomies varied a great deal, including anywhere from 2 to 2000 different racial groups. Montague himself identified some 40 different races (1960, 1964).

In South Africa, the laws of apartheid ("aparthood") recognized four racial categories: white (those of European descent),

---

[2]Polygenistic theories (that is, theories that claim that people of different races evolved from different genetic stock) have been invoked in many cultures to justify discrimination against minorities. In Japan, for example, there are minorities—little known to outsiders—called the *hinin* and the *eta*, or "heavily polluted." Now called the *burakumin*, or "people of the hamlet," these people were long treated as if they were not quite human, and certainly not Japanese. As recently as 1965 a government survey in Japan revealed that 70 percent of the people polled believed that members of the *burakumin* "were of a race and lineage different from the Japanese" (Hane 1982, 40). Yet no empirical evidence can be found to support such a theory.

[3]Blumenbach's classification was widely accepted among scientists, but conventional observers tended to modify his taxonomy. For example, for the first several decades of the twentieth century, it was illegal for foreigners of Asian descent to buy property. In 1920 a group of Armenians in the United States (whom Blumenbach's scheme had classified as Caucasian) had to go to court to prove they were not of "Mongolian" or Asian descent and thus could legally purchase property.

coloured (mixed), Asiatic (including those of Indian descent), and African (called *Bantu*). The categories were strict, but they were not entirely based on physical differences. For example, Japanese (who tended to be fairly affluent) could be classified as white.

In the United States, persons of European, African, and North American ancestry are divided into three races: white, black, and Native American. In Mexico, however, the same population would be divided into at least six groups: *Negro* (black), *Indio* (Indian), *Hispano* (white), *mestizo* (Indian and white), *lobo* (Indian and black), and *mulatto* (white and black). The term *mestizo/ mestiza* is particularly revealing with respect to the social nature of race. Originally, it meant strictly mixed Indian and white heritage; by the end of the seventeenth century, however, "any person of the lower or intermediate classes who adopted Spanish culture was considered mestizo/mestiza, regardless of his or her [biological] descent" (Appiah and Gates 1997, 455).

Even within the United States, there has been disagreement about who qualifies as what race. In the days when segregation was legal and intermarriage forbidden, it was quite important to know who belonged to which race. But one's race could vary from state to state. Who, for example, was black?

> In Kentucky, anyone having one-fourth or more Negro blood (at least one grandparent)
>
> In Indiana and Maryland, anyone having one-eighth or more Negro blood (at least one great-grandparent)
>
> In Louisiana, anyone having one-sixteenth or more Negro blood (at least one great-great-grandparent)

Still, in other states the law was quite simple. In Arkansas, for example, the law stated, "The words 'persons of negro race' shall be held to apply to and include any person who has in his or her veins any negro blood whatever." Likewise, in Georgia, "The term 'white person' shall include only persons of the white or Caucasian race, who have no ascertainable trace of either Negro, African, West Indian, Asiatic Indian, Mongolian, Japanese, or Chinese blood in their veins" (Kennedy 1959, 48–50). These states, then, followed the "one-drop rule"—meaning that a "single drop of 'black blood' makes a person black" (Davis 1991, 51).

What, then, is race? Although the concept of race is not very useful to biologists, it continues to be an important one for sociologists—but only because people's assumptions about race have tremendous consequences for individuals. Race is a socially constructed attribute that is tied to beliefs about differences in the physical makeup of different individuals.

Ethnicity is different. When most people speak of "ethnic differences," they are referring specifically to *cultural* differences.

Thus, *ethnicity has to do with shared cultural heritage.* The ties that bind people together into ethnic groups may be varied and frequently include religion, language, dress, music, and food preferences. Sometimes ethnicity has less to do with shared culture than with how people in a social group are perceived. That is, sometimes ethnicity is imposed upon a people. One example involves Italian Americans. Many of the people who emigrated to the United States in the 1880s were surprised to find that they were "Italian." They had thought of themselves as Venetians, Neopolitans, Calabrians, Sicilians, or Corsicans. To them there was no such person as an Italian. But when they came to the United States, their ethnic distinctions were treated as meaningless by members of the dominant group, who lumped all Italians into a single ethnicity. As Nancy Lurie put it, "Immigrant communities were not communities when they came; their ethnic identities were, to a surprising extent, constructed in America" (1982, 143). In other words, "The Sicilians, the Neopolitans, and the Calabrians thus became conscious of their common destiny in America" (Schermerhorn 1949, 25). Likewise, it was white Americans who created "Indian" and "African" as ethnicities out of an incredible diversity of cultures.[4]

In conventional language, ethnic labels are not neutral, technical devices. If they were, it would make sense to say that everyone has an ethnicity. But as it is used in society, the concept of ethnicity has connotations of something foreign or exotic. Think about it—what is stocked in the supermarket in the aisle marked "ethnic foods"? If those are ethnic foods, what is it that is stocked throughout the rest of the store?

Gender

Gender is a social construction as well. If differences between men and women were biologically determined, then they would be the same across cultures. But they aren't.

In 1935 the American anthropologist Margaret Mead published her famous study *Sex and Temperament in Three Primitive Societies.* This book contained an account of the differences between men and women among the Arapesh, the Mundugumor, and the Tchambuli (pronounced "cham-bully")—small societies in New Guinea.[5] As Mead later explained, she had set out to study the degree to which differences in male and female temperaments

---

[4]The imposition of ethnicity on a minority group by a dominant group is called *ethnogenesis* (Greeley 1971).

[5]New Guinea is the second largest island in the world (only Greenland is larger). It's located north of Australia.

(that is, personalities) were a result of socialization rather than physical or biological factors. Mead and her colleagues found that there was what she called a standardized male personality and a standardized female personality in each culture. But the differences across these three cultures were amazing. Here is how Mead summarized the nature of male and female in each society:

> We found the Arapesh—both men and women—displaying a personality that, out of our historically limited preoccupations, we would call maternal in its parental aspects, and feminine in its sexual aspects. We found men, as well as women, trained to be cooperative, unaggressive, responsive to the needs and demands of others. We found no idea that sex was a powerful driving force for men or for women. In marked contrast to these attitudes, we found among the Mundugumor that both men and women developed as ruthless, aggressive, positively sexed individuals, with the maternal cherishing aspects of personality at a minimum. Both men and women approximated to a personality type that in our culture we would find only in an undisciplined and very violent male. Neither the Arapesh nor the Mundugumor profit by a contrast between the sexes; the Arapesh ideal is the mild, responsive man married to the mild, responsive woman; the Mundugumor ideal is the violent aggressive man married to the violent aggressive woman. In the third tribe, the Tchambuli, we found a genuine reversal of the sex-attitudes of our own culture, with the woman the dominant, impersonal, managing partner, the man the less responsible and the emotionally dependent person. (1935/1950, 205)

What to make of these findings? To Mead it was clear: "If those temperamental attitudes which we have traditionally regarded as feminine—such as passivity, responsiveness, and a willingness to cherish children—can so easily be set up as the masculine pattern in one tribe, and in another be outlawed for the majority of women as well as for the majority of men, we no longer have any basis for regarding such aspects of behavior as sex-linked." And, she added, "This conclusion becomes even stronger when we consider the actual reversal in Tchambuli of the position of dominance of the two sexes" (1935/1950, 205).

There are, of course, physical differences between men and women, and most societies divide their own population into two groups—male and female—on the basis of these physical characteristics. What sociologists have found most fascinating, however, is what different societies have made of these sex differences. Mead's research in New Guinea brought home the fact that we may have overlooked the real source of most differences between men and women. More specifically, many of the differences between men and women that people conventionally assume are related to biological factors turn out to be products of socialization. Physically females among the Arapesh, Mundugumor, and

Tchambuli were the same, as were the men among the three tribes. Nonetheless, what it meant to be a woman or a man varied tremendously across these groups.

Today sociologists frequently distinguish between *sex differences* (the physical and biological differences between males and females) and *gender differences* (which have to do with social expectations about how males and females ought to act and their respective rights and duties). To put it another way, *sex* is a biological or physical attribute while *gender* is a social/cultural attribute.

Which of the differences that we see between men and women are related to sex and which are related to gender? In other words, which of the differences between men and women have to do with their innate biological selves and which have to do with the kind of socialization they receive? The evidence increasingly shows that gender differences tend to override sex differences— that social expectations, for example, are much more powerful determinants of people's behaviors than their physical attributes.

> Summarizing the differences between women and men is not an easy task, once one leaves the obvious biological domains [that is, differences in reproductive capacities]. . . . The basic repertoires of women and men are quite similar, particularly when it comes to social behaviors. Both women and men know how to be aggressive, how to be helpful, how to smile, and how to be rude. What they actually do is determined less by differential abilities than by the context in which they are acting. Attitudes and actions of others affect what people do. Societal norms and expectations are also influential. So, too, do people alter their own behavior from one situation to another, depending on their goals and objectives.
>
> Comparisons of women and men cannot be analyzed in a vacuum, independent of their social context. Even in the area of cognitive abilities, the differences between women and men have shifted over time. Now there are fewer differences than there were twenty years ago. . . .
>
> No doubt people will continue to ask how men and women differ. But the answers will never be simple ones. Nor can observed differences between the sexes be used as a simple explanation for the broader gender roles of women and men [for example, the fact that in our society, women are regarded as having more responsibility for nurturing children]. Indeed, the causal direction may be just the reverse: Accepted roles may channel men and women into different patterns of behavior. Whatever the patterns observed, most sex differences will continue to reflect a gendered environment and be subject to further change. (Deaux 1992, 1753)

14.4 Explain the difference between *sex* and *gender*.

14.5 When a sociologist says that some phenomenon is a *social construction*, what does he or she mean?

Chapter Review

1. Make a list of the sociological concepts that you learned in this chapter. Define each term. (*Hint:* You will learn the most from this exercise if, in addition to defining each concept, you create an example of it in your own words.)

2. Each of the following jokes is an example of sex-based discrimination, but which are examples of sexism? Explain how you distinguished sexism from sex-based discrimination.
   1. Q: What's the difference between a sorority girl and an elephant? A: About 10 pounds.
   2. Q: Why did the blonde get fired from the M&M factory? A: Because she threw out all the w's.
   3. Q: Why was the blonde happy when she completed the puzzle in two hours? A: Because it said on the puzzle box "two to four years."
   4. Q: What's the difference between men and government bonds? A: Bonds mature.
   5. Q: What did God say after creating man? A: I can do better.
   6. Q: What is gross stupidity? A: 144 men in a room.

3. Just a few decades ago, African American adult males were frequently referred to as "boys." Today, adult males of all races are generally referred to as "men." However, adult women are frequently referred to as "girls." In your judgment what are some of the implications of this for women?

4. How important is your gender to the way you live your life? Imagine that tomorrow morning you woke up and discovered that, overnight, you had changed from female to male (or male to female). Describe how the next few days would go for you. Will there be any change in what you do or how you behave? (Assume that everyone around you acted as if your new sex was the one you had always had.) What lessons would you learn from this experience?

STOP & REVIEW

Answers and Discussion

14.1 Prejudice is a negative and persistent judgment, based on incorrect information, about people in a particular group. Discrimination involves treating someone differently because of membership in some group. The essential difference between them is that prejudice involves attitudes and beliefs while discrimination involves behaviors.

14.2 Individual discrimination occurs when a single person discriminates against another (for example, an owner of a building refuses to rent to someone because of his or her race, religion, or whatever). Institutional discrimination is discrimination that is built into the system; the person who acts out the discrimination (for example, the bank loan officer or the college admissions officer) may not intend to discriminate (or even know that he or she is discriminating).

14.3 Any act that discriminates against another based on his or her race is race-based discrimination. However, not all race-based discrimination qualifies as racism. Determining which acts are racist and which are not requires that one look at the social context in which the act occurs.

If a white building owner discriminates against a Japanese renter, that is racism, because whites are the dominant group in U.S. society. On the other hand, if a Japanese building owner discriminates against a white renter in Tokyo, that would be racism, because whites are in the minority in Japan.

There is no difference between the actual behavior (and, to the conventional observers, they both are bad). How "bad" the behaviors are, of course, is not of interest to sociologists. Sociologists distinguish between the two kinds of acts because of the different kinds of effects they have on the people who are discriminated against.

Michael Schwalbe (quoted in the chapter) says that it is important to take into account power differences—that it is perverse to regard all race-based discrimination as the same, because not all people have institutional power to make life difficult for others.

14.4 Sex has to do with physical attributes (such as a person's genitalia). Gender has to do with the meaning that a particular society attaches to those physical attributes. For example, long hair on women and short hair on men are gender attributes (and may vary from society to society).

14.5 To say that something is socially constructed is to say that it is made by people in society. A norm is a social construction (it has no other reality). Similarly, according to sociologists, race is a social construction—the main reality of race is not biological or physical. Race is a social construction, as is gender.

References

Ackernecht, Erwin H. 1982. *A Short History of Medicine*. Baltimore: Johns Hopkins University Press.

Alba, Richard D. 1985. *Italian Americans*. Englewood Cliffs, NJ: Prentice-Hall.

Allport, Gordon W. 1954. *The Nature of Prejudice*. New York: Doubleday/Anchor Books.

Appiah, Kwame Anthony, and Henry Louis Gates, Jr. 1997. *The Dictionary of Global Culture*. New York: Knopf.

Axtell, Roger E. 1991. *Gestures: The Do's and Taboos of Body Language Around the World*. New York: Wiley.

Ayres, Ian. 1991. "Fair Driving: Gender and Race Discrimination in Retail Car Negotiations." *Harvard Law Review* 104: 817–872.

Barber, Bernard. 1968. "Social Stratification." Pp. 288–295 in David Sills (ed.), *Encyclopedia of Social Science*. New York: Macmillan.

Becker, Howard S. 1963. *Outsiders: Studies in the Sociology of Deviance*. New York: Free Press.

Berger, Peter. 1963. *Invitation to Sociology: A Humanistic Perspective*. New York: Anchor.

Berger, Peter L., and Thomas Luckmann. 1967. *The Social Construction of Reality: A Treatise in the Sociology of Knowledge*. Garden City, NY: Anchor Books.

Berkow, Robert, ed. 1987. *The Merck Manual of Diagnosis and Therapy*, 15th ed. Rahway, NJ: Merck Sharp & Dohme Research Laboratories.

Bierstedt, Robert. 1960. "Sociology and Humane Learning." *American Sociological Review* 25: 3.

Birdwhistell, Ray L. 1970. *Kinesics and Context: Essays on Body Motion Communication*. Philadelphia: University of Pennsylvania Press.

Bishop, Morris. 1968. *Middle Ages*. Boston: Houghton Mifflin.

Black, Henry Campbell. 1979. *Black's Law Dictionary*. St. Paul, MN: West.

Blumenbach, Johann F. 1775. "On the Natural Variety of Mankind." Reprinted in *Anthropological Treatise*. Trans. T. Bendyshe. London: Anthropological Society, 1865.

Boxer, Sarah. 1995. "The United States Is the New Bastion of Inequality." *New York Times,* April 23.

Bouglé, Célestin. 1908/1971. *Essais sur le Régime des Castes (Essays on the Caste System).* Trans. D. F. Pocock. Cambridge: Cambridge University Press.

Brace, Emma. 1894. *The Life of Charles Loring Brace.* New York: Author.

Braun, Denny. 1997. *The Rich Get Richer—The Rise of Income Inequality in the United States and the World.* Chicago: Nelson-Hall.

———. 1995. "Negative Consequences to the Rise of Income Inequality." *Research in Politics and Society* 5: 3–31.

Bremner, John B. 1980. *Words on Words.* New York: Columbia University Press.

Bryson, Bill. 1990. *The Mother Tongue: English and How It Got That Way.* New York: Avon Books.

Bureau of Justice Statistics. 1993. *Highlights from 20 Years of Surveying Crime Victims.* Washington DC: U.S. Government Printing Office.

———. 1992. *Criminal Victimization in the United States.* Washington DC: U.S. Government Printing Office.

Campbell, Frederick L., Hubert M. Blalock, Jr., and Reece McGee (eds.). 1985. *Teaching Sociology: The Quest for Excellence.* Chicago: Nelson-Hall.

Carmichael, Stokely, and Charles Hamilton. 1967. *Black Power.* New York: Vintage Books.

Carroll, Chas. 1900/1991. *The Negro a Beast.* Salem, NH: Ayer.

Chagnon, Napoleon A. 1977. *Yanomamö: The Fierce People.* New York: Holt, Rinehart & Winston.

Chambliss, William. 1973. "The Saints and the Roughnecks." *Society* 11: 24–31.

Clark, Kenneth B. 1967. *Dark Ghetto.* New York: Harper Torchbooks.

Cleaver, Eldridge. 1968. Interview. *Playboy,* December, pp. 89–108, 238.

Cloward, Richard, and Lloyd E. Ohlin. 1960. *Delinquency and Opportunity: A Theory of Delinquent Gangs.* New York: Free Press.

———. 1959. "Illegitimate Means, Anomie, and Deviant Behavior." *American Sociological Review* 24: 164–176.

Cooley, Charles H. 1909. *Social Organization.* New York: Scribner.

———. 1902. *Human Nature and the Social Order.* New York: Scribner.

Corcoran, Margaret. 1995. "Rags to Rags: Poverty and Mobility in the United States." *Annual Review of Sociology* 21: 237–267.

Coser, Lewis A. 1971. *Masters of Sociological Thought: Ideas in Historical and Social Context.* New York: Harcourt Brace Jovanovich.

Craig, Albert M., William A. Graham, Donald Kegan, Steven Ozment, and Frank M. Turner. 1986. *The Heritage of World Civilizations.* New York: Macmillan.

Cummings, Scott, and Del Taebel. 1978. "The Economic Socialization of Children: A New Marxist Analysis." *Social Problems* 26: 198–210.

Curtiss, Susan. 1997. *Genie: A Psycholinguistic Study of a Modern-Day "Wild Child."* New York: Academic Press.

Darwin, Charles. 1859/1962. *The Origin of Species by Means of Natural Selection of the Preservation of Favoured Races in the Struggle for Life.* New York: Collier Books.

Davis, Allison. 1948. *Social Class Influences upon Learning.* Cambridge, MA: Harvard University Press.

Davis, James F. 1991. *Who Is Black? One Nation's Definition.* University Park: The Pennsylvania State University Press.

Davis, Kingsley. 1947. "Final Note on a Case of Extreme Isolation." *American Journal of Sociology* 50: 432–437.

———. 1940. "A Case of Extreme Social Isolation of a Child." *American Journal of Sociology* 45: 554–564.

Deaux, Kay. 1992. "Sex Differences." In Edgar F. Borgatta and Marie L. Borgatta (eds.), *Encyclopedia of Sociology.* New York: Macmillan.

Della Fave, Richard. 1980. "The Meek Shall Not Inherit the Earth: Self-Evaluation and the Legitimacy of Stratification." *American Sociological Review* 45: 955–971.

Deutch, Morton P. 1964. "The Disadvantaged Child and the Learning Process." Pp. 172–187 in Frank Reissman, Jerome Cohen, and Arthur Pearl (eds.), *Mental Health of the Poor.* New York: Free Press.

Douglas, Mary. 1986. *How Institutions Think.* Syracuse, NY: Syracuse University Press.

Downs, A. 1970. *Racism in America and How to Combat It.* Washington DC: U.S. Commission on Civil Rights.

Dumont, Louis. 1970. *Homo Hierarchicus: The Caste System and Its Implications.* Chicago: University of Chicago Press.

Durkheim, Émile. 1904/1950. *The Rules of the Sociological Method.* Trans. Sarah A. Solovay and John H. Meuller. Glencoe, IL: Free Press.

———. 1897/1951. *Suicide.* Trans. John A. Spaulding and George Simpson. Glencoe, IL: Free Press.

———. 1893/1933. *The Division of Labor in Society.* Trans. George Simpson. New York: Free Press.

Dushkin, Lelah. 1972. "Scheduled Caste Politics." In Michael Mahar (ed.), *The Untouchables in Contemporary India.* Tucson: University of Arizona Press.

Eder, Donna. 1995. *School Talk: Gender and Adolescent Culture.* New Brunswick, NJ: Rutgers University Press.

Entwisle, Doris R., and Karl L. Alexander. 1993. "Entry into School: The Beginning School Transition and Educational Stratification in the United States." *Annual Review of Sociology* 19: 401–423.

Farb, Peter. 1993. *Word Play: What Happens When People Talk.* New York: Vintage Books.

Feagin, Joe R. 1991. "The Continuing Significance of Race: Anti-Black Discrimination in Public Places." *American Sociological Review* 56: 101–116.

Fussell, Paul. 1983. *Class: A Guide Through the American Status System.* New York: Touchstone/Simon & Schuster.

Gamoran, Adam, and Robert D. Mare. 1989. "Secondary School Tracking and Educational Inequality: Compensation, Reinforcement, or Neutrality?" *American Journal of Sociology* 94: 1146–1183.

Gates, David. 1993. "White Male Paranoia." *Newsweek,* March 29, pp. 48–53.

Gleick, James. 1987. *Chaos.* New York: Viking/Penguin.

Goffman, Erving. 1963. *Stigma: Notes on the Management of Spoiled Identity.* Englewood Cliffs, NJ: Prentice-Hall.

———. 1961. *Asylums: Essays on the Social Situation of Mental Patients and Other Inmates.* Garden City, NY: Doubleday/Anchor Books.

Greeley, Andrew. 1971. *Why Can't They Be Like Us?* New York: Dutton.

Greenberg, David F. 1988. *The Construction of Homosexuality.* Chicago: University of Chicago Press.

Hallinan, Maureen T. 1988. "Equality of Educational Opportunity." *Annual Review of Sociology* 14: 249–268.

Hallinan, Maureen T., and Richard A. Williams. 1987. "The Stability of Students' Interracial Friendships." *American Sociological Review* 52: 653–664.

Hane, Mikiso. 1982. *Peasants, Rebels and Outcastes: The Underside of Modern Japan.* New York: Pantheon Books.

Holmes, Oliver Wendell. 1891. *Medical Essays, 1842–1882.* Boston: Houghton Mifflin.

Hughes, Everett C. 1945. "Dilemmas and Contradictions of Status." *American Journal of Sociology* 50: 353–359.

Hyde, J. S. 1979. *Understanding Human Sexuality.* New York: McGraw-Hill.

James, C. L. R. 1967. "Black Power." Pp. 362–374 in Anna Grimshaw (ed.), *The C. L. R. James Reader.* Oxford: Basil Blackwell.

Johnson, Charles S. 1941/1967. *Growing Up in the Black Belt.* New York: Schocken Books.

Johnson, Clifford M., Leticia Miranda, Arloc Sherman, and James D. Weill. 1991. *Child Poverty in America.* Washington DC: Children's Defense Fund.

Kennedy, Stetson. 1959. *Jim Crow Guide to the U.S.A.: The Laws, Customs and Etiquette Governing the Conduct of Nonwhites and Other Minorities as Second Class Citizens.* London: Lawrence & Wishart.

Kerbo, Harold R. 1991. *Social Stratification and Inequality: Class Conflict in Historical and Comparative Perspective,* 2nd ed. New York: McGraw-Hill.

Kluegel, James R., and Eliot R. Smith. 1981. "Beliefs About Stratification." *Annual Review of Sociology* 7: 29–56.

Kottak, Conrad P. 1992. *Assault on Paradise: Social Change in a Brazilian Village.* New York: McGraw-Hill.

Kozol, Jonathan. 1991. *Savage Inequalities: Children in America's Schools.* New York: Crown.

Kroeber, A. L., and Clyde Kluckhohn. 1952. *Culture: A Critical Review of Concepts and Definitions.* Papers of the Peabody Museum of American Archaeology and Ethnology. Vol. 47, no. 1.

Lederer, Richard. 1987. *Anguished English.* New York: Bantam/Doubleday/Dell.

Lemert, Edwin M. 1967. *Human Deviance, Social Problems and Social Control.* Englewood Cliffs, NJ: Prentice-Hall.

Levine, Robert A., and Donald T. Campbell. 1972. *Ethnocentrism: Theories of Conflict, Ethnic Attitudes, and Group Behavior.* New York: Wiley.

Lewis, Oscar. 1966. "The Culture of Poverty." *Scientific American,* October, pp. 7–25.

Liebow, Elliot. 1967. *Talley's Corner.* Boston: Little, Brown.

Linton, Ralph. 1945. *The Science of Man in the World Crisis.* New York: Columbia University Press.

Liska, Allen E. 1987. *Perspectives on Deviance,* 2nd ed. Englewood Cliffs, NJ: Prentice-Hall.

Lurie, Nancy Destreich. 1982. "The American Indian: Historical Background." Pp. 131–144 in R. Yetmen and C. H. Steele (eds.), *Majority and Minority*, 3rd ed. Boston: Allyn & Bacon.

Mannheim, Karl. 1929/1936. *Ideology and Utopia: An Introduction to the Sociology of Knowledge*. Ed. and trans. Louis Wirth and Edward Shils. New York: Harcourt Brace Jovanovich.

Marx, Karl, and Friedrich Engels. 1845–6/1963. *The German Ideology*. New York: International.

McLeod, Jane D., and Michael J. Shanahan. 1993. "Poverty, Parenting and Children's Mental Health." *American Sociological Review* 58: 351–366.

McNeill, William Hardy. 1987. *A History of the Human Community*, 2nd ed. Englewood Cliffs, NJ: Prentice-Hall.

Mead, George H. 1934. *Mind, Self and Society: From the Standpoint of a Social Behaviorist*. Chicago: University of Chicago Press.

Mead, Margaret. 1935/1950. *Sex and Temperament in Three Primitive Societies*. New York: Morrow.

Merton, Robert K. 1976. *Sociological Ambivalence and Other Essays*. New York: Free Press.

———. 1949/1968. "Manifest and Latent Functions." In R. K. Merton, *Social Theory and Social Structure*. New York: Free Press.

———. 1938. "Social Structure and Anomie." *American Sociological Review* 13: 672–682. Reprinted in Merton, *Social Theory and Social Structure*. New York: Free Press, 1949.

Miller, Joanne. 1988. "Jobs and Work." Pp. 327–359 in Neil Smelser (ed.), *Handbook of Sociology*. Newbury Park, CA: Sage.

Mills, C. Wright. 1959. *The Sociological Imagination*. New York: Free Press.

Mishel, Laurence, and Jared Bernstein. 1993. *The State of Working America, 1992–1993*. New York: Sharpe.

Montague, M. F. Ashley. 1964. *The Concept of Race*. New York: Free Press.

———. 1960. *Introduction to Physical Anthropology*, 3rd ed. Springfield, IL: Thomas.

Morrill, John. 1984. "The Stuarts (1603–1688)." Pp. 286–351 in Kenneth O. Morgan (ed.), *The Oxford Illustrated History of Britain*. Oxford: Oxford University Press.

Muller, Edward N. 1985. "Income Inequality, Regime Repressiveness and Political Violence." *American Sociological Review* 50: 47–61.

Murdock, George Peter. 1957. "World Ethnographic Sample." *American Anthropologist* 59: 664–697.

Murdock, George P. 1945. "The Common Denominator of Culture." In Ralph Linton (ed.), *The Science of Man in the World Crisis*. New York: Columbia University Press.

Nelson, M. D., Jr. 1992. "Socioeconomic Status and Childhood Mortality in North Carolina." *American Journal of Public Health* 82: 1131–1133.

Newman, Graeme. 1967. *Comparative Deviance: Perceptions and Law in Six Cultures*. New York: Elsevier.

Newman, Katherine, and Chauncy Lennon. 1995. "The Job Ghetto." *The American Prospect*, Summer.

Oakes, Jeannie. 1994. "More Than Misapplied Technology: A Normative and Political Response to Hallinan on Tracking." *Sociology of Education* 67: 84–89.

Parsons, Talcott. 1966. *Societies: Evolutionary and Comparative Perspectives.* Englewood Cliffs, NJ: Prentice-Hall.

———. 1985. *Keeping Track: How Schools Structure Inequality.* New Haven, CT: Yale University Press.

Patterson, Orlando. 1982. *Slavery and Social Death.* Cambridge, MA: Harvard University Press.

Pattullo, E. L. 1992. "Straight Talk About Gays." *Commentary,* December.

Payne, Stanley L. 1951. *The Art of Asking Questions.* Princeton, NJ: Princeton University Press.

Pollock, Frederick, and Frederic William Maitland. 1898/1968. *The History of English Law Before the Time of Edward I.* 2 vols. Cambridge: Cambridge University Press.

Quint, Michael. 1991. "Mortgage Race Data Show Gap. Fed Has Apprised Bankers of Disparity in Loan Approvals." *New York Times,* October 14.

Radcliffe-Brown, A. R. 1922/1948. *The Andaman Islanders.* Glencoe, IL: Free Press.

Rank, Mark P. 1989. "Fertility Among Women on Welfare: Incidence and Determinants." *American Sociological Review* 54: 296–304.

Rheingold, Harriet L. 1969. "The Social and Socializing Infant." Pp. 779–790 in D. H. Goslin (ed.), *Handbook of Socialization Theory and Research.* Chicago: Rand McNally.

Robertson, Ian. 1987. *Sociology.* New York: Worth.

Rose, Peter I., Myron Glazer, and Penina Migdal Glaser. 1979. "In Controlled Environments: Four Cases of Intensive Resocialization." Pp. 323–325 in Peter I. Rose (ed.), *Socialization and the Life Cycle.* New York: St. Martin's Press.

Rosenthal, Robert, and Lenore Jacobson. 1968. *Pygmalion in the Classroom: Teacher Expectations and Pupils' Intellectual Development.* New York: Holt, Rinehart & Winston.

Ryan, William. 1971. *Blaming the Victim.* New York: Vintage Books.

Sadker, Myra, and David Sadker. 1994. *Failing at Fairness. How Our Schools Cheat Girls.* New York: Touchstone.

Schermerhorn, Richard A. 1949. *These Are Our People.* Boston: Heath.

Schur, Edwin M. 1971. *Labelling Deviant Behavior.* New York: Harper & Row.

Schwalbe, Michael. 1996. *Unlocking the Iron Cage: The Men's Movement, Gender Politics, and American Culture.* New York: Oxford University Press.

Smith, Huston. 1958. *The Illustrated World's Religion: A Guide to Our Wisdom Traditions.* New York: HarperCollins.

Sorokin, Pitirim A. 1928. *Contemporary Sociological Theories.* New York: Harper.

Speilberg, Nathan, and Bryon D. Anderson. 1987. *Seven Ideas That Shook the Universe.* New York: Wiley.

Spencer, Herbert. 1852. "A Theory of Population, Deduced from the General Law of Animal Fertility." *Westminster Review* LVII.

———. 1864. *Social Statics.* New York: Appleton.

Spitz, René A. 1945. "Hospitalism: An Inquiry into the Genesis of Psychiatric Conditions in Early Childhood." *Psychoanalytic Study of the Child* 1: 53–74.

Sprecher, Susan, and Rachita Chandak. 1992. "Attitudes About Arranged Marriages and Dating Among Men and Women of India." *Free Inquiry in Creative Sociology* 20, 1: 59–69.

Sullivan, Andrew. 1995. *Virtually Normal.* New York: Knopf.

Sumner, William G. 1934. *Essays of William Graham Sumner.* 2 vols. Ed. Albert G. Keller and Maurice R. Davie. New Haven, CT: Yale University Press.

———. 1906. *Folkways.* Boston: Ginn.

Thernstrom, Abigail. 1992. "Tracking: The Drive for Racially Inclusive Schools." Pp. 131–143 in Harold Orland and June O'Neill (eds.), *Affirmative Action Revisited, The Annals,* September.

Thurow, Lester C. 1996. *The Future of Capitalism: How Today's Economic Forces Shape Tomorrow's World.* New York: Morrow.

Tittle, Charles R., and Robert F. Meier. 1990. "Specifying the SES Delinquency Relationship." *Criminology* 28: 271–279.

Tittle, Charles R., W. J. Villenez, and D. A. Smith. 1978. "The Myth of Social Class and Criminality: An Empirical Assessment of the Empirical Evidence." *American Sociological Review* 43: 643–656.

Tönnies, Ferdinand. 1898/1963. *Gemeinschaft and Gesellschaft.* Trans. and ed. Charles P. Loomis. New York: Harper & Row.

United Nations Human Development Programme, 1994. *Human Development Report.* New York: Oxford University Press.

Visser, Margaret. 1986. *Much Depends on Dinner.* New York: HarperCollins.

Webb, Eugene J., Donald T. Campbell, Richard D. Schwartz, and Lee Sechrest. 1966. *Unobtrusive Measures: Nonreactive Research in the Social Sciences.* Chicago: Rand McNally.

Weber, Max. 1904–1905/1958. *The Protestant Ethic and the Spirit of Capitalism.* New York: Scribner.

———. 1918/1958. "Inconvenient Facts." Pp. 145–147 in H. H. Gerth and C. W. Mills (eds.), *From Max Weber.* New York: Oxford University Press.

———. *Bureaucracy.* Pp. 196–266 in H. H. Gerth and C. W. Mills (eds.), *From Max Weber.* New York: Oxford University Press.

Williams, Lena. 1991. "When Blacks Shop, Bias Often Accompanies Sale." *New York Times,* April 30.

Williams, Robin M., Jr. 1970. *American Society: A Sociological Interpretation.* New York: Knopf.

Wirth, Louis. 1945. "The Problem of Minority Groups." In Ralph Linton (ed.), *The Science of Man in the World Crisis.* New York: Columbia University Press.

Glossary/Index

achieved status: A status earned by the individual through his or her own efforts. In the United States, bank robber, college professor, carpenter, and husband are achieved statuses, 112. *See also* ascribed status; social status

active discrimination. *See* discrimination, Allport's typology of

Ackernecht, Edwin, 11

Addams, Jane, 23, 24

agents of socialization: Groups in which socialization takes place, 150–156. *See also* peer group; schools; socialization; work place

aggregate, social: Not a social group, but a collectivity of people who happen to be in the same place at the same time, 118.

Allport, Gordon W., 222–224

altruistic suicide, 165n

American Sociological Association, 23

Anderson, Bryon, 36

animism, 138

anomic suicide: As described by Durkheim, a kind of suicide that increases when society fails to exercise adequate regulation over individuals' desires and goals, 164–165

anomie, as cause of deviance: According to Robert Merton, a situation that occurs when there is a disjuncture between the goals promoted by society and the availability of legitimate means to achieve those goals, 166–169

anticipatory socialization: The process of learning about the role requirements of a particular status prior to actually acquiring that status, 135. *See also* socialization

antilocution, as a form of discrimination, 224

apartheid, 231

aristocracy: Rule by the best few, 138

Arkwright, Richard, 10

artifact, 86. *See also* cultural artifact

ascribed status: A status that is bestowed upon an individual, regardless of his or her efforts or wishes. In the United States, sex, race and ethnicity are ascribed statuses, 112. *See also* social status

atavists, 161, 161n

attribute: A characteristic that describes a thing, 53

authority: According to Weber, legitimate power, 191. *See also* power

avoidance. *See* discrimination, Allport's typology of

Axtell, Roger, 104

Ayres, Ian, 219

Baker vs Nelson, 137

Baker vs State of Vermont, 137n

Barber, Bernard, 181

B.C.E.: Before common era, 6n

Becker, Howard, 170–173

beliefs, cultural: Shared ideas about what is real, 102. *See also* ideology

247

Bellarmine, Robert, 8
Berger, Peter, 135
Birdwhistell, Ray, 104
Bishop, Morris, 187
blaming the victim: Unjustly stating or believing that the cause of a problem resides in the individuals or groups who experience the problem, when the real source or cause of the problem is not within the individual but in the social environment, 206
Blumenbach, Johann Friedrich, 230–231
bourgeoisie: Marx's term for the class of people who own the means of production in modern society, the capitalists, 20, 189. *See also* proletariats
Boxer, Sarah, 200
Brace, Charles Loring, 22
brahmans, 184, 194
Broun, Heywood, 158
Bryson, Bill, 47, 51
bureaucracies, ideal type, 121–124; as iron cages, 124; bureaucratic personality, 29
Butterfly effect, 37

Campbell, Donald T., 48
capitalists. *See* bourgeoisie
Carmichael, Stokely, 225
Carroll, Chas., 231
caste system, 182–185; legitimating rationale of, 182
cause and effect, 57
Chagnon, Napoleon, 49–50, 104n
Chambliss, William, 174
Chandrak, Rachita, 139
chaos theory, 37
Clark, Kenneth B., 206
Cleaver, Eldridge, 76
Cloward, Richard, 169
collective conscience: Durkheim's term for the shared ideas, values, norms, and goals of people within a particular society, 13; and deviance, 163–164. *See also* mechanical solidarity; organic solidarity
Communist Manifesto, The, 20
Comte, Auguste, 11–12; law of three stages, 11
conflict paradigm: Model of the social world that assumes that society is composed of people or groups of people who are in competition for scarce resources, 21, 39, 40–41
conformity, as response to anomie, 168
consensus paradigm. *See* functionalist paradigm
content analysis, 87–88
control group: In an experiment, the group that does not receive the experimental treatment, 82–84. *See also* experimental group
convenience sample: A type of nonrandom sample, 90. *See also* random sample
Cooley, Charles H., on primary groups, 119–120; on looking glass self, 145–147. *See also* looking glass self; primary group
Copernicus, Nicolaus, 6–7, 25
Corcoran, Margaret, 200–201
Coser, Lewis, 12
counterculture: Subculture whose values and beliefs set it not only apart from but in opposition to the dominant culture, 107. *See also* subculture
crime and justice, effects of social class on, 202
cultural artifact: By-products of human behavior 95, 95n. *See also* material culture
cultural diffusion: Process by which people of different cultures borrow elements of material or nonmaterial culture from one another, 107
cultural leveling: Occurs when different cultures come to seem alike as a result of a great deal of cultural diffusion, 107
cultural relativism: The belief that other people and their ways of doing things can be understood only in terms of the cultural context of those other people; an antidote to ethnocentrism, 50–51
cultural wisdom, 106
culture: The set of ideas and things handed down from generation to generation in a particular group or society; culture is both a product of people's actions and a constraint on their actions, 94; material and nonmaterial culture, 95
culture of poverty. *See* poverty, cultural explanations of
culture shock, 104
Cummings, Scott, 199
Curtiss, Susan, 144n

Darwin, Charles, 21, 183n

data: Observations, pieces of information, 59; distinguished from datum, 61n

Davis, Allison, 203

Davis, James F., 232

Davis, Kingsley, 144

Deaux, Kay, 235

degradation ceremony: Ritual used by total organizations to degrade a person's sense of self, 157. *See also* total institutions

democracy: Rule by the people, 138

Democracy in America, 213

demography: Study of populations, 77, 77n

dependent variable: A variable that is thought to be influenced by another variable, 56–58. *See also* variable

depersonalization, 157

Deutsch, Morton, 203–204

devil's response to sociology, 44

dharma, 183

Diderot, Denis, 158

diffusion. *See* cultural diffusion

discreditable identity: The social identity of one who hides a stigma and is thereby vulnerable to being found out and discredited, 176. *See also* stigma

discredited identity: A social identity that has been marred owing to stigma, 176. *See also* stigma

discrimination: Unfavorable treatment of people based on their membership in some ill-favored group, 223–230; Allport's typology of, 224. *See also* individual discrimination; institutional discrimination; *ism*; prejudice

Division of Labor in Society, 12–13

dollars, different value to different people, 218–222

dominant group: The group in society with the most institutionalized power, 230–231. *See also* minority groups

Douglas, Mary, 135

Downs, A., 225

DuBois, W. E. B., 24

Durkheim, Emile, 12–15, 24, 47; on social facts, 14, 74; suicide as a social issue, 28–29, 162–166; on functions of deviance, 177

Dushkin, Lelah, 228n

dys, as a prefix, 32n

dysfunctions: Outcomes of social action that have a negative impact on the well-being of people in society, 32. *See also* functional; latent functions; manifest functions

ectomorph: Individual with tall, thin, and fragile physique, 162

education, effects of social class on, 201, 208, 218–219; as an investment, 218–219

egoistic suicide: Durkheim's term for a type of suicide whose rates increase when people are not well integrated into society; when people lack strong bonds to one another, 164–165

Einstein, Albert, 36

empirical: Something that can be observed through the use of one's physical senses, 44–45

endogamy: Norm that requires an individual to marry someone from within his or her own kinship, religious, or social class group, 195. *See also* exogamy

endomorph: Individual with a tendency to be short and heavy, 62

Engels, Friedrich, 20

epiphenomenon: A phenomenon that reflects the influence of some, more important, phenomenon; a secondary phenomenon, 20. *See also* Marx

Erikson, Kai T., 177–178

estate system, 9, 185–188; legitimating rationale of, 187

Eta, 231n

ethics, professional: Rules for the behavior of professions that are specifically oriented to the welfare of the larger society and not to the self-interest of the professional, 91

ethnic group: People who have in common a history and identity, shared customs, language, and, frequently, religion; people who see themselves as, or are seen by others as, a distinct group, 232

ethnocentrism: Tendency to use one's own culture as a standard against which to judge other people's cultures, 46–50. *See also* cultural relativism

ethnogenesis: Process by which members of the dominant group impose an ethnic label on members of a particular minority group, 233, 233n

exogamy: Norm that requires an individual to marry someone from outside of his or her own kinship, religious, or social class group, 195. *See also* endogamy

experiment: Research technique that involves manipulating the independent variable and then observing the effects on the dependent variable, 84; independent and dependent variables in, 83–84

experimental group: In an experiment, the group that receives the experimental treatment, 82–84. *See also* control group

Farb, Peter, 104

Feagin, Joe R., 228–230

Flexner, Abraham, 30

folkways: The most gentle of norms, 98. *See also* mores; norms; taboos

formal organization: Group created and formally organized to achieve some specific goal or set of goals, 121. *See also* goal displacement

fourth estate: The press, 187

Freud, Sigmund, 162

functional: Outcome of social action that has a positive effect on the well-being of society, 32

functionalist paradigm: Model that assumes that parts of society work interdependently and in harmony with one another, 38–39, 40–41

functions, manifest and latent, 30–32; of deviance, 177

Fussell, Paul, 198–199

fuzzy objects, 34–36

Galilei, Galileo, 7–8

games: As used by Mead, organized activities in which activity is guided by rules and in which each individual player has a specific role to carry out; role in socialization, 149–151

Gandhi, Mohandas, 184n

Gates, David, 227–228

Gemeinschaft: Tönnies' term for social relationships that are ends in and of themselves, 16–17; related to Cooley's conception of primary group, 119

gender: Social expectations about the attributes and behaviors of males and females; as a social construction, 233; in socialization, 153–154; cross-cultural differences in, 233–235; differences in income, 219–220

generalized other: According to G. H. Mead, "the attitude of the generalized other is the attitude of the whole community," 149–150. *See also* role-taking

genocide: The murder of an entire people, 47n, 224

geocentric view of cosmos: View that the earth is the center of the universe, 7

Gesellschaft: Tönnies' term for social relationships that are entered into as means to an end, 16–17, 119

gestures: Physical acts that convey shared meanings, 103–104

Gleick, James, 37

goal displacement: Occurs when scrupulously following procedures becomes more important than achieving the goals that those procedures were designed to achieve, 124. *See also* bureaucracies

Goffman, Erving, on total institutions, 156; on stigma, 176

Goring, Charles, 162

Greenberg, David F., 46

group, social: Two or more individuals who regularly interact with one another, share goals and a sense of identity, 118. *See also* primary group; secondary group

Guillard, Achille, 77n

habitualized behavior: An action that is repeated frequently and becomes cast into a pattern, 134; compared to institutionalized behavior, 135

Hallinan, Maureen T., 46, 207

Hamilton, Charles, 225

Hawthorne effect: Changes that occur in people's behavior because they are involved as research subjects; can occur when any obtrusive research technique is used, 85–88. *See also* unobtrusive research

health, effects of social class on, 201

Hegirae, 6n

Heisenberg, Werner, 36

heliocentric view of cosmos: Model of the universe that holds that the sun is at the center, 7. *See also* geocentric view of cosmos

Heraclitus, 5

hidden curriculum in schools: The latent functions of education, 153

homogeneous: Not diverse, 89

heterogeneous: Diverse, 89

Hindu religion, 139, 183

Holmes, Oliver Wendell, 47

horizontal mobility: Movement within a particular social stratum, 194. *See also* intergenerational mobility; mobility, social; vertical mobility

Hughes, Everett C., 117

Hull House, 23

Hyde, J. S., 47

hypothesis: A testable statement about the relationship between two or more variables, 54–56

I and Me: G. H. Mead's conception of how individuals acquire and maintain their social selves. The Me is the self as an object (as perceived to be seen by others); the I is one's unique response to a situation, 147–150

ideal types: A methodological strategy made famous by Max Weber. An ideal type is an "analytic construct" (it exists only in the abstract); it is created by listing only the fundamental attributes of some thing. The result is a portrait of the ideal type of that thing that can be used as a standard against which to measure the thing as it exists in the real world. Ideal types do not exist in the real world, 121, 131, 195

ideology: Beliefs that are shaped by the self-interest of some group of people, 101. *See also* beliefs, cultural

illegitimate means: Socially disapproved means of achieving desired goals, 169. *See also* anomie, as cause of deviance

income: The amount of money that an individual or family group receives each year (from wages, salary, investments, and so on), 199, 199n. *See also* wealth

incumbent, status. *See* status incumbent

independent variable: A variable that is thought to cause a change in another variable, 56–58. *See also* variable

individual discrimination, 224–225

individualism, as a threat to society, 11

industrial revolution, 10–11, 23, 188; effect on stratification, 217

inequality. *See* discrimination; gender; poverty; prejudice; race; stratification; tracking

informed consent: Consent that is obtained after the research subject has been informed of the possible risks and benefits of participating in a research project, 91

innovation, as response to anomie, 168

Inquisition, 8, 8n

institution. *See* social institution

institutional, total. *See* total institution

institutional discrimination: Discriminatory treatment of certain people that is built into the social system; individuals who carry out institutional discrimination may not intend to discriminate, 224–225. *See also* ism

institutional racism, 29, 224–225

Institutional Review Board, 91

institutionalized behavior compared to routine behavior, 135

intellectual anarchy, 11

intergenerational mobility: Social mobility that occurs across generations. For example, when a daughter achieves a higher social status than her father, she has experienced intergenerational mobility, 194–195; and social change, 213–214

interviews, 77–81

ism: Suffix generally applied to any type of discrimination that is consistent with patterns of institutional discrimination, 225–230

James, William, 99

jati, 184, 195
Johnson, Lenore, 210–211
jokes, as discrimination, 226

karma, 183
Kennedy, Stetson, 232
Kluckhohn, Clyde, 94
Kluegel, James, 188
Kopernik, Mikolaj. *See* Copernicus, Nicolaus
Kozol, Jonathan, 204–206
Kroeber, Al, 94
kshatriyas, 184
Kuznet, Simon, 190
Kuznet's curve, 190

labeling theory, 174–177
language, 96–97, 103
latent functions: Consequences of social actions that are unintended or hidden, 30–32. *See also* functional; dysfunctions; manifest functions
Lederer, Richard, 97
legitimate means: Socially approved means of achieving desired goals, 169. *See also* anomie, as cause of deviance
legitimating rationales: Explanations for why social arrangements are right and proper, 182. *See* caste system; estate system; social class
Lemert, Edwin, 175–176
Lemkin, Raphael, 47n
Lennon, Chauncy, 212–213
level of analysis, 37–42. *See also* macro-sociology; microsociology
leveling. *See* cultural leveling
Levine, Robert A., 48
Lewis, Oscar, 203
Liebow, Elliot, 204
life chances: The probabilities concerning the fate an individual can expect in life, 189n
lifestyle: Distinctive ways in which people consume goods and services; the social customs associated with each class, 189n
Linton, Ralph, 46
literature review, as a phase in the research process, 75–77
Lombroso, Cesare, 161–162

looking glass self: Cooley's term for the process by which individuals acquire and maintain their social selves through reflective interaction with others, 145–147
Luckmann, Thomas, 135

macrosociology: Approach to the study of society that focuses on relationships between social structures and institutions rather than between individuals themselves, 41–42
Maitland, Frederic William, 186
manifest functions: Consequences of social acts that are intended and obvious, 30–32. *See also* functional; dysfunctions; latent functions
Mann, Horace, 206
Mannheim, Karl, 101
manumission: Process by which a slave is granted freedom, 193
marriage, 136–138
Marshall, Thurgood, 116
Marx, Karl, 20–21, 24; on ideology, 101; on social class, 189–190
master status: The status that others deem most telling about an individual; acts as a filter through which the individual's actions are judged, 117–118
material culture: Things that humans make or adapt from the raw stuff of nature, 95. *See also* artifact; culture
matrix questions, 79. *See also* surveys
Matthew effect: The notion that people who have wealth, fame, or other scarce social goods find it easier to accumulate more of these compared to those with no wealth, fame, or other social goods, 202
McNeill, William Hardy, 183
Mead, George H., 147–151
Mead, Margaret, 233–235
mechanical solidarity: Durkheim's term for a kind of solidarity based on the likeness of people in a society, associated with a simple division of labor, 13. *See also* collective conscience; organic solidarity
Meier, Robert, 202
Merton, Robert K., 30–31; on deviance, 166–169, 170; on discrimination, 223–224. *See also* goal displacement; Matthew effect

mesomorph: An individual with a physique that is muscular and athletic, 162

microsociology: Approach to the study of society that focuses on the nature of people's interactions within particular groups, 41–42

Mills, C. Wright, 27–29, 201

minority groups: Groups whose members are singled out from others in society for differential treatment owing to their physical or cultural characteristics, 230–233

mobility, social: Movement of individuals within the society's stratification system, 194–196, 213–214; changes in rates as a result of structural factors, 214. *See also* horizontal mobility; intergenerational mobility; vertical mobility

monarchy: Rule by a king or queen, 138

monogamy, 139. *See also* serial monogamy

monotheism: Belief in a single God or deity, 138

morbidity rates: Rates of illness, 201

mores: Important norms, 98. *See also* folkways; norms; taboos

Morrill, John, 187

mortality rates: Rates of death, 201

Murdock, George, 129

National Association for the Advancement of Colored People, 24

negative relationship: A type of relationship between two variables in which they vary in opposite ways. For example, if as variable A gets bigger or faster, variable B gets smaller or slower, the relationship between A and B is negative, 58–59. *See also* positive relationship

nepotism: Process in which one gives preferences (usually on the job) to friends or relatives, 122

Newman, Katherine, 212–213

Newton, Isaac, 8–9

Newton's Laws of Motion and Gravitation, 9

nonrational behavior: Weber's term for behavior that is enjoyed or appreciated for its own sake, with no ulterior goal, 18–19. *See also* rational behavior

nonreactive research. *See* unobtrusive research

norms: Socially accepted rules for behavior, 97–98, 159; place in social institutions, 130; relativity of, 159–160. *See also* folkways; mores; taboos

Oakes, Jeannie, 206–207

observation: Research technique in which the researcher directly observes people's behavior in its natural context, 84

occupational prestige, 191–192

Ohlin, Lloyd E.,169

one-drop rule, 232–233

operational definition: Defining a variable in such a way that it can be observed and measured; often accomplished by listing the variable's attributes, 59–61. *See also* attribute

organic solidarity: Durkheim's term for a type of solidarity based on the dissimilarity and interdependence of people in a particular society, 13. *See also* collective conscience; mechanical solidarity

organization, formal. *See* formal organization

paradigm: A particular approach to the study of some phenomenon; a model of the thing under study that includes a set of assumptions about the nature of that thing, 37–42. *See also* conflict paradigm; functionalist paradigm; symbolic interaction paradigm

Parks, Rosa, 178

Parsons, Talcott, 129

participant observation: Research technique in which the researcher covertly or openly participates in the lives of research subjects, 84–85

Patterson, Orlando, 193–194

Payne, Stanley L., 80

peer group: Associates of approximately the same age and social situation; as agents of socialization, 153

personal troubles: Mills' term for problems whose causes originate within the individual, 27–29. *See also* social issues; sociological imagination

Plato, 217

play: Term used by G. H. Mead to refer to the simple imitative behaviors of small children; role in socialization, 148–151

Pollock, Frederick, 186

polyandry: Marriage between one wife and two or more husbands, 139

polygamy: Marriage to more than one husband or wife, 139

polygenicism: Belief that people of different races evolved from different genetic stock, 231, 231n

polygyny: Marriage between several wives and one husband, 139

polytheism: Belief in more than one god or deity, 139

Pope, Alexander, 9

positive relationship: A type of relationship between variables in which they vary in the same direction. For example, if as variable A gets bigger or faster, variable B gets bigger or faster, the relationship between A and B is positive, 58–59. *See also* negative relationship

poverty, cultural explanations of, 203–204; structural explanations of, 204

power: According to Weber, "the probability that one actor within a social relationship will be in a position to carry out his or her own will despite resistance," 191. *See also* authority

prejudice: Negative and persistent judgment based on scant or incorrect information about people in a particular group; an unjustified pre-judgment, 222–223. *See also* discrimination; Merton, on discrimination; stereotypes

primary deviance: The kind of deviant acts that most everyone does from time to time; frequently, may go unnoticed and unsanctioned, 175. *See also* secondary deviance

primary group: Term coined by C. H. Cooley to refer to small, intimate groups in which relationships tend to be *Gemeinschaft*, 119–120, 146

proletariats: Marx's term for the class of people who survive in modern society by selling their labor to the bourgeoisie, 20, 189. *See also* bourgeoisie

Ptolemy, Claudius, 6–7

Purusha, 184

Pygmalion, 210n

Pygmalion effect: Effect of teachers' expectations on students' performance, 210–211

pyramiding effect, 230

qualitative research: Interpretative research; seeks to gain an understanding of things from the point of view of the people being studied, 74–75. *See also* quantitative research

quantitative research: Research approach that gathers data that is easily expressed in numbers; generally not concerned with understanding the meanings that people attach to their behaviors, 74–75. *See also* qualitative research

questionnaires, 77–81

questions, closed ended and open ended, 78–80

race, as a social construction, 230–232

racism. *See* discrimination; *ism*

Radcliffe-Brown, A. 135

random sample: A sample in which each element of the population has the same chance of being included, 90

rational behavior: Weber's term for behavior that is calculating, means to an end behavior, 18–19. *See also* nonrational behavior

rebellion, as response to anomie, 168

reincarnation, 183

Reissman, Leonard, 199

relativism. *See* cultural relativism

resocialization: Intense socialization process that involves stripping away the individual's existing social self and then requiring him or her to learn new roles, 156. *See also* total institution

retreatism, as response to anomie, 168

rickets, 144, 144n

Rig Veda, 184

rites of passage: Ceremonies or rituals that mark important transitions from status to status within the life cycle, 155

ritualism, as response to anomie, 168

role: The sum total of expectations about the behavior of people who occupy a particular status, 114–115; place in social institutions, 130

role conflict: Occurs when an individual occupies two or more statuses which have roles that are contradictory or in conflict, 116–117

role strain: Occurs when the demands of a particular role are such that the individual is hard pressed to do all that is expected, 115

role-taking: Process of taking on the role of another and seeing how things look from his or her point of view; the variety of experiences one has with role-taking helps generate the generalized other; the term is sometimes used in the more specialized sense to refer to the process in which children learn to see things from the perspectives of others, 149–150. *See also* generalized other

Rose, Peter I., 156–157

Rosenthal, Robert, 210–211

Russell, Bertrand, 94

Ryan, William, 206

Sadker, David, 87–88

Sadker, Myra, 87–88

sample: A portion of the population that is studied in order to make inferences about the entire population, 89–90. *See also* random sample

sanctions: Visible responses to behavior; may be positive or negative, formal or informal, 98–99, 131

Sanskrit, 183n

Scase, Richard, 199

scheduled castes, 184

schools, impact on socialization,153

Schur, Edwin, 177

secondary deviance: Deviant behavior that occurs after and because of the fact that the individual has been labeled as deviant, 175–176. *See also* primary deviance

secondary group: Nonintimate group of people; relationships tend to be *Gesellschaft*-type, 119–120

self-fulfilling prophecy: When the very prediction of an event causes that event to happen. For example, if the media predict a shortage of heating oil for the coming winter, many individuals may hoard heating oil in anticipation of the shortage. This hoarding behavior will result in a shortage of heating oil. Likewise, if Lisa is convinced that she will never pass the sociology exam and spends all of her time worrying about flunking instead of studying, she will flunk the class, 175. *See also* Thomas Theorem

self-sufficiency. *See* society

serial monogamy, 139n

SES: Socioeconomic status. Sociologists' shorthand for the multiple factors that go into determining one's overall status in the social system. *See* social class

sex, 235

sexism. *See* discrimination; *ism*

Shaw, George B., 210n

Sheldon, William, 162

shudras, 184

slavery, 193–194

Smith, D. A., 202

Smith, Eliot, 188

Smith, Huston, 194

social change, and culture, 107; and institutions, 139–140; and deviance, 177; and social inequality, 213

social class, as type of stratification system, 188–192; legitimating rationale, 188; cultural explanations of, 203–204; structural explanations of, 204; perceptions of, 199; Marx's definition of, 189–190; Weber's definition of, 189–191; as a touchy issue, 198–199. *See also* poverty; SES

social Darwinism, 21–22

social facts: According to Durkheim, "manners of acting, thinking, and feeling external to individuals, which are invested with coercive power over individuals," 14, 89

social institution: A set of ideas about the proper response to an important societal problem, 106; an accepted and persistent constellation of statuses, roles, values, and norms that respond to important societial needs, 129–139; and social change, 139–140

social issues: Mills' term for problems whose causes are properly found in the larger social environment and not within the individuals who experience these problems, 27–29. *See also* personal troubles; sociological imagination

social self: The values, beliefs, ideas, and decision-making strategies, and the general way in which people live their lives, 143, 146

social status: One's place in the social system, 112–114; ascribed and achieved, 112, 151; place in social institutions, 130; and parental expectations, 151–152; the concept as used by Weber, 191

social structure: An abstraction; made up of statuses and attached roles, 114n; as enduring and repetitive, 128–129

socialization: Lifelong process by which people acquire cultural competency and through which society perpetuates the fundamental nature of existing social structures and institutions, 143; agents of, 150–156. *See also* resocialization

socialization, anticipatory: The process of learning about the role requirements of a particular status prior to actually acquiring that status, 155

society: The totality of people and social relations in a given geographic space, 129

sociological imagination: Mills' term for a kind of outlook on the world which allows one to look beyond the circumstances of the individual and see the effects of larger historical and social factors, 27–29. *See also* personal troubles; social issues

sociological topics, 37–42

sociology: The scientific study of interactions and relations among human beings, 2; origins of the term, 11; as social engineering, 23; as an interpretative science, 75

solidarity: The social glue; a sense of community and togetherness; that which binds a community, 13. *See also* mechanical solidarity; organic solidarity

Sorokin, Pitirim, 75–76

Speilberg, Nathan, 36

Spencer, Herbert, 21–23, 24

Spitz, René, 144–145

Sprecher, Susan, 139

Starr, Ellen Gates, 23

status. *See* social status

status inconsistency: Occurs when an individual's ascribed and achieved statuses are deemed (by others) to be inconsistent, 115–116

status incumbent: Individual who occupies a particular status. For example, Dr. Jones is an incumbent of the occupational status of physician, 113

status symbols: Visible clues to an individual's status; for example, a police officer's badge, a wedding ring, a priest collar, 113

stereotypes: Oversimplified generalized images of members of a particular group, 223

stigma, 176–177, 176n. *See also* discreditable identity; discredited identity

stratification, social, 181; open versus closed systems, 194–197; *See also* caste system; estate system; social class

structural mobility. *See* mobility, social

structural strain, theories of deviance, 164–169

subculture: A group of people whose shared specialized values, norms, beliefs, or use of material culture sets them apart from other people in society, 107–109. *See also* counterculture

sui generis: Latin term, meaning unique and of its own kind, 15

Suicide, 164

Sullivan, Andrew, 46

Sumner, William G., 23, 24; on norms, 98

superego, 172

surveys: Research technique that involves asking a series of questions of a set of people, 77–81

survival of the fittest: Spencer's term for the notion that unfettered social competition will lead to the betterment of society since, without help, the weak will lose that competition and die out, 22, 23

symbol: Anything that represents something else to more than one person, 95–96

symbolic interaction paradigm: Model of the social world that assumes that how people act depends in large part on how they see and evaluate reality and that reality is a social construction, 39, 40–41

syntax, 96n

tables and figures, how to read, 61–64

taboos: Society's most important social norms; even the thought of violating a taboo is deeply repugnant, 98. *See also* folkways; mores; norms

Taebel, Del, 199

Tawney, R. H., 198

technological change, 10–11, 23, 137

theocracy: Rule by God, or God's representatives, 138

Thomas, Dorothy, 215

Thomas, W. I., 3

Thomas Theorem: "If people define situations as real, they are real in their consequences," 3, 215. *See also* self-fulfilling prophecy

Thurow, Lester, 202

Tittle, Charles R., 202

Tocqueville, Alexis de, 213

Tönnies, Ferdinand, 16–18, 119. *See also* Gemeinschaft; Gesellschaft

total institution: Erving Goffman's term for a place of "residence and work where a large number of like-situated individuals, cut off from the wider society for an appreciable period of time, together lead an enclosed, formally administered round of life," 156–157

tracking, in schools, 206–210

transmigration, 183

triangulation: Research strategy in which different research methods are brought to bear on a single research problem; different methods are chosen so that their respective strengths and weaknesses complement one another, 88–89

tyranny: Rule by a tyrant, 138

uncertainty principle, 36

unobtrusive research: Strategies for studying behavior that do not affect the behavior of research subjects, 85

vaishyas, 184

values: Abstract ideas about what is good and what is bad; shared by people in a society, 100–102; place in social institutions, 130

variable: A thing that is thought to influence or be influenced by another thing, 52–53; independent and dependent, 56; operationalizing, 60–61; in experiments, 81–82

varna, 184, 195

verbal rejection, as a form of discrimination, 224

vertical mobility: Movement (up or down) from one social stratum into another, 194; and social change, 213–214. *See also* horizontal mobility; intergenerational mobility; mobility, social

villein, 185

Villenez, W. J., 202

Visser, Margaret, 108

Voltaire, 8n

Washington, Booker T., 24

Washington, George, 31n

wealth: The total value of the assets owned by an individual or family group, 199, 199n. *See also* income

Weber, Max, 16, 18–20, 21; on rational and irrational behavior, 18–19; on inconvenient facts, 45; on research, 74–75; on bureaucracy, 121–123; on ideal types, 121, 131, 195; on social class, 189–191; on social status, 191

Weltanschauung, 101

William the Conqueror, 185

Williams, Richard, 46

Wittgenstein, Ludwig Josef, 35

working life, effects of social class on, 201

workplace, as agent of socialization, 154–157

Yanomamö, 49–50

Credits

Chapter 7 Page 108 From *Much Depends Upon Dinner*. Published by HarperCollins Publishers, Ltd. Copyright © 1986 by Margaret Visser. Reprinted by permission.

Chapter 8 Page 148 From *Mind, Self, and Society* by Charles W. Morris (ed.), University of Chicago Press, 1934. Copyright © 1934 University of Chicago Press. Reprinted with permission of the publisher.